OXFORD IB DIPLOMA PROGRAMME

GLOBAL POLITICS

COURSE COMPANION

Max Kirsch

OXFORD
UNIVERSITY PRESS

OXFORD
UNIVERSITY PRESS

Great Clarendon Street, Oxford, OX2 6DP, United Kingdom

Oxford University Press is a department of the University of Oxford. It furthers the University's objective of excellence in research, scholarship, and education by publishing worldwide. Oxford is a registered trade mark of Oxford University Press in the UK and in certain other countries

© Oxford University Press 2017

The moral rights of the authors have been asserted

First published in 2017

British Library Cataloguing in Publication Data

Data available

978-0-19-830883-6

7 9 10 8

Paper used in the production of this book is a natural, recyclable product made from wood grown in sustainable forests. The manufacturing process conforms to the environmental regulations of the country of origin.

Printed and bound by CPI Group (UK) Ltd, Croydon, CR0 4YY

Acknowledgements

The publishers would like to thank the following for permissions to use their photographs:

p1: RTimages/Alamy Stock Photo; **p4**: National Geographic Creative/Alamy Stock Photo; **p5**: Ryan Heffernan/Getty Images; **p7**: Gianni Muratore/Alamy Stock; **p10**: Albin Lohr-Jones/Pacific Press/LightRocket/Getty Images; **p11t**: Peter Probst/Age Fotostock ; **p11b**: Khin Maung Win/AFP/Getty Images; **p14**: Images & Stories/Alamy Stock Photo; **p15**: World History Archive/Alamy Stock Photo; **p16-17**: Rtimages/Shutterstock; **p18**: ImageBROKER/Alamy Stock Photo; **p19t**: Yann Arthus-Bertrand/Earth from Above/UNESCO; **p19b**: AFP/Stringer/Getty Images; **p20**: Kuni Takahashi/Getty Images News; **p22**: French School/Getty Images; **p24**: DEA Picture Library/Getty Images; **p25t**: Peter Probst/Age Fotostock; **p25b**: General Electric; **p26**: Peter Probst/Alamy Stock Photo; **p27**: Trevor Collens/Alamy Stock Photo; **p31**: Hector Mata/AFP/Getty Images; **p34**: Epa European pressphoto agency b.v./Alamy Stock Photo; **p44-45**: Granger, NYC./Alamy Stock Photo; **p46**: PHAS/UIG/Getty Images; **p47**: Nelson Almeida/AFP/Getty Images; **p49t**: Beryl Peters Collection/Alamy Stock Photo; **p49b**: World History Archive/Alamy Stock Photo; **p51**: Grafissimo/Getty Images; **p52**: Universal Declaration of Human Rights; **p53**: Granger, NYC./Alamy Stock Photo; **p56**: The Print Collecto/Alamy Stock Photo; **p57**: Archivart/Alamy Stock Photo; **p59t**: Benoit Gysembergh/Paris Match/Getty Images; **p59m**: Peter Northall/EPA; **p59b**: David Ball/Alamy Stock Photo ; **p60**: Realimage/Alamy Stock Photo; **p61t**: Image Source/Alamy Stock Photo; **p61b**: ullstein bild/Getty Images; **p62t**: Peter Probst/Alamy Stock Photo; **p62br**: TP/Alamy Stock Photo; **p62bl**: Imagebroker/Alamy Stock Photo; **p63**: TP/Alamy Stock Photo; **p66t**: Central Press/Stringer/Getty Images; **p66l**: Julio Etchart / Alamy Stock Photo; **p66r**: Luis Zabreg/EPA; **p67**: INTERFOTO/Alamy Stock Photo; **p69**: The Washington Post/Getty Images; **p70**: Loop Images Ltd/Alamy Stock Photo; **p78-79**: Ideeone/Getty Images; **p80**: TP/Alamy Stock Photo; **p82**: Ben Wyeth/Alamy Stock Photo; **p84**: Don Emmert/AFP/Getty Images; **p96**: John Darkow/Columbia Daily Tribune, Cagle Cartoons ; **p88**: Bettmann/Getty Images; **p92**: Urbanmyth/Alamy Stock Photo; **p94**: David R. Frazier Photolibrary, Inc./Alamy Stock Photo; **p95r**: Mustafa Abdi/AFP/Getty Images; **p95b**: China Daily; **p98**: Timothy A. Clary/AFP/Getty Images; **p108**: Robertharding/Alamy Stock Photo; **p109**: Alissa Everett/Alamy Stock Photo; **p116**: Jake Lyell/Alamy Stock Photo; **p117**: Saurabh Das/AP Photo; **p120l**: Subir Halder/India Today Group/Getty Images; **p120r**: Roberto Serra - Iguana Press/Contributor/Getty Images; **p129**: De Visu/Shutterstock; **p140-141**: Ssouf Sanogo/AFP/Getty Images; **p142**: Rolls Press/Popperfoto/Getty Images; **p145**: United Nations Photo ; **p146t**: Peter Probst/Alamy Stock Photo; **p146b**: AFP/Getty Images; **p150**: Aizar Raldes/Stringer/AFP/Getty Images; **p152**: Joseph Eid/AFP/Getty Images; **p153**: Bell Bajao; **p159**: Mohamed Nureldin Abdallah/Reuters; **p162**: AP Photo; **p165**: Evelyn Hockstein/Newscom; **p168**: Evan Schneider/UN Photo; **p170**: Rey T. Byhre/Alamy Stock Photo ; **p173**: Zapiro Cartoons; **p174**: Copyright © The Granger Collection, New York / The Granger Collection; **p177**: Richard Levine/Alamy Stock Photo; **p188**: The Asahi Shimbun via Getty Images; **p189**: Pierre Crom/Getty Images.

The author and publisher are grateful for permission to reprint extracts from the following copyright material:

Human Rights

Excerpt from *Universal Human Rights in Theory and Practice* (Second Edition), by J. Donnelly, 2003, reprinted by permission of Cornell University Press.

Excerpts from *Europe and the People without History* by Eric R. Wolf, University of California Press © 1982, 1997, 2010 by The Regents of University of California, reprinted by permission.

'The Universal Declaration of Human Rights' by United Nations, © 1948 United Nations, reprinted with the permission of the United Nations.

Entry on Human Rights from Encyclopædia Britannica, reprinted with permission from Encyclopædia Britannica, © 2016 by Encyclopædia Britannica, Inc.

Excerpts from 'Human rights, the midlife crisis' by Michael Ignatieff in *New York Review of Books*, Vol. 46, no. 9, p. 5, Copyright © 1999 by Michael Ignatieff, reprinted by permission.

Excerpt from p. 390 of *The Human Rights Reader* by Micheline Ishay, 2007, London, Routledge, reprinted by permission of Taylor and Francis Group LLC Books, permission conveyed through Copyright Clearance Center, Inc.

Excerpts from 'The Recent History of Human Rights' by Kenneth Cmiel in *The American Historical Review*, February 2004, reprinted by permission of Oxford University Press and the Estate of Kenneth Cmiel.

Excerpts from 'Do Human Rights Increase Inequality?' by Samuel Moyn, 26 May 2015, *The Chronicle of Higher Education, The Chronicle Review*, pp. 7–8, reprinted by permission of The Chronicle of Higher Education, Copyright © 2016, all rights reserved.

Development

Excerpt from speech by Rt. Hon. Helen Clark, 'Beyond the Millennium Development Goals: What could the next global development agenda look like?' 19 August 2013, Auckland, copyright United Nations Development Programme, www.hdr.undp.org, reprinted under the Creative Commons Attribution 3.0 IGO licence, https://creativecommons.org/licenses/by-nc-nd/3.0/us/.

Excerpt from 'Democracy, Human Rights and Development', European Commission - Democracy and Human Rights, http://www.eidhr.eu/democracy-human-rights-development, © European Union, https://ec.europa.eu/info/legal-notice_en#copyright-notice.

Excerpt from 'Sustainable Development Knowledge Platform', https://sustainabledevelopment.un.org/, © United Nations, reprinted by permission of the United Nations.

Excerpts from *The Idea of Poverty* by Paul Spicker, Policy Press, © 2007, reprinted by permission of the author.

Excerpt from 1990 Human Development Report '*Concept and Measurement of Human Development*', Human Development Report Office, copyright United Nations Development Programme, www.hdr.undp.org, reprinted under the Creative Commons Attribution 3.0 IGO licence, https://creativecommons.org/licenses/by-nc-nd/3.0/us/.

Excerpts from 'Our Common Future' by The World Commission on Environment and Development, 1990, by permission of Oxford University Press, USA.

Excerpt from 'Remarks to the World Economic Forum Session on Redefining Sustainable Development' by Ban Ki-moon, 28 January 2011, © (2011) United Nations, reprinted with the permission of the United Nations.

Excerpt from *World Development Report 2011: Conflict, Security, and Development* by World Bank, https://openknowledge.worldbank.org/handle/10986/4389, p. 4: WDR team calculations based on Ravallion, Chen and Sangaula. 2008 Poverty Data available on PovcalNet (http://iresearch.worldbank.org), © World Bank, reprinted under the terms of the Creative Commons Attribution license (CC BY 3.0 IGO), https://creativecommons.org/licenses/by/3.0/igo/.

Excerpt from *Religion and Economic Growth* by Robert J. Barro and Rachel M. McCleary, Working Paper 9682, http://www.nber.org/papers/w9682. National Bureau of Economic Research. May 2003, © 2003 by Robert J. Barro and Rachel M. McCleary, all rights reserved.

Excerpts from 'The Fate of Sustainable Development Under Neo-Liberal Regimes in Developing Countries' by M. Shamsul Haque, in *International Political Science Review*, April 1999, 20: 197-218, copyright SAGE Publications.

Excerpt from *The What, Why, and How of Privatization: A World Bank Perspective* by Mary M. Shirley, 60 Fordham Law Review S23 (1992), reprinted by permission.

Excerpt from 'State Capitalism Comes of Age: The End of the Free Market' by Ian Bremner, *Foreign Affairs*, May/June 2009, reprinted with permission of *Foreign Affairs*, from www.foreignaffairs.com, copyright 2009, permission conveyed through Copyright Clearance Center, Inc.

Excerpts and information from 'The World's Women 2010: Trends and Statistics' © 2010 United Nations, reprinted by permission of the United Nations.

Continued on last page

Course Companion definition

The IB Diploma Programme Course Companions are resource materials designed to support students throughout their two-year Diploma Programme course of study in a particular subject. They will help students gain an understanding of what is expected from the study of an IB Diploma Programme subject while presenting content in a way that illustrates the purpose and aims of the IB. They reflect the philosophy and approach of the IB and encourage a deep understanding of each subject by making connections to wider issues and providing opportunities for critical thinking.

The books mirror the IB philosophy of viewing the curriculum in terms of a whole-course approach; the use of a wide range of resources, international mindedness, the IB learner profile and the IB Diploma Programme core requirements, theory of knowledge, the extended essay, and creativity, activity, service (CAS).

Each book can be used in conjunction with other materials and indeed, students of the IB are required and encouraged to draw conclusions from a variety of resources. Suggestions for additional and further reading are given in each book and suggestions for how to extend research are provided.

In addition, the Course Companions provide advice and guidance on the specific course assessment requirements and on academic honesty protocol. They are distinctive and authoritative without being prescriptive.

IB mission statement

The International Baccalaureate aims to develop inquiring, knowledgable and caring young people who help to create a better and more peaceful world through intercultural understanding and respect.

To this end the IB works with schools, governments and international organizations to develop challenging programmes of international education and rigorous assessment.

These programmes encourage students across the world to become active, compassionate, and lifelong learners who understand that other people, with their differences, can also be right.

The IB learner Profile

The aim of all IB programmes is to develop internationally minded people who, recognizing their common humanity and shared guardianship of the planet, help to create a better and more peaceful world. IB learners strive to be:

Inquirers They develop their natural curiosity. They acquire the skills necessary to conduct inquiry and research and show independence in learning. They actively enjoy learning and this love of learning will be sustained throughout their lives.

Knowledgable They explore concepts, ideas, and issues that have local and global significance. In so doing, they acquire in-depth knowledge and develop understanding across a broad and balanced range of disciplines.

Thinkers They exercise initiative in applying thinking skills critically and creatively to recognize and approach complex problems, and make reasoned, ethical decisions.

Communicators They understand and express ideas and information confidently and creatively in more than one language and in a variety of modes of communication. They work effectively and willingly in collaboration with others.

Principled They act with integrity and honesty, with a strong sense of fairness, justice, and respect for the dignity of the individual, groups, and communities. They take responsibility for their own actions and the consequences that accompany them.

Open-minded They understand and appreciate their own cultures and personal histories, and are open to the perspectives, values, and traditions of other individuals and communities. They are accustomed to seeking and evaluating a range of points of view, and are willing to grow from the experience.

Caring They show empathy, compassion, and respect towards the needs and feelings of others. They have a personal commitment to service, and act to make a positive difference to the lives of others and to the environment.

Risk-takers They approach unfamiliar situations and uncertainty with courage and forethought, and have the independence of spirit to explore new roles, ideas, and strategies. They are brave and articulate in defending their beliefs.

Balanced They understand the importance of intellectual, physical, and emotional balance to achieve personal well-being for themselves and others.

Reflective They give thoughtful consideration to their own learning and experience. They are able to assess and understand their strengths and limitations in order to support their learning and personal development.

A note on academic honesty

It is of vital importance to acknowledge and appropriately credit the owners of information when that information is used in your work. After all, owners of ideas (intellectual property) have property rights. To have an authentic piece of work, it must be based on your individual and original ideas with the work of others fully acknowledged. Therefore, all assignments, written or oral, completed for assessment must use your own language and expression. Where sources are used or referred to, whether in the form of direct quotation or paraphrase, such sources must be appropriately acknowledged.

How do I acknowledge the work of others?

The way that you acknowledge that you have used the ideas of other people is through the use of footnotes and bibliographies.

Footnotes (placed at the bottom of a page) or endnotes (placed at the end of a document) are to be provided when you quote or paraphrase from another document, or closely summarize the information provided in another document. You do not need to provide a footnote for information that is part of a 'body of knowledge'. That is, definitions do not need to be footnoted as they are part of the assumed knowledge.

Bibliographies should include a formal list of the resources that you used in your work. The listing should include all resources, including books, magazines, newspaper articles, Internet-based resources, CDs and works of art. 'Formal' means that you should use one of the several accepted forms of presentation. You must provide full information as to how a reader or viewer of your work can find the same information. A bibliography is compulsory in the extended essay.

What constitutes misconduct?

Misconduct is behaviour that results in, or may result in, you or any student gaining an unfair advantage in one or more assessment component. Misconduct includes plagiarism and collusion.

Plagiarism is defined as the representation of the ideas or work of another person as your own. The following are some of the ways to avoid plagiarism:

- Words and ideas of another person used to support one's arguments must be acknowledged.

- Passages that are quoted verbatim must be enclosed within quotation marks and acknowledged.

- CD-ROMs, email messages, web sites on the Internet, and any other electronic media must be treated in the same way as books and journals.

- The sources of all photographs, maps, illustrations, computer programs, data, graphs, audio-visual, and similar material must be acknowledged if they are not your own work.

- Works of art, whether music, film, dance, theatre arts, or visual arts, and where the creative use of a part of a work takes place, must be acknowledged.

Collusion is defined as supporting misconduct by another student. This includes:

- allowing your work to be copied or submitted for assessment by another student

- duplicating work for different assessment components and/or diploma requirements.

Other forms of misconduct include any action that gives you an unfair advantage or affects the results of another student. Examples include, taking unauthorized material into an examination room, misconduct during an examination, and falsifying a CAS record.

Contents

About the authors

Max Kirsch is Professor of Anthropology and UNESCO Chair in Human and Cultural Rights at Florida Atlantic University. He is the author of four books and many journal articles, including, *In the Wake of the Giant, Queer Theory and Social Change, Rethinking Disney: Private Control, Public Dimensions, and Inclusion and Exclusion in the Global Arena.* He is currently working on two monographs, one an analysis of current global effects on our daily lives entitled *The Way We Live Now*, and the second is an ethnography concerning rapid social change, redevelopment, and internal colonialization in the Florida Everglades.

The author would like to thank the following:

For substantial contributions to Unit 3, Arpita Mathur.

Dr. Arpita Mathur is an independent research scholar currently based in Singapore. She was formerly Research Fellow, S. Rajaratnam School of International Studies, Nanyang Technological University, Singapore, where she was also course instructor for a post-graduate level course conducted by the Institute. Prior to her assignment with the RSIS at Singapore, she worked as an Associate Fellow at the Institute for Defense Studies and Analyses in New Delhi, India. Arpita has a doctorate in international relations from Jawaharlal Nehru University, New Delhi (India). She has authored a monograph on 'India-Japan Relations: Drivers, Trends and Prospects' and numerous book chapters, papers in peer-reviewed journals, policy briefs and commentaries. She is a recipient of the Japan Foundation Fellowship, the Saburo Okita Fellowship and invited to Japan under the Program for Opinion Leaders by the former Japan Defense Agency in 2004.

For substantial contributions to Unit 4, Michael (Chiel) Mooij.

Chiel Mooij studied the History of International Relations (MA) at Utrecht University and International Organisations and International Relations (BA) at the University of Groningen, both in the Netherlands. He introduced Global Politics during the pilot phase at UWC Atlantic College, after first having taught Peace and Conflict Studies there, one of the subjects that laid the foundations for the Global Politics course. An experienced examiner, he currently teaches at United World College Maastricht, where he has also introduced Global Politics. He leads face-to-face and online workshops for Global Politics teachers for the IBO and affiliated organisations.

For the TOK features, Jenny Gillett, IBO.

The International Baccalaureate and the DP Program Developers

The International Baccalaureate Guide to Global Politics, Final for Assessment, May 2017

Syllabus content

Unit 1 Power, sovereignty and international relations

This unit focuses on the dynamics of power and how it is manifested and legitimised at various levels. The roles of state and non-state actors are examined, their interactions in global politics are discussed and their success in achieving their aims and objectives are evaluated.

Key concepts: power, sovereignty, legitimacy, interdependence

Learning outcome	Prescribed content	Possible examples (intended as a starting point only: for many topics, local and current examples will be more appropriate than the ones listed, and many more examples are listed than are expected to be covered during the course)
Nature of power	Definitions and theories of power	• Definitions and theories of power, e.g. Nye, Mearsheimer, Gramsci, Lukes, Wolf
	Types of power	• Types of power, e.g. hard vs. soft; economic, military, social, cultural; individual vs. collective; unilateral vs. multilateral

Operation of state power in global politics	States and statehood	• States and statehood, e.g.
		
		  ○ State, nation, nation-state, stateless nation, types of state (e.g. unitary states, federal states, confederations)
		
		  ○ Democratic states
		
		  ○ Militarised states
		
		  ○ Fragile / failed states
		
		  ○ Rising states

	The evolving nature of state sovereignty and legitimacy of state power	• The evolving nature of state sovereignty and legitimacy of state power, e.g.
		
		  ○ The Westphalian conception of state sovereignty and present-day challenges to this (e.g. globalization, supra-nationality, humanitarian intervention, indigenous rights)
		
		  ○ Domestic and international sources of legitimacy for state power (e.g. possession and use of force, international law and norms, recognition by other states due to economic and balance of power considerations, consent of the governed through political participation – or not)

Function and impact of international organizations and non-state actors in global politics	The United Nations (UN)	• The UN, e.g. UN Charter, General Assembly, Security Council, other organs and agencies
	Intergovernmental organizations (IGOs)	• IGOs, e.g. World Trade Organisation (WTO), International Monetary Fund (IMF), European Union, African Union, Arab League, ASEAN
	Non-governmental organisations (NGOs), multinational corporations (MNCs) and trade unions	• NGOs, e.g. Red Cross/ Red Crescent, Amnesty International, Human Rights Watch, Greenpeace, BRAC • MNCs, e.g. Unilever, Philips, IKEA, Lenovo, Tata • Trade unions, e.g. International Trade Union Confederation
	Social movements, resistance movements and violent protest movements	• Social movements, e.g. Occupy, Avaaz.org, Billion Voices • Resistance movements, e.g. Arab Spring, Orange Revolution in Ukraine, Zapatista Rebellion • Violent protest movements, e.g. FARC, Hezbollah, Naxalites, Al Qaeda
	Political parties	• Political parties, e.g. the Republican and Democratic parties in the US, CDU and SPD in Germany, the Communist Party in China
	Informal forums	• Informal forums, e.g. G20, G8, G2, World Economic Forum, World Social Forum
Nature and extent of interactions in global politics	Global governance	• Global governance, e.g. UN Security Council resolutions, climate change agenda, Basel accords on financial regulation, WTO trade agreements, regional decision-making
	Cooperation: treaties, collective security, strategic alliances, economic cooperation, informal cooperation	• Treaties, e.g. Nuclear Non-Proliferation Treaty, Montreal Protocol • Collective security, e.g. NATO, Organization of American States • Strategic alliances, e.g. China's alliances in Latin America and Africa, US-Taiwan, US-Israel, India-Afghanistan • Economic cooperation, e.g. bi- and multilateral trade agreements, regional economic integration, facilitation and regulation of international production • Informal cooperation, e.g. extraordinary rendition, technology harmonization, cultural exchange
	Conflict: interstate war, intrastate war, terrorist attacks, strikes, demonstrations	• Interstate war, e.g. Iraq, Afghanistan, Sudan and South Sudan • Intrastate war, e.g. Syria, Ukraine • Terrorist attacks, e.g. 9/11, Mumbai bombings • Strikes and demonstrations: local examples

Unit 2: Human Rights

This unit focuses on the nature and practice of human rights. Debates surrounding human rights are examined.

Key concepts: human rights, justice, liberty, equality

Learning outcome	Prescribed content	Possible examples

Nature and evolution of human rights	Definitions of human rights
	
	The UN Universal Declaration of Human Rights (1948)
	
	Developments in human rights over time and space
		• Definitions of human rights, e.g. through notions such as inalienability, universality, indivisibility, equality, justice, liberty
		• Developments in human rights over time and space, e.g.
		  ○ Human rights milestones, e.g. civil and political rights, economic, social and cultural rights, gender rights, children's rights, indigenous people's rights, refugee rights
		  ○ Internationalization of human rights, e.g. universal jurisdiction, international humanitarian law

Codification, protection and monitoring of human rights	Human rights laws and treaties Protection and enforcement of human rights at different levels Monitoring human rights agreements	• Human rights laws and treaties, e.g. role of custom, human rights in constitutions (e.g. South Africa, Brazil), International Covenants on Civil and Political Rights and on Economic, Social and Cultural Rights, Convention on the Protection of the Rights of Migrant Workers, Rome Statute • Protection and enforcement of human rights at different levels, e.g. national courts and police, International Court of Justice, International Criminal Court, Inter-American Commission on Human Rights, Cambodia Tribunal • Monitoring human rights agreements, e.g. ombudsmen, Human Rights Watch, Amnesty International, Red Cross/ Red Crescent, monitoring elections
Practice of human rights	Claims on human rights Violations of human rights	• Claims on human rights, e.g. labour rights, indigenous land claims, movements for gender equality, debates about same sex marriage • Violations in human rights, e.g. forced labour, human trafficking, forced relocation, denial of prisoners of war rights, child soldiers, violations of freedom of speech, violations in the name of prevention of terrorism, gender discrimination
Debates surrounding human rights: differing interpretations of justice, liberty and equality	Individual vs. collective rights Universal rights vs. cultural relativism Politicization of human rights	• Individual vs. collective rights, e.g. Western, Asian and African conceptions, indigenous conceptions • Universal rights vs. cultural relativism, e.g. Sharia law, honour killings, hate crime laws, consumer rights • Politicization of human rights, e.g. use of human rights for political gain, humanitarian arguments, responsibility to protect, use of sanctions

Unit 3: Development

This unit focuses on what development means, how it can be pursued and what may help or stand in the way of people, communities and countries becoming better off in a comprehensive sense. Debates surrounding development are examined.

Key concepts: development, globalization, inequality, sustainability

Learning outcome	Prescribed content	Possible examples
Contested meanings of development	Different definitions of development, including sustainable development and well-being	• Economic growth, a fairer income distribution, reduction in poverty, meeting basic needs, improved capabilities, achievement of political and social freedoms, well-functioning institutions, lifestyles that respect the ecological constraints of the environment
	Measuring development	• Gross National Product, Gini Index, Human Development Index, Human Poverty Index, Gender-related Development Index, Genuine Progress Indicator, Inclusive Wealth Index, Happy Planet Index, corruption indices, trust indices
Factors that may promote or inhibit development	Political factors	• Ideologies, history of and persistence of conflict, stability, accountability, transparency, legal frameworks, political consequences of different development paths, decisions about the allocation of aid, political culture, culture of bureaucracy, vested interests
	Economic factors	• Access to resources, increasing resource constraints, infrastructure, debt, access to capital and credit, aid, trade, foreign direct investment (FDI), income distribution, informal economy, vested interests
	Social factors	• Values, cultures, traditions, gender relations, migration
	Institutional factors	• UN, IMF, World Bank, WTO, partnerships between developing countries
	Environmental factors	• Geography, resource endowment, consequences of climate change on people and communities' lives
Pathways towards development	Models of development	• Modernization and post-modernization theories (e.g. Rostow, Inglehart), dependency theories (e.g. Cardoso, Wallerstein), neoliberalism (e.g. Washington consensus), state capitalism (e.g. China, Russia), capability theories (e.g. Sen, Nussbaum)
	Approaches for developing the economy	• Trade liberalization, export orientation, commodity-led growth, tourism, entrepreneurship, knowledge economy, circular economy, complementary currencies
	Approaches for developing society	• Concern for citizenship skills and engagement, improving education and healthcare, changing roles of women, more ecological living, indigenous revitalization movements
Debates surrounding development: challenges of globalization, inequality and sustainability	Globalization: wins and losses	• Facts about development of standard of living and assessment of realization of human rights, well-being and opportunity for different groups of people within and between societies, environmental impacts of globalization
	Inequality: how important a factor in development?	• Opportunities for and limits of state, IGO and NGO action, (e.g. global regulation of MNCs and cross-border financial flows, role of local regulation of conditions of work, power of lobbies)
	Sustainable development: which way forward?	• Opportunities for and limits of state, IGO and NGO action (e.g. progress in global climate change negotiations, role of regional, national and local policies for sustainable development)

Unit 4: Peace and Conflict

This unit focuses on what peace, conflict and violence mean, how conflicts emerge and develop, and what can be done to build a lasting peace.

Key concepts: peace, conflict, violence, non-violence

Learning outcome	Prescribed content	Possible examples

Contested meanings of peace, conflict and violence	Different definitions of peace, conflict and violence, including positive peace and structural violence	• Different definitions of
		  ○ Peace: e.g. negative peace, balance of power, peace in different political traditions and religions, feminist peace
		  ○ Conflict: e.g. through scale of conflict from e.g. disenfranchisement through to interstate war
		  ○ Violence: e.g. direct violence, cultural violence

	Types of conflict	• Types of conflict, e.g.
		  ○ Territorial conflict (e.g. Western Sahara, Russian claims, disputes in the South China Sea)
		  ○ Interest-based conflict (e.g. weapon sales, positive discrimination on the factory floor)
		  ○ Ideological conflict (e.g. political ideologies, free market versus state-led economy)
		  ○ Identity conflict (e.g. indigenous populations, more heterogeneous populations in previously homogeneous states)

	Justifications of violence, including just war theory	• Justifications of violence, e.g. humanitarian intervention, self-defence, religiously or culturally condoned violence
Causes and parties to conflict	Causes of conflict	• Causes of conflict, e.g. greed vs. grievance (e.g. Colombia, Sierra Leone), territorial control, material interest, resource scarcity, ideology, threatened identity, perception
	Parties to conflict	• Parties to conflict, e.g. states, intrastate groups, protest groups, individuals
Evolution of conflict	Manifestations of conflict, including non-violence	• Manifestations of conflict, e.g. demonstrations, civil disobedience, violent protests, guerrilla warfare, terrorism, genocide, civil war, interstate war
	Conflict dynamics	• Conflict dynamics, e.g. Galtung's conflict triangle, positions-interests-needs, conflict cycles
	Third-party involvement in conflict, including humanitarian intervention	• Third-party involvement, e.g. weapon embargoes, NATO involvement, election observers
Conflict resolution and post-conflict transformation	Peacemaking, including negotiations and treaties	• Peacemaking, e.g. UN peace enforcement, imposed settlement, ceasefires, truces, arbitration, mediation, peace treaties, peacekeeping, peace enforcement, military victory
	Peacebuilding, including reconciliation and work of justice institutions	• Peacebuilding, e.g. truth and reconciliation commissions (e.g. Sierra Leone), courts (e.g. Cambodia, International Criminal Court), forgiveness

Key concepts

The following sixteen key concepts (with brief explanations provided below) weave a conceptual thread throughout the course. They should be explored both when working with the core units and the HL extension in order to equip students with a conceptual framework with which to access and understand the political issues examined.

The concepts below are listed in the order in which they appear in the core units, with four concepts attached to each unit. This unit affiliation indicates where the concepts are most likely to surface, but the intention is that any of them can and should be addressed at any point of the course where they add value to the discussion.

Concept	Explanation
Power	Power is a central concept in the study of global politics and a key focus of the course. Power can be seen as ability to effect change in the world and, rather than being viewed as a unitary or independent force, is as an aspect of relations among people functioning within various social organizations. Contested relationships between people and groups of people dominate politics, particularly in this era of increased globalization, and so understanding the dynamics of power plays a prominent role in understanding global politics.
Sovereignty	Sovereignty characterises a state's independence, its control over territory and its ability to govern itself. How states use their sovereign power is at the heart of many important issues in global politics. Some theorists argue that sovereign power is increasingly being eroded by aspects of globalization such as global communication and trade, which states cannot always fully control. Others argue that sovereign states exercise a great deal of power when acting in their national interest and that this is unlikely to change.
Legitimacy	Legitimacy refers to an actor or an action being commonly considered acceptable and provides the fundamental basis or rationale for all forms of governance and other ways of exercising power over others. The most accepted contemporary source of legitimacy in a state is some form of democracy or constitutionalism whereby the governed have a defined and periodical opportunity to choose who they wish to exercise power over them. However, even within an overall framework of legitimacy, individual actions by a state can be considered more or less legitimate. Other actors of global politics and their behaviours can also be assessed from the perspective of legitimacy.
Interdependence	For global politics, the concept of interdependence most often refers to the mutual reliance between and among groups, organizations, areas and states for access to resources that sustain living arrangements. Often, this mutual reliance is economic (such as trade), but can also have a security dimension (such as defence arrangements) and, increasingly, a sustainability dimension (such as environmental treaties). Globalization has increased interdependence, while often changing the relationships of power among the various actors engaged in global politics.
Human rights	Human rights are basic rights and entitlements which many argue one should be able to claim simply by virtue of being a human being. Many contemporary thinkers argue that they are essential for living a life of dignity, are inalienable, and are universal. The Universal Declaration of Human Rights adopted by the United Nations in 1948 is recognized as the beginning of the formal discussion of human rights around the world.

Justice	There are a number of different interpretations of the term justice. It is often closely associated with the idea of fairness and with each getting what he or she deserves, although what is meant by desert is also itself contested. The term justice is also closely associated with rights and what individuals can legitimately demand of one another or their government.
Liberty	The term liberty refers to having freedom and autonomy. It is often divided into positive and negative liberty, with negative liberty often defined as freedom from external coercion and positive liberty defined as a person having the freedom to carry out their own will. Some scholars reject this distinction and argue that in practice one cannot exist without the other.
Equality	Egalitarian theories are based on a concept of equality where all people, or groups of people, are seen to have the same intrinsic value. Equality is therefore closely linked to justice and fairness, as egalitarians argue that justice can only exist if there is equality. Increasingly, with growing polarization within societies, equality is also linked to liberty, as different people have different opportunities to carry out their own will.
Development	Development is a broad based and sustained increase in the standard of living and well-being of a level of social organization. Many consider it to involve increased income, better access to basic goods and services, improvements in education, healthcare and public health, well-functioning institutions, decreased inequality, reduced poverty and unemployment and more sustainable production and consumption patterns. Although the focus of development debates in global politics is on issues faced by developing countries, all societies and communities face questions about how to best promote well-being and reduce ill-being. Development is typically measured through indicators such as longevity and literacy as well as income per head, but other measures, such as carbon footprint and subjective well-being, are being included in many metrics.
Globalization	Globalization is a process by which local, regional and national economies, societies and cultures are becoming increasingly integrated and connected. The term refers to the reduction of barriers and borders, as goods, services and ideas flow more freely between different parts of the world and people. Globalization is a process which has been taking place for centuries but the pace has quickened in recent decades, facilitated by developments in global governance and technology and powered by cheap energy. By now, it is widely acknowledged that globalization has both benefits and drawbacks and that its proceeds are not evenly distributed.
Inequality	Inequality refers to the unequal access to resources that are needed to sustain life and communities. It is closely connected to discussions of power in a globalized world and who holds the rights to these resources and their proceeds. Inequality can be examined both as a phenomenon within and between societies.
Sustainability	Definitions of sustainability begin with the idea that development should meet the needs of the present without compromising the ability of future generations to meet their needs. Sustainability today has three fields of debate – environmental, sociopolitical and economic. In global politics, mechanisms and incentives required for political institutions, economic actors and individuals to take a longer term and more inclusive well-being perspective in their decision-making are particularly important.
Peace	Peace is often defined as a state of both non-conflict and harmonious relations. Many also refer to peace as a state of non-conflict among personal relations, particularly with oneself and one's relationship with others. Peace is the ultimate goal of many organizations that monitor and regulate the relationships among states.

Conflict	Conflict is the dynamic process of actual or perceived opposition between individuals, groups or countries. This could be opposition over positions, interests or values. Most theorists would distinguish between non-violent and violent conflict. In this distinction, non-violent conflict can be a useful mechanism for social change and transformation, while violent conflict is harmful and asks for conflict resolution.
Violence	Violence is often defined as physical or psychological force afflicted upon another being. In the context of global politics it could be seen as anything manmade that prevents someone from reaching their full potential (e.g. structural violence). This broader definition would encompass unequal distribution of power and discriminatory practices that exclude entire groups of people from accessing certain resources.
Non-violence	Non-violence is the practice of advocating one's rights without physically harming the opponent. It often involves actively opposing the system that is deemed to be unjust, through for example boycotts, demonstrations and civil disobedience. It is argued by theorists that non-violence can often draw international attention to a conflict situation and that it could provide a fertile basis for post-conflict transformation.

The nature of Global politics

The twenty-first century is characterized by rapid change and increasing interconnectedness, impacting people in unprecedented ways and creating complex global political challenges. The study of global politics enables students to critically engage with different and new perspectives and approaches to politics, in order to better make sense of this changing world and their role in it as active citizens. Global politics is an exciting dynamic subject that draws on a variety of disciplines in the social sciences and humanities, reflecting the complex nature of many contemporary political issues.

The Diploma Programme global politics course explores fundamental political concepts such as power, equality, sustainability and peace in a range of contexts. It allows students to develop an understanding of the local, national, international and global dimensions of political activity, as well as allowing them the opportunity to explore political issues affecting their own lives. The course helps to understand abstract political concepts by grounding them in real-world examples and case studies. It also invites comparison between such examples and case studies to ensure a transnational perspective.

The core units of the course together make up a central unifying theme of "people, power and politics". The emphasis on people reflects the fact that the course explores politics not only at a state level but also explores the function and impact of non-state actors, communities and individuals. The concept of power is also emphasized as being particularly crucial to understanding the dynamics, tensions and outcomes of global politics. Throughout the course issues such as conflict, migration or climate change are explored through an explicitly political lens, politics providing a uniquely rich context in which to explore how people and power interact.

Global politics and international-mindedness

Developing students' international-mindedness and awareness of multiple partial perspectives and approaches – including their own – is at the heart of the global politics course. The course encourages dialogue, discussion and debate. Nurturing the capacity to listen to themselves and to others in order to understand where each is coming from is important for interpreting competing and contestable claims, but also for appreciating that political beliefs and positions are contextual and deeply held. By engaging in dialogue, discussion and debate in a respectful and attentive spirit, it is hoped that students will progress towards forming their own, well-informed provisional viewpoints. They will be better equipped to understand the hurdles of and opportunities for political progress in the real world, to build relationships with others and to resolve conflicts in a peaceful way.

The course also encourages students to reach an awareness and appreciation of both their own civic responsibility at a local level and our shared responsibility as citizens of an increasingly interconnected world. The inclusion of an engagement activity in the course reflects the importance given to not only appreciating and understanding the complex issues facing the world today, but also of engaging with them in an active and personal way.

The global politics course develops international-mindedness in students through an examination of fundamental political concepts and debates that have global significance. The course considers contemporary examples and case studies at a variety of levels, from local to global, as well as encouraging comparison between such examples and case studies. Throughout the course teachers have the opportunity to choose relevant examples and case studies to ensure that the course appropriately meets their students' needs and interests, whatever their location or cultural context.

– Global politics guide,
International Baccalaureate Organization, 2015

Introduction to the course

The global politics course is a unique examination of the significant changes that have taken place in world politics in contemporary times. The course is an interdisciplinary and multidisciplinary exploration of rapid social change, while also covering the issues that are now dominating the world stage. With the explanatory subtitle of "people, power and politics", the course focuses on four areas that are major issues of our time: power, sovereignty and international relations; human rights; development; and peace and conflict.

The course presents concepts and case studies that can be adapted to the specific interests of teachers and students. These concepts present a broad framework for a wide range of definitions and ideas about our current world; the examples and case studies ground the investigations in material that can serve as a guide for exploring how politics in the world now functions and how it has evolved and changed over time.

Individual and group perspectives

Throughout the course it is also useful to approach the key political concepts and contemporary political issues through various individual and group perspectives. This can help you to develop an appreciation of multiple points of view, and deepen your understanding of the complexity of many issues encountered in the study of global politics: our unique personalities, life experiences and the social and cultural environments we are a part of influence how we act in global politics. Three examples of important perspectives are gender, ethnicity and religion; additional individual and group perspectives will be relevant depending on the issue at stake.

Gender

Gender is an important form of identity, and can be socially constructed as well as biologically determined. Gender values can also change dramatically over time. In the last century, feminist movements successfully drew attention to women's inequality in education, employment, the home and in politics, and these issues remain pertinent in all human societies. Today, gender relations in global politics refers to contested and changing power relations between men and women in which men often dominate. Many key aspects of global politics such as human rights, development and conflict remain highly gendered, and issues such as literacy, migration, sexual violence and disease continue to impact on men, women and children differently.

Increasingly gender theorists argue that dominant understandings of masculinity may be the key to making sense of how gender relations in global politics affect us all. International organizations such as the United Nations continue to promote both gender awareness and combat discrimination towards women through the policy of gender mainstreaming. However, it is important to remember that many countries and communities still have different ideas about the rights and roles of men and women and that learning about gender can be seen to be a political act in itself.

What is a concept?

Always used as a noun, a concept is an abstract idea that includes categories of experiences or phenomena that are of the same set of thoughts, impressions and beliefs. For example, a concept album could be an album made with similar songs that express similar thoughts or styles of music. A concept car is defined by the design of the car, often of an experimental variety, creating a new set of presumptions and expectations of how the car will perform and be designed.

In global politics, concepts are bundles of ideas that refer to phenomena or experiences. Each unit has key concepts that represent what is emphasized in that section. The experiences, thoughts and phenomena they refer to are always connected to the other concepts and units in the course, and should always be seen as part of the whole of global politics.

Ethnicity

Ethnicity is a form of identity in terms of membership of an ethnic group. Individuals within an ethnic group share common characteristics, for example, cultural and societal similarities such as language, beliefs and history. Although there may be no formal agreement about what makes an ethnic identity different, many people describe themselves as descendants of a particular ethnic group and wish to preserve this status and their rights. Categories based on ethnicity may overlap with both national identities and racial identification.

Religion

Religion refers to a diverse set of belief systems. Religious identity usually has both a personal and a social dimension. On one hand, religions provide answers to questions about life, death, origins of the world and so forth, and are a way for people to find or generate meaning in their own lives. On the other hand, members of a religion share these narratives, certain rituals and, often, social norms and a moral code; being a member of the religious community is an important aspect of most religions. The powerfulness of both the personal and social dimensions of religion to devotees combined with the fact that religions assert authority from divine sources serves to strengthen the influence of religious identities and communities in global politics.

Globalization

"Global", or "globalization", has often been considered within both specialized and more public circles as a simple concept. It is often seen as a natural process that has integrated the world, with winners and losers that correspond to the centres of power and the regions controlled by those powerful countries. It is, however, important to remember that the global system is not new, and has existed for centuries through trade and exploratory missions of peoples from all over the globe. The existence of the Spice Trade or the trading posts of the Silk Road are common

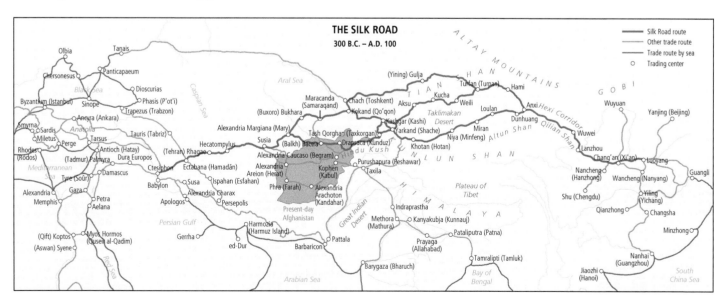

▲ The Silk Road was an ancient trade network that stretched from China to the Mediterranean. Trade along this route greatly enhanced the development of Europe, the Indian subcontinent, Persia and China.

examples of how people have long traveled great distances to interact with other cultures and communities.

The city states of the Inca Empire or the Kingdoms of Egypt are other examples of peoples spread over thousands of miles, traveling to far-away places to trade and interact for social purposes.

Globalization and social change

What has changed is the speed and distance at which these transactions take place and at which politics now functions. The world has changed more in the past 50 years than in all of human history before it: global population has grown more than tenfold since 1700, our environment no longer resembles that which existed in the pre-industrial age, military technology has advanced to the point at which one bomb can instantly vaporize every human on earth. As well as big changes, there are also smaller changes. We can now instantly communicate from one point of the globe to the other, wars and disasters are seen by populations in real time rather than days or weeks later and there are no humans on earth who have not been in contact with other groups and cultures.

▲ The ruins of Machu Picchu, sacred city of the Inca Empire

Groups ranging from small communities to governments have had to adapt to the changes in worldwide production, as local areas and indigenous peoples have reacted and often rebelled against changes occurring from outside their boundaries. Climate change has affected all populations on earth, but countries have differed in the way that they have reacted. At the same time, changes in investment by those with capital have undermined the authority of poorer governments and government policy.

This course recognizes that politics is now a complex social process and that it is almost always integrated on various levels of geographic organization. From the local, to regional, to national and global, politics affects all facets of society and plays a part in the cycles and changes in geographic organization. Global politics has become a major player in the daily social life of all of the world's citizens as it is constantly reorganizing communities, regions and nations.

This course will observe and analyse these changes through the actions of people, power and politics. Together, these add up to an integrated whole that is not a monolith but a starting point for the discussion and analysis of the way the world has changed and where it is moving towards. The course has been designed with options for teachers and students to explore their own interests as they develop and change; as you explore the course, we hope that it will help bring together the many complex facets of the world as it is today.

TOK

Global politics falls within the area of knowledge known as the human sciences. How are the methods used to gain knowledge in global politics similar or different to the methods used in other disciplines in the social sciences, such as economics or psychology? How are they similar or different to the methods used in the natural sciences?

Introduction to the Course Companion

This book is designed to accompany and supplement the IB Diploma Course in global politics. It will introduce you to meanings of global politics and its components, focusing on key concepts and issues that we now encounter on a day-to-day basis. The primary content of the Companion, like the course, is contemporary. However, humans have always been travellers, interacting with those near and far, and integrating peoples and cultures. As a result there has been a constant transformation of human cultures

Trade routes and commerce have always encouraged social and cultural interaction, from the beginnings of theatre in Ancient Rome and Athens to the Victorian merchants who encouraged London theatre that fostered Shakespeare and Marlowe, and the Japanese Kabuki that thrived in Tokyo (Edo). Particularly since the fourteenth century onward, the Silk Road, mostly used for trade from the East to the West and then to Africa and India (long before the West was exporting to the East), the expansion of Europe from the Cape of India to the Americas, and the growth of the media that started with printing and the printing press have all been spurred on by human travel and trade, their growth accompanied by a growing specialization of goods among cultures. It was not until the twentieth century, however, that we encounter "globalization" as we know it today, and it has touched and changed all humans living on earth.

Change continues to occur on all levels. Can you now imagine life without a mobile phone, radio, television or headphones? Can you imagine having to find a telephone on a street corner to make a phone call? What if did not work (as most did not in New York City, USA, in the 1970s, for example, when people had physical fights over their use)?

The lives that we live now – whether our home is on the seventy-eighth floor of a residential tower in Tokyo or a shack protected only by the pieces of tin gathered by its inhabitants – look very different from the way that most of our settled communities have lived previously. Even the tribes that continue to change their settlements, such as the nomadic Maasai of Kenya, or the simple lifestyles of the few remaining hunting and gathering groups found in remote parts of the world, are very different from how the world's peoples lived in the past.

> **ATL Thinking and communication skills**
>
> With a partner, discuss how the world has changed since you were born.

▲ Maasai warriors look out over the Laikipia Plateau, Kenya

The Massai journey along roads with SUVs and their cattle are often hit by high-speed vehicles; the remotest peoples of highland New Guinea use tools that are made in urban centres and wear clothing that may come from almost anywhere. Globalization, as you will see in the following pages, both creates more diversity in some places and encourages a similarity in daily life in others.

The course assumes that politics is a result of complex social organization and that it is almost always integrated on multiple levels of geographic organization. From the local, to regional, to national and global, politics affects all facets of geographic space and plays a part in the cycles and changes in geographic organization as change takes place. Global politics has become a major player in the daily social life of all of the world's citizens as it is constantly reorganizing communities, regions and nations.

The current integration of the world's peoples has often made understanding peoples on their own terms more difficult, as global politics is transforming the world around them. Globalization is a complex subject, requiring us to look beyond the assumptions and to examine instead the possible meanings behind what we observe. Globalization has taught us to appreciate diversity and to recognize that differences are not dangerous and should be celebrated. Most importantly, studying global politics helps us to find solutions to the problems of being human in an ever-changing contemporary world.

Many of us in today's world will be required to travel, conduct business and participate in the global economy. At the same time, peoples around the globe are experiencing rapid and extreme changes as whole communities are forced to migrate to other areas to make a living, to find necessities (such as water and food), to look for subsistence, or to avoid dangerous conflicts.

The challenge facing all of us in our world is setting aside our own beliefs in an effort to understand the beliefs and practices of others. We must learn to describe, understand and interpret meaning as we approach contemporary issues such as poverty, racism, and environmental disasters.

Recent contributions to the study of global politics have broadened the scope of our studies of human communities. Globalization has changed the way we produce daily goods; for example, a lot of the basic production of goods for consumption has shifted from the Eurocentric countries to the former colonial states. At the same time as the face of re-industrialization in former colonial states mimics the look of early industrialization in the capital-intensive countries – a good example is the role of women in early industrialization in the United States – the phenomenon of globalization has exposed the populations of the West to different forms of social organization, bringing in experiences and visions that went unnoticed during colonial rule. The voices and cultures of formerly colonialized peoples became a subject for students of globalization, providing corrections to assumptions about peoples outside of the dominant West.

As another example, the reaction of indigenous peoples that are now threatened by the power and authority of outside forces are now

TOK

Are there times when we are morally obliged to act on what we know?

frequently taking the world stage. From the Zapitistas in Southern Mexico to the cultures in Indonesia and New Guinea which are endangered by the economics of globalization, these groups are now fighting to maintain ways of life that may go back hundreds or even thousands of years. June Nash (1994) tells us that the role of the researcher has become more complex and the ethics of study more of a concern. For professional academic organizations it means that much thought must be put into how we carry out our work and who it benefits or potentially harms. All academic organizations have a code of ethics, the primary tenant of which is to "do no harm". Likewise, all colleges, universities and other institutions conducting research are required to have an Institutional Review Board (IRB), which reviews research proposals to make sure that the subject, whether animal or human, is not harmed or put in danger by the research or after the research is concluded.

The sections in this Companion follow the primary units of the course and their key concepts and themes. They may or may not be followed in order according to the teacher's arrangement of topics. Learning ways to place yourself within the context of global politics is one of the major objectives of this book.

An EZLN banner draped across a gate in Mexico City; the text reads "Everything for everyone!" The Ejército Zapatista de Liberación Nacional (Zapatista Army of National Liberation, commonly known as the Zapatistas) are a revolutionary militant group based in Chiapas, the southernmost state of Mexico.

Political issues: When we think of politics[1]

Politics, as most of us have been taught, refers to the actions taken in the formation and maintenance of the state or other governing entity. Traditional definitions assume, for example, that there are no politics without that governing entity, so hunting and gathering (band) groups do not have internal politics. With state formation, politics play the role of maintaining the power of the state by the inclusion and exclusion of peoples and competing formations. The goal of the state is to produce, as the political philosopher Antonio Gramsci elaborated, hegemony, a stable agreement between ruling entities and the rest of society. "Political issues", given this definition, would be any events or actions that are in the arena of state power and its maintenance.

The level that this definition works on is that of the state. What is missed are the actions on the global, international, regional, local or community level. The "state" definition of politics was accepted by academic disciplines and assumed as popular knowledge through the Second World War and particularly through the 1950s, when states consolidated their power and their influence over less powerful (and particularly less developed) social formations.

More recently, however, and particularly with the onset of a growing globalization of industry and development, both "politics" and "political issues" have taken on a broader and more inclusive meaning. Given the transformative changes in global social organization that has taken place during the past 50 years, politics and political issues have come to have meaning on numerous levels not included in traditional definitions. Regional conflicts, multinational organizations, an

---

[1] This discussion is from the *Global politics guide*, International Baccalaureate Organization, 2015

increase in poverty and violence, indigenous rights and the effects of climate change, as examples among many, have all come to the world stage. Politics is now part of our everyday lives as communities and international bodies compete for labour and resources, and geographic entities are often confronted with power and influence from outside their boundaries. Politics is no longer simply a state phenomenon but a global reality.

For global politics, a political issue is any question of global interaction that permits, invites and calls for critical examination. Political issues populate the agendas of politicians and policy-makers; they occupy the minds of CEOs of global corporations and local social entrepreneurs; they are discussed in media and over a cup of coffee; they motivate art, they are deeply grounded in history and culture, and they are a part of our daily lives. Importantly for the central unifying theme of the course, political issues reveal how power is distributed and operates in a social organization and how people think about and engage in their communities and the wider world on matters that affect their well- or ill-being, including survival.

Political issues can be found on all levels of global politics. Taking the example of the political theme of climate change, relating issues permeate all aspects of politics.

Defining an interesting political issue in the wider real-world situation they are studying is often an early and key step for students in making progress towards their understanding of global politics. This is particularly important in order for you to see the connections between the key concepts and examples in the core units, to determine an appropriate reflective focus for the engagement activity and to select an engaging aspect of the higher level case studies for oral presentation.

Geographic levels and levels of analysis

In this course, a level refers to a *unit of analysis* of the inhabited world. For global politics, levels run from the geographic whole of the political world to the smallest area under study, and the unit of analysis is the major entity, or the "what" or "whom" that is being analysed. The most common levels now found in the study of global politics are global, international, national, regional, and local, with the concept of community intersecting all of the levels as discussed below. In addition, the global systems theorist Immanuel Wallerstein (1974) also argued that a world system separated the geographic spaces of the world into "cores", "peripheries" and "semi-peripheries", depending on their roles in the world economy, and, until recently, these designations were the most commonly found in the analysis of global politics.

The core economies were the most capital-intensive and powerful countries, the peripheries were the least capital-intensive countries and the areas most readily exploited by the core economies by

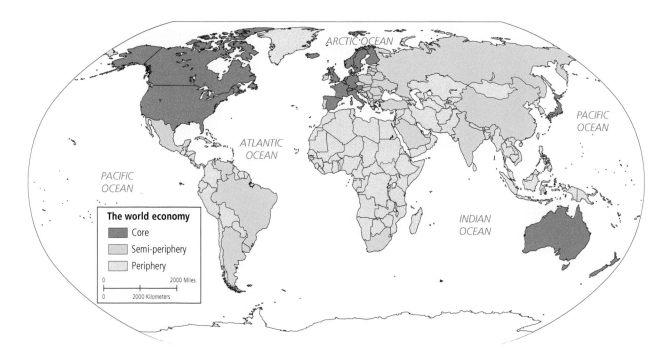

the extraction of labour, capital and commodities, and the semi-peripheral countries represented the developing nations. The problem with these units of analysis was that they assumed unidirectional relationships that underplayed the role of the people in the peripheries and semi-peripheries in shaping the practices of the core. Many also questioned the sudden emergence of the world system in Wallerstein's analysis, arguing that a world system existed long before the birth of global capitalism in the 1600s, the starting point of his observation.

The terms defined below are more inclusive and recognize that these designations are meant to represent interrelations that affect each other in the world today. While stronger and more capital-intensive regions may dominate local ones, the local areas also affect the strategies and functioning of the dominating forces. So, for example, while until recently the Soviet Union dominated Eastern Europe, the countries and cultures of Eastern Europe had a strong influence on the economy, politics and culture of the Soviet Union. The loss of Eastern Europe from Soviet domination was a major cause for political change in both regions, just as (former) colonial states influenced the day-to-day operations of colonial powers.

Below are the terms most commonly used as units of analysis of the global system. Levels are most easily seen through institutional forms; global institutions, such as the United Nations or the World Bank, clearly illustrate the level on which they are functional, just as national legislatures or city governmental departments portray local levels of operations. They distinguish among geographic areas but are not discrete units. There are, however, many issues and questions that are not institutional in nature and operate on varying levels. Depending on the question considered or the study conducted, one or more of these terms

TOK

How can we judge whether one model is better than another?

will be employed as descriptive mechanisms and key concepts within the sphere of global politics. The illustrations provided are only examples among many that could be used for these terms.

Global

In the context of global politics, the term global describes events and trends that have far-reaching and long-term impact across the globe, cutting geographic areas. Examples include economic globalization, climate change, appeals to human rights, water depletion, global governance (the United Nations), and the organization of corporations.

▲ The United Nations Climate Change Conference, 2016

National

National refers to the geographic boundaries of a particular state. Topics that could be studied under this level include (but are not limited to) economic crisis or economic change, political and legal reforms, changes in governance, questions of cultural practice (education, languages) and geographic borders.

International

For our purposes, the term international represents events and trends that have a narrower impact than global events and trends. Nonetheless, they have implications for several geographic areas, for example, a particular region (see below), but not only limited to that region. Examples include various international organizations, Non-governmental organizations (NGOs), multi-national corporations (MNCs), international law, and international trade, diasporas and migratory movements.

Regional

Regional for our discussion refers to units of analysis that cover specific geographic areas, such as the Middle East, Central Asia, Western and Eastern Europe, sub-Saharan Africa, South Asia, Asia-Pacific, Latin America, among others. Topics that could be studied under this level could include (but are not limited to) the European Union, North American Free Trade Agreement, the Arab League, the African Union, and movements that cross geographic boundaries (such as indigenous claims to land, or the re-emergence of languages) and ecological dimensions.

▲ The logo of the African Union

Local

Local in the context of global politics is the geographic area where social organization is created and where culture is transmitted from one generation to the next. It is always in relation to larger geographic spheres, and it is the place where cultural practices are defended against outside intrusion. This level can represent a geographic space as small as a gated community or as large as a city or region. "Local" is defined by its inhabitants and the practices of its residents. The incorporation of globalization and its consequences on time, access to resources and control over labour and social reproduction have altered the way that social scientists think about the local. In the attempt to integrate shifts in political influence resulting from global processes, globalization studies have tended to marginalize the local and its role in determining the course of globalization and global politics.

▲ Aid is handed out following a typhoon in the Philippines

Place

In the context of global politics and its analysis, place is the geographic location where action occurs. It can be the position of bounded communities, states and countries where peoples live and reproduce over generations or it may be the locale of conflict grounded in ethnic rivalry or economic competition. It is a site of affiliation and by definition, either positive or negative, of common interests. Its particular usefulness as a concept for the study of global politics is in the discussion of boundaries, settled populations, migration and immigration. Place is often the unit of analysis for peoples fighting for their autonomy against the demands and power of external forces, and the politics of place is integral to the discussion of space and the destruction of political, economic and cultural boundaries.

Space

Space as a unit of analysis in global politics has increasingly become a term of debate in the analysis of the autonomy of peoples, regions and nations around the globe. As with "local" and "place", space is a social construct. Many now claim that "place" is an outdated term as the concept of space argues against geography as a unit of analysis in the study of political power and capital accumulation. The increasing movement of peoples around the globe has also questioned the importance of place as a key concept in the analysis of global politics, but it is often forgotten that while global strategies are frequently aimed at controlling geographic spaces, they may also reinforce the resistance of local struggles based on the politics of place. What is important to consider, however, is that both place and space are social constructs and may be integrated according to the actions and social organization of populations. While unions and multi-national corporations, as examples, exist over space, their membership and management is deeply grounded in the politics of place.

The concept of community

The idea of community is one of the most debated concepts in the social sciences. Until the 1980s, the definition of community had remained relatively stable as geographically based groups of people with similar interests, mutual support, cultural traits and transmission that featured interaction on a face-to-face basis and the intention of reproducing the community over time. The most commonly held view was that communities must include not only spatial and ecological dimensions but institutional and emotional ones, or those aspects of social life (schools) that transmitted culture from one generation to the next. In these terms, it is the basis for the analysis of human identity and solidarity. During the past 25 years, however, processes of globalization have led social scientists to rethink standard and assumed definitions. Can we talk of community outside the constraints of territory or, further, without place? With the introduction of satellite communication technologies, and the advent of diverse methods of maintaining interest groups that spread similar interests beyond boundaries and across physical landscapes, the definition of community has become intertwined with debates about globalization and the role and place of peoples within it.

The debates around the concept of community include the role of migration and diasporas in maintaining and reproducing interest groups and the spread of technologies such as the Internet that can keep people with similar interests connected by affiliation rather than face-to-face interaction. Whether these "communities of taste", as the French anthropologist Jane Jacobs has referred to them, have the ability to reproduce themselves and maintain their interactions over time has become part of the debate around the definition of community. Communities have traditionally been viewed as long-term and the maintenance of community has become one of the rallying cries of resistance movements fighting intrusion from the outside. By putting the emphasis on affiliation rather than physical association, space, place and time become contested. Space in the sense of territory and place; time in the sense of maintenance, stability and social reproduction. These "communities of taste" or "taste cultures" are most often driven by the market and, as such, change often. So then, according to this reasoning, do communities.

With this broadening and opening-up of the definition of community in recent years, the question arises about the usefulness of the term for describing groups of people under specific conditions. There is agreement among many social scientists that the term remains useful as long as it is defined under specific circumstances. The creation of short-term communities over the Internet is not the same as geographically based communities founded on face-to-face interaction that have existed over time, many of which are fighting to maintain their existence under increasingly difficult circumstances as the forces of globalization encourage and/or force the movements of people around the globe. The possibilities of redefining or eliminating boundaries in our studies have raised questions of voice and agency for the people of the world that are the vessels of global politics and has altered the narratives that they can provide.

Ultimately, the use of the concept of community as a unit of analysis will depend on the topic studied. Those who are interested in the creation of communities by use of the Internet as a vehicle for communication will be different from those defending their land against outside forces and the destruction of culture and social organization. Some have advocated for the elimination of the term as it is too loaded with past definition and meaning, while others have insisted that the position of "community" as a vehicle for organization and the defence of culture and social reproduction still plays an extremely important role in the discussion of the dynamics of power, globalization and global politics, boundaries, space and place.

People, power and politics

An introduction to the study of globalization and politics

This Companion has been organized so that each of the sections begins with the key concepts and themes that will be discussed in the following pages. Each section brings with it a contemporary example or description of a set of circumstances, and how others have explored the particular topic under discussion, either through excerpts from monographs that emphasized the topic or examples of discussions and debates that relate to the topic's focus. As the tables on pages ix–xiv show, you will find that all units relate back to the first section which focuses on people, providing an integration that emphasizes the current experience of peoples around the globe as it gives us insight into change, both social and structural. While providing material for discussion, the sections then conclude with suggestions for further research and reading, including references that have been used in the section or can be investigated for further work.

Examples of the study of globalization

Our discussion of globalization has thus far emphasized that this worldwide interaction of peoples is not a new process. Humans as traders, travellers, and members of nomadic communities reveals our condition as social animals; it is the type of globalization under discussion and the contemporary changes that have occurred that is the basis of our course and this Companion.

Class discussion

What would constitute good evidence in global politics?

Our knowledge of the presence of global relations in the forms of trade routes and exchange transactions stretches back as early as 1200 to 1400 AD; definitions of this form of globalization are in the description of economic relations among and between communities. We also have records from traveling missionaries, especially Jesuits, who made detailed and careful notes about the communities they encountered and in which they worked. They also provided descriptions of daily life and organization and culture, enabling a whole field of study we now refer to as *ethnohistory.* Scholars of ethnohistory such as Eleanor Leacock and Richard Lee countered many assumptions we made about life before the market and capitalist society, providing a counter-balance to accepted lore.

The consistent scholarly study of globalization began in the late twentieth century, particularly after the Second World War, when trade and the international division of labour changed on a radical scale. Karl Polanyi's *The Great Transformation* (1944) and Eric Wolf's *Europe and the People without History* (1981), as well as Immanual Wallerstein's *The Modern World System* (1974) are recognized as seminal works in this discussion, as is David Harvey's *The Condition of Postmodernity* (1991). Polanyi traces the history of economic evolution and the division of labour, or how communities assign and complete labour tasks required for living. The most significant change, in Polanyi's view, is the transition from "production for use", meaning that people produced goods for their own and their communities' use, to "production for exchange", in which production was organized so that objects could be produced that would then be traded with others for goods not found in the local community. Polanyi takes this distinction in how the community is organized for production from Karl Marx, who saw that this change would necessitate a major reorganization of community life as well as signify an evolution of economic trade.

▲ Şavaklar nomadic tribe in Keşiş Mountain, Erzincan, Turkey

The colonial period (circa 1800 to 1950+)

While the course is about current events and circumstances, it often helps to have some historical background to the events of today. It is important to remember that the course is based on contemporary global politics. However, these notes will provide the background to which these politics emerged. The colonial period in world history significantly changed the way that civilizations were evolving all over the globe. Most of the colonizers were European, while the colonized ranged from Latin America and Africa to the Caribbean and South Pacific. The colonizers travelled the world looking for free labour and resources; in many places it was brutal and close to, if not outright, genocide. Other civilizations experienced a more nuanced and paternalistic rule, although it was clear who was in power and who was not. Most of the resources and goods left the colonized country and were shipped back to the ruling power, while slavery accounted for much free labour in the more powerful economies such as the United States and some European countries.

▲ The colonized and their French colonizers

What's important to remember here is that the colonized were functioning societies with their own cultures, rules and ways of producing the goods that kept them alive and trading with others. Colonization put an immediate stop to self-rule and began the movement from simple to more complex societies.

References and further reading

Goody, Jack 2006, "Globalization and the Domestic Group," in M. Kirsch, *Inclusion and Exclusion in the Global Arena,"* pp. 31-41, London: Routledge.

Harvey, David. 1991. *The Condition of Postmodernity.*

Kirsch, Max 2006. *Inclusion and Exclusion in the Global Arena,* New York: Routledge

Leacock, Eleanor and Lee, Richard. 1982. *Politics and History in Band Societies,* Cambridge: Cambridge University Press.

Leacock, Eleanor. 1982. *Myths of Male Dominance,* New York: Monthly Review Press

Nash, June 1984 *Women, Men and the International Division of Labor,* Albany New York: SUNY Press

Polanyi, Karl. 1944. *The Great Transformation.*

Wallerstein, Immanual. 1974. *The Modern World System.*

Wolf, Eric. 1981. *Europe and the People without History.*

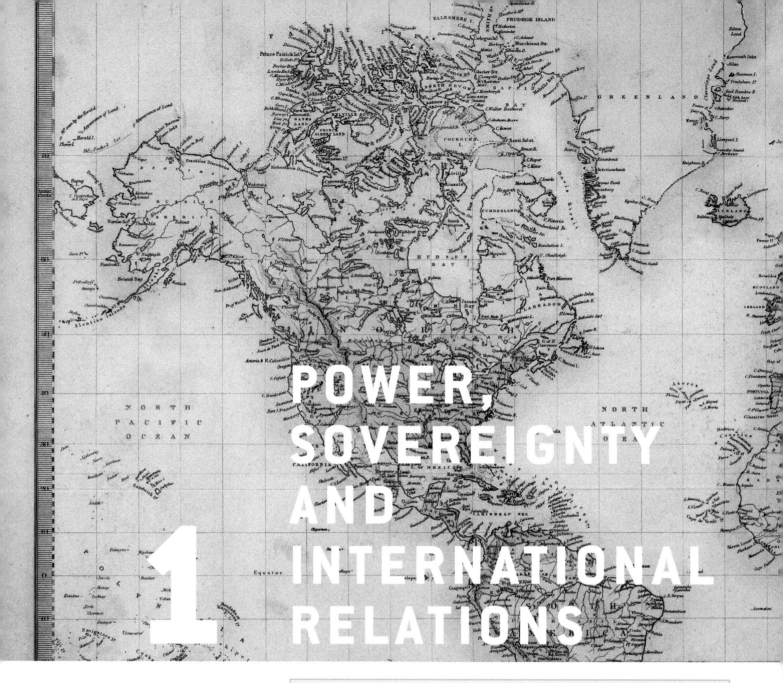

POWER, SOVEREIGNTY AND INTERNATIONAL RELATIONS

1

Key concepts

→ Power

→ Sovereignty

→ Legitimacy

→ Interdependence

Learning outcomes

→ Nature of power

→ Operation of state power in global politics

→ Function and impact of international organizations and non-state actors in global politics

→ Nature and extent of interactions in global politics

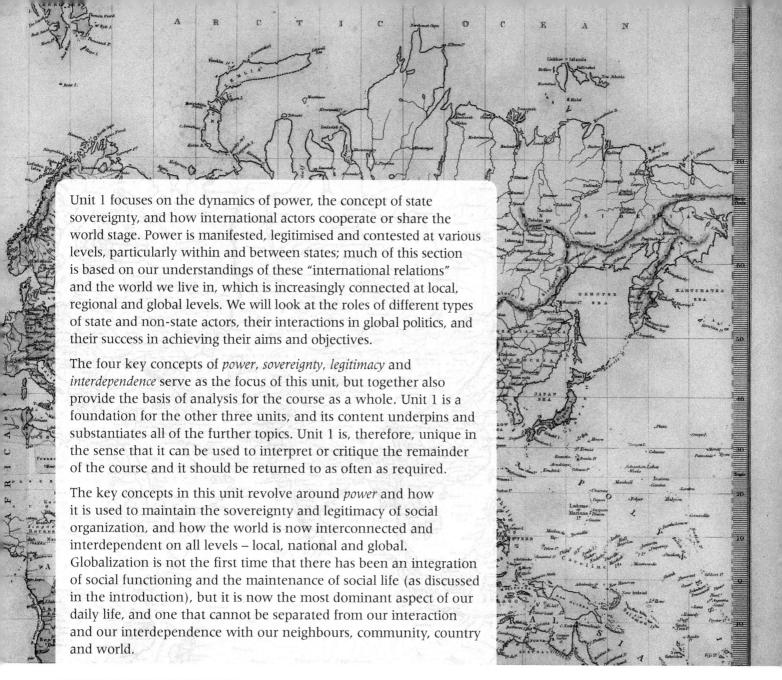

Unit 1 focuses on the dynamics of power, the concept of state sovereignty, and how international actors cooperate or share the world stage. Power is manifested, legitimised and contested at various levels, particularly within and between states; much of this section is based on our understandings of these "international relations" and the world we live in, which is increasingly connected at local, regional and global levels. We will look at the roles of different types of state and non-state actors, their interactions in global politics, and their success in achieving their aims and objectives.

The four key concepts of *power*, *sovereignty*, *legitimacy* and *interdependence* serve as the focus of this unit, but together also provide the basis of analysis for the course as a whole. Unit 1 is a foundation for the other three units, and its content underpins and substantiates all of the further topics. Unit 1 is, therefore, unique in the sense that it can be used to interpret or critique the remainder of the course and it should be returned to as often as required.

The key concepts in this unit revolve around *power* and how it is used to maintain the sovereignty and legitimacy of social organization, and how the world is now interconnected and interdependent on all levels – local, national and global. Globalization is not the first time that there has been an integration of social functioning and the maintenance of social life (as discussed in the introduction), but it is now the most dominant aspect of our daily life, and one that cannot be separated from our interaction and our interdependence with our neighbours, community, country and world.

Key questions

1   How is power expressed in global politics?

2   On what geographic levels does global politics operate?

The nature of power

Power is a matter of relationships. Power is also situational. It cannot be viewed as a unitary or independent force but as an aspect of relations among people. The ability to direct another's actions or a country's economy is always situated within a context that has increasingly become the subject matter of social inquiry. Power cannot be assumed, but needs to be explored and studied in order to discover the patterns and bases on which it operates.

Eric Wolf, one of the most prominent scholars in the study of the concept of power and its application to social analysis, outlined four types of power. In his words, "power works differently in interpersonal relations, in institutional arenas and on the level of whole societies" (1999: 5).

For global politics, it is Wolf's *structural power* that is the most useful in studying the relationships between key concepts and units in this course. Structural power includes the people, power and politics that feature in global politics. There are other types of power that also fit into our study. These include theories of power and types of power, such as military, social and cultural, unilateral and multilateral, hard and soft, which all present differing kinds of power relevant to the particular example under study, and will be discussed throughout this Companion.

▲ A collection of international flags in Munich, Germany

Power in context

The past century has been an era of revolutions, genocides and major wars in almost every part of the globe. Millions have died from violence in conflicts over religion, ethnicity and colour, and what all of these conflicts have in common are the adversarial claims over the resources that support the basic ability to reproduce life. There are many communities that are today in danger of extinction and many more that are in dire poverty. Over the past 50 years, the configuration of the world's resources has changed dramatically. More than half of the world's population now lives on less than US$2.00 per day, and one child (under five) dies every three seconds from poverty – that is some 60 million between 2000 and 2006. How did this happen?

When we observe the world today, we notice first the many divisions based on physical geography, but quickly revealed are also divisions based on race, ethnicity, religion and the many ways by which people and communities reproduce themselves and the contexts of their daily living. These contexts are interwoven with divisions based on nations, power, politics and claims to authority. Every day the news – available by radio in even the remotest of villages – tells stories of conflicts and quests for peace, of battles and genocides and attempts at reconciliation, of crises and the hopes of peace by the citizens of a globe who are now all interconnected in ways that we have never been before. There are no longer isolated peoples, regions or countries, and one region's

TOK

Can we have beliefs or knowledge that are independent of our culture? Does global politics seek to discover truths about human nature, or is it based on assumptions about human nature?

wars over oil are another's crises over food and basic resources. The ways in which the world's resources are used have become issues of power and authority. Scientists now predict that the current conflicts over energy resources will be dwarfed by future claims over water, as desertification takes away livable spaces and famines are initiated by increasing droughts brought on by industrialization and global warming. Dams, for example, often affect the availability of water thousands of miles away, while pollution is making more of the Earth's water unusable for food production.

A number of questions may immediately be raised:

- How do decisions affecting the global and local distribution of resources get made?

- How is authority determined?

- Who decides who has the right to build dams or burn forests, or worse, allow the genocide of an area's population?

- What is a government, and who decides what it does?

Anthropology tells us that there are many different types of government and ways of reproducing human social life, and that in the context of human history, government is a relatively recent development. Egalitarian societies have been a common thread throughout most of human history, characterized by equality between men and women, between groups, and among communities. The earliest forms of the differentiation of people is based on age and sex, but even these divisions do not necessarily mean that there is an inequality between older and younger or between men and women. These early differences are *task* oriented, with older and younger people performing different aspects of labour to maintain community life, or they are biologically necessitated, such as the case with women bearing children.

So how did we get to this point of ever more complex forms of social hierarchy, power, and authority? What is the difference that people experience in a simple or a complex society? We have seen in the introduction chapter that earlier societies are not just societies and cultures minus some of the characteristics of more modern ones. They are *qualitatively* different from the societies and culture that most of us live in today, and our experience of daily life is, by definition, very different from those who lived hundreds or thousands of years ago. We are unique, indeed.

▲ Desertification necessitates permanent crop protection in many parts of the world

TOK

Can a person or group of people know what is best for other people?

▲ A Somali National Government soldier walks past burning debris following a suspected suicide bombing

States and statehood in the contemporary world

In contemporary society states are the best-known mechanisms of social control and social integration. Designed to promote and protect "the will of the people", they have their own internal dynamics. There are many and varied kinds of states in the contemporary world, and not all have been successful. We have many examples of failed states in our world today – states that can no longer maintain social control over their populations. A few recent examples include Libya and Somalia, and there are others that are fast approaching that point. As the *New Yorker* reports (2016), Tunisia is the only country to emerge from the Arab revolutions of 2011 as a functioning democracy. Mexico has become dangerously close to becoming a failed state with the influx and violence of drugs and cartels, as has Colombia and other countries of that region for the same reason.

Many claim that the term "states" has become outdated as boundaries are no longer legitimate, and the sovereignty of states has been questioned by trade agreements and large multi-national corporations. Also, the porous nature of many states with the immigration and migration of millions of people around the globe questions the stability of territory as it has been traditionally defined.

▲ 9 March 2011: Rebel soldiers fighting against Colonel Muammar Gaddafi fire a Katyusha rocket near Ras Lanuf, Libya

Other types of power

Beyond those discussed above, other descriptions and reference to power have come into play as analysts try to understand the nature of power and its sources. Joseph Nye, for example, in his book, *Bound to Lead: The Changing Nature of American Power* (1990), uses the terms "hard" and "soft" power as descriptors of kinds of interventions that are designed to bring about the desired change, whether coming from the outside or within a geographic level. As their names suggest, "hard" power refers to the use of force and threats of force to influence the decision-making of those in charge; "soft" power lies more in the realm of negotiation, promises of aid, cooperation and other non-military means of influencing change. Recently, the descriptor of "smart" power has been added to this matrix, and although there is debate about its first use and who used it, there seems to be some consensus that it came from speeches made by Hillary Clinton as she ran for President in the 2016 election in the USA. "Smart" refers to the combination of hard and soft power, the ability to use both when called for, or one or the other when necessary.

Other kinds of power used in this Companion include military power, economic power, political power, social power, individual versus collective power, and universal versus multilateral power. It is important to remember that these are descriptors, not analyses, and that the type of power described must be part of a larger discussion and analysis of power and its uses. For example, Wolf's structural power refers to social conditions and the use of labour to maintain social realms. Soft power is a descriptor for a kind of approach to the use of power, and needs to be connected to the analysis of particular situations and the strategies that are being employed.

Violence and structural violence

What is violence? As citizens, we customarily assume a commonplace definition that encompasses physical acts among individuals, groups or nations. However, there are subtler and less obvious forms of violence that are inherent in the diverse forms of inequality and unequal access to social resources. In today's world, violence is inherently integrated into the larger process of political economy and social life. Derived from liberation theologians, structural violence is the situated place characterized by social inequality that is exerted systematically – "that is, indirectly – by everyone who belongs to a certain social order… The concept of structural violence is intended to inform the study of the social machinery of oppression" (Farmer, 2004).

Along with that violence and oppression, however, is the need to integrate the power that generates and maintains structural violence, and by which society is kept operationally functional. States often employ structural violence through laws and other mechanisms that would make it seem that the cause of this kind of violence occurs naturally. If poverty is a major problem, then, the reason for it becomes one of individual failure rather than problems with the system. The state thus protects itself from becoming the object of blame for the unequal access to resources that often causes the violence of poverty and the silence of those in poverty.

Social scientists have been interested in structural violence as part of a study of power to analyse events associated with globalization, and that includes an analysis and reconstruction of events around the world, on scales that vary from the household to regional and continental organization. One of the more insidious characteristics of structural violence, as Farmer points out, is the erasure of history and the machinery of suffering, and how suffering and poverty generate violence (Farmer, 2004).

ATL **Research skills**

Research the first use of the term "smart power" and why it was introduced.

Class discussion

What is violence? Discuss your individual interpretations of the term.

The nation state, the result of a complex division of labour and exchange relationships, is a political and territorial entity. "Nation" implies that there is a common ethnicity and cultural characteristics, such as language, while "state" most often refers to the sovereign nature of the area in which a state has been formed. While we know that state formations are the result of stratified socio-economic classes that have developed formal legal authority backed by force, it is less clear when a state becomes a nation state, or whether the nation can exist before state formation takes place. Nationalism has historically been a mechanism by which peoples are united under common characteristics with a sense of identity, generally backed by a government that defines a state. Whether nations existed before a state is formed is a research question, and many theories exist on both sides of the issue.

States are classified as sovereign if they are independent entities not controlled by other territories or entities. They are political entities governed by a single form of government. People living within a sovereign state are subject to the rules, laws and duties as citizens of the state entity. Here we also have to consider internal sovereignty, for in order for sovereignty to exist, there has to be an agreement within the nation's population that the state is legitimate and the holders of the will of the people. Here is where sovereignty can become very complicated, for while the nation's leaders may assert to others around the globe that the sovereignty of the nation is stable and real, those inside that nation may not agree with their leaders, and conflict within the state can be a problem for the wishes of its leaders, elected or not.

The French Revolution

During the French Revolution less than 50 per cent of the population spoke French, and even fewer spoke it well. Here is an example where the state clearly did come before the nation. The French Revolution solidified the role of the state as a generator of common identity, creating policies and mandates that united the "French People" under a dominant language, culture, and territory.

Nations and states have goals to unite people under a single rubric of political rule. The Italian philosopher Antonio Gramsci (2011), in his *Prison Notebooks*, coined the term *hegemony*: the goal of harmony through the agreement of the peoples under state control. However, this is not always possible, and he states that when the creation of hegemony becomes impossible, then the state often uses force. The elites that are the beneficiaries of state unity generate their own ideologies to justify their positions as managers and leaders, as well as rally the population for war when it is to the advantage of state organization or when the state is threatened by internal or external forces. They are also the generators of what is now often referred to as *structural violence*, or the institutional mechanisms by which people are discriminated against or oppressed because of their particular ethnicity, race or gender. The object of the managers of a state is to provide legitimacy for its existence that incorporates its peoples and resources. Other definitions of states represent the political realities of the area and its history. The present circumstances that are transforming areas, territories, legitimacy and social control are transforming past circumstances with the realities of the rapidly changing world system.

At the start of the twentieth century, there were approximately 50 acknowledged states (Crawford, 2007: 3). Crawford tells us that before the Second World War there were approximately 75. He continues:

> The emergence of so many new States represents one of the major political developments of the twentieth century. It has changed the character of international law and the practice of international organizations. It has been one of the most important sources of international conflict (2007: 3).

The most common forms of states are unitary states, federal states, confederations, democratic states, militarized states, fragile/failed states and rising states. The differences between these types of states are predominately political: unitary states, for example, are organized by a centralized power that incorporates various territories and resources central to its functioning; confederations are unions of countries and territories with a centralized authority; militarized states are groups of territories organized for military action, and so on.

In the contemporary world, types of states are changing often, with confederations coming together to defend territorial resources. There is an evolving nature of state sovereignty that is militated by stronger states and, importantly, multi-national corporations. These states must continually justify their legitimacy with the people under their governance. It is not unusual in the contemporary world to witness changes of governments, wars between states that were formerly close allies, and changing allegiances among governments and other non-governmental entities. Some of these changes are influenced by international law, challenges to the Westphalian conception of state sovereignty, or the ultimate power of the central administration. There has been much debate about the possibility of this sort of state, given the interactions of trade and challenges to centralized law, such as supra-nationality, humanitarian intervention, indigenous rights, and social movements. It is better conceptualized as an ideal that never quite comes into full completion as competing stakeholders keep the politics of states in motion.

TOK

To what extent do the language and concepts we use shape or determine, rather than just describe, the world?

Research skills

Research the Westphalian concept of state. With a partner, discuss whether this a model that most countries follow today.

Social order, ideology and power

In order for power to be sustained, it must be justified, either by convincing people that existing forms of power are justified and good, or by force – whether that be the blocking and prevention of resistance against the existing forms of power or by all-out warfare. This justification of relationships of power is accomplished through the application of *ideology,* or "ideas in the service of power".

Wolf distinguishes between *ideas* and *ideology,* for, as he notes,

> *the term "ideas" is intended to cover the entire range of mental constructs rendered manifest in public representations, populating all human domains…"ideology" needs to be used more restrictively, in that "ideologies" suggest unified schemes or configurations developed to underwrite or manifest power.* (1999: 4)

In simple terms, *ideology* means a way of thinking about a situation, a context, or the world. When we are told, for example, that the pursuit of life, liberty and happiness is best brought about by supporting the policies of a current administration (whether that be national, local or institutional), we are being presented with an ideology that hopes to direct our thinking and our action. The goal of ideology, according to Antonio Gramsci (1891–1937), the Italian political theorist and resistance leader who fought the Fascist government of Mussolini, is to create a peaceful state of social stasis through *hegemony,* where the dominating world-view is integrated throughout society as a whole. The object of hegemony is to convince all within a society that the government is working towards their best interests, and this is accomplished in a number of ways, including education, the Church, military ideology, the penal system (Foucault, 1975) and the control over media and everyday cultural life. Where hegemony cannot be achieved through the incorporation or co-optation of competing ideologies, force is used, as we can see from the brutal actions of Mussolini in the 1930s. Gramsci, prolific in his writing, died in 1937 as a political prisoner, having been in prison since 1926. The point that Gramsci made clear was that ideologies represent powerful agendas, providing a "social cement" (Therborn, 1980: 4).

The sophistication of an ideology, then, is found in its ability to construct a convincing logic that *includes* the reservations and resistance of its critics, thereby creating the lack of conflict that leads to hegemony. When force becomes necessary the actual seizure may only be momentary; it is an act that is necessary to gain power and domination. In other words, to exercise power, there must be mechanisms in place to keep it going, to keep social tensions from tearing the domination apart. The successful implementation of hegemony creates a "common sense" that all understand and share, it becomes an integral part of the culture. It is this "common sense" in a community that we look for to understand the mechanisms by which the interplay between power and its exercise takes place (Kirsch, 2001: 43).

▲ Antonio Gramsci, 1891–1937, wrote widely on philosophy, politics and linguistics; he was also a founding member of the Communist Party of Italy

1.3 Non-state actors

Along with the authority of nations and states, non-state actors, from the United Nations to smaller organizations, are playing a larger role on the world stage. We can refer to these types of actors as civil society, or the portion of society that acts as an alternative to coercive state power. In simple terms, non-state actors are those that operate outside the sphere of governmental control. Unit 3 has many good examples of non-state actors and their contributions to social movements and to politics. Some good examples of these types of actors are Human Rights Watch, Amnesty International, the United Way and academic discipline associations such as the American Anthropological Association. These organizations often take positions on the debates around the local, regional, international and global actions and policies of the day, and are often more useful in the struggle to change long-held positions than states themselves.

Another type of non-state actor that has gained much attention are the interrelated state organizations or IGOs (intergovernmental organizations), the most prominent being the United Nations. We will refer more to the United Nations below, and Unit 2 also uses the United Nations as a focal point for the discussion of human rights. Other IGOs that have gained prominence are the trade unions that exist on almost every continent, such as the African Union, and more government-related organizations such as the World Bank and the International Monetary Fund. The Union of International Organizations (UIO) lists 68,000 international organizations, adding somewhere in the area of 1,200 per year. Not all of these organizations are active (the UIO estimates that about half are active and half are not), and these include both NGOs and IGOs. Other prominent organizations that play a large role in global politics are multi-national (sometimes referred to as transnational) corporations (MNCs), such as General Electric, Westinghouse, BP, Exxon Mobil and, more recently, Facebook and Twitter. As these companies operate in many different countries and interact with their governments, they can exert strong influences on every level of global politics. *The Economist* reported that in 2012, for example, General Electric held more assets than any other financial firm in the world (10 June 2012). As they report:

> *Of the 100 companies with the most foreign assets, 17 hold over 90% of their assets abroad, including ArcelorMittal, Nestlé, Anheuser-Busch InBev and Vodafone. Their share of foreign sales is also substantially larger than GE's. More than half of GE's 300,000-strong workforce is based outside America; Toyota, which has slightly more employees, only has 38% of its 326,000 workers abroad.* (2012; accessed 16 June 2016)

These new realities, created in the midst of globalization, have their clearest effect on the local level. This is demonstrated by empty streets where stores and factories used to be, abandoned houses that people have forsaken in their quest to find work in other areas where, they

▲ The logo of the African Union

▲ The logo of General Electric

hope, production has not yet moved outside the country, a drastic dip in the population that affects the ability of families to maintain ties as generations split apart in the movement of peoples, and the rise of poverty generated by a lack of jobs and the entitlements such as healthcare and retirement benefits that jobs provide.

For example, in Kirsch's 1988 ethnography, *In the Wake of the Giant*, he shows how a healthy, family-dominated town in the north-east of the United States became torn apart as parts of its major employer, General Electric, went overseas or closed down. Pittsfield, Massachusetts, USA, where this ethnography was carried out, was part of a deindustrialization that blanketed much of the north-east and Midwest of the United States in the 1970s and 1980s, splitting generations as younger members of the community moved away in search of work, and creating crises as sources of pollution from the General Electric plant resulted in health crises that the company would not take responsibility for. The irony in this particular case is that the head of General Electric at that time, Jack Welsh, was born and raised in Pittsfield, and his direct orders to close down most of the plant not only destroyed the strong ties between corporation and community that has existed for the previous 100 years, but left a community that had, for the most part, been designed and run by the corporation so they lacked the knowledge of how to organize themselves or attract other industry when General Electric fled the scene.

Also operating on global levels are large media corporations, 96 per cent of which are owned by four multi-national companies. Social movements and resistance movements are now more visible on an international scale, sometimes as a result of Internet access or because of actions by organizations such as Amnesty International. The legitimacy and sometimes even the survival of states are tied into these multi-national organizations and forums, as the following units will show.

The United Nations

The United Nations and its members and activities are referenced throughout the course and throughout this Companion. It is an organization of interrelated states that was created shortly after the Second World War as a way to generate cooperation among the world's states and, some would argue, as a direct reaction to the horrors of the Holocaust (more of this will be discussed in the next unit on human rights). Before the United Nations there was the League of Nations, established after the First World War by the Treaty of Versailles. It was, like the United Nations, created to maintain peace and security among nations, but was designated a failure when the Second World War started.

The term "United Nations" was coined by Franklin D. Roosevelt in 1942. The United Nations emerged as a pledge by 26 nations to band together and prevent major conflicts, especially with what were called the "Axis Powers", which consisted of Germany, Italy and Japan. They were joined by 24 other countries directly after the Second World War ended, meeting in San Francisco to draft the UN Charter, which was initially signed by 51 countries. The remaining assets of the League of Nations

TOK

How has technology changed the way in which knowledge is produced? What role does the media play in shaping people's views of issues in global politics?

▲ The logo of the League of Nations

were turned over to the United Nations, as the League formally dissolved.

Today, most of the countries of the world are members of the United Nations, and its organization is a monolith that reaches out in all directions, touching almost every citizen on the planet. With agencies and research organizations as part of its outreach, the United Nations holds a potential power that no individual country could possibly assemble. Its major constituent parts are the General Assembly, the Security Council, the Economic and Social Council, the Trusteeship Council, the International Court of Justice, and the Secretariat. Its 193 member countries agree in principle to abide by the UN

▲ The Security Council chamber at the UN headquarters in New York

Charter and to obey the rulings of the Security Council, which often deals with major conflicts and disasters around the world. As an intergovernmental organization it provides universal ideals for nations to follow, sometimes intervening in conflicts. The range of its power is a subject of ongoing debate, as are the constitution of the Security Council and the prosecution of individuals and nations through the International Criminal Court.

The essence of the debates about the United Nations centre on its ability to challenge the sovereignty of the nation state, and if any of its treaties and covenants are enforceable at all. There have been many objections to the rule of the Security Council and its effect on smaller and less-developed nations. A developed, industrialized country has never been brought before the International Criminal Court, and in particular the United States, Russia, China, India and Israel, as members of the Security Council, are almost never challenged on their actions in their own countries or globally. Interestingly, these countries are often the major nations that do not sign agreements on issues such as the environment, the abuse of women and children, and human rights.

Many, then, bring into question the place of the United Nations in world politics and as an example of good global governance. The next unit on human rights discusses these issues in more detail as Franklin D. Roosevelt's wife, Eleanor, initiated and founded the commission that drew up the Universal Declaration of Human Rights. The debates around this declaration and the inability to enforce human right precepts are ongoing problems that attract attention from every part of the globe. Importantly, the United Nations operates by assembling nations together, while the daily realities of local and global politics takes place on levels far below the chambers of the United Nations in New York.

1.4 Communities

In the introduction the community was defined as a geographic level on which we work and analyse the global arena. Both NGOs and IGOs are most active on community – or, perhaps more precisely, local – levels. However, given the influence of outside forces such as IGOs, MNCs and the United Nations, the viability of communities has come into question. The existence and definition of communities have become increasingly a subject of debate in the academic and the public sectors, and a further discussion of its present use and the surrounding debates can be helpful in defining our basic units of study.

Class discussion

Has the Internet created equality among citizens?

The basic question is whether we can define communities outside the constraints of territory, or taken a step further, without place. Those promoting the primacy of cyberspace would seem to suggest that the community in space and time has become a relic of the past. The often referenced "virtual community" assumes something post-community, or at least a reformulation of community. Andrew Sullivan, in a story for the *New York Times Magazine* (2000, Section 6: 30–34), makes a claim that the Internet has generated an equality among citizens that Marx could have only dreamed of. If we are to accept his premise, "virtual communities" promise eqalitarian interaction, requiring only a computer and a modem. What is forgotten, of course, is who has access to a computer and a modem and who does not.

Cyberspace communities are based on technology, and in the words of Gillespie and Robins (1989),

> *In considering the extent to which the new communications technologies challenge or reinforce existing monopolies of information, and the associated spatial hierarchies and interdependencies, we need to ascertain in whose interests they are developed and whose interests they serve.* (1989: 11)

They conclude that the

> *"distance-shrinking" characteristics of the new communications technologies, far from overcoming and rendering insignificant the geographic expressions of centralized economic and political power, in fact constitute new and enhanced forms of inequality and uneven development.* (1989: 7)

The new definitions of community emphasize space over physical place and are more pronounced in the capital-intensive countries, in which the role of technology has been more decisive in everyday life. Even within these countries, however, in Bourdieu's (1982) terms, the effect has been uneven, as those with the resources to access and to own technology have been more willing to redefine themselves as novel and distinct from those who are forced to rely on more traditional means of communication and identification.

The Internet *has* proved to be an enormous asset to those, with certain means, who are isolated and unable to communicate freely with their would-be peers. What has occurred with the rise of the Internet and other communications technologies is the ease at which, for some populations, communication over space is possible. However, while the ability to express one's thoughts and feelings in novel modes of communication has helped some to reinforce self-identification, it can also contribute to an isolation that potentially works against the same process of self-discovery that the Internet engenders. The validation that the Internet provides exists in isolation from the physical, and the body, in postmodern terms, becomes an abstraction that is secondary to the working of the imaginary. Composed of text, cyberspace acts as a particularly relevant example of the primacy of space over place, where reality is inferior to perception (Mihalache, 2000).

What can we say about the state of our communities, then, as we have traditionally known them, and what is the outlook for their continued survival? We have noted that the need for the community as a basis for socializing the next generation has diminished. Nevertheless, from independence movements in less capital-intensive countries to the resurgence of cultural identities, communities have continued to assert group identification and affiliation. There are no shortages of examples of geographic communities that have acted as sites of resistance against oppression, and of community revolts that have broadened into larger revolutions. How do we reconcile the lessons of history with the realities of change that are represented in "the problem of place"? David Harvey argues:

> *... we cannot go back... we cannot reject the world of sociality which has been achieved by the interlinking of all peoples into a global economy... we should somehow build upon this achievement and seek to transform it into an unalienated experience. The network of places constructed through the logic of capitalist development, for example, has to be transformed and used for progressive purposes rather than be rejected or destroyed.* (1993: 13)

Should this position be uncritically accepted? Is increasing globalization inevitable? Even if we accept the premise that we cannot resist globalization, how this understanding and call for action is put into use remains an open question, tied to our understanding of place and space. Citing Young, Harvey further posits:

> *The 'desire for unity or wholeness in discourse'... 'generates borders, dichotomies and exclusions'. In political theory, furthermore, the concept of community 'often implies a denial of time and space distancing' and an insistence on 'face-to-face interaction among members within a plurality of contexts'. Yet there are 'no conceptual grounds for considering face-to-face relations more pure, authentic social relations than relations mediated across time and distance.'* (1993: 15)

However, the extreme cases where communities are presented as being exclusionary and, by implication, promoting discriminatory practices (and, in the worst cases, atrocities), run the risk of "blaming the victim". We cannot ignore the enormous pressures to which communities have been subjected in a period of rapid globalization. The conflict between and among communities has often led to a tragic outcome. Other consequences have been the loss of livelihood, the alienation of community members from each other, and the loss of a sense of being. Further, the "new communities" of virtual reality and other forms of communication over networked space often exclude

---

Class discussion

Is increasing globalization inevitable?

TOK

How can we decide between the opinions of experts when they disagree with one another? Are there different amounts of disagreement in the different areas of knowledge? In what ways might disagreement be helpful to the production of knowledge?

the very people who are most subject to the purposeful fragmentation created by a growing capitalist market: those without the resources to have access to electronic communication networks. Populations without resources, and particularly those exploited in less capital-intensive countries, are hardly able to participate in these new forms of community definition.

Unsurprisingly, the argument concerning exclusion is the same that has been used against "identity politics". This argument envisions "all human beings with universal human rights" as Duberman (2001) explains the complaint. The logic ignores the fact that communities and identities are being challenged rather than legitimated, dissolving the common bases for resistance with other attacked minorities and communities, the bases for building bridges (Kirsch, 2000).

There is a difference between communities of exclusion, often generated by conflict from the outside, and communities as centres of cultural transmission and inclusion. While not all relations may be alienating, the very changes in time and space to which Harvey refers have often come as a reaction to community resistance to domination that causes the "alienation, bureaucratization and degradation" experienced by many around the world. When the basis for this identification is destroyed and the individual is left on his or her own, alienation results. As Maria Dalla Costa (1996: 113) tells us,

> It is significant that, according to Italian Press reports in 1993–94, many cases of suicide in Italy are due to unemployment or to the fact that the only work available is to join a criminal gang. While, in India, the 'tribal people' in the Narmada valley have declared a readiness to die by drowning if work continues on a dam which will destroy their habitat and, hence, the basis of their survival and cultural identity.

Suicide, of course, is not the only way out. Violence is often a part of the threat to communities, precipitated by a perceived need to maintain a past, even if idealized. Young's complaints about the attributes of communities are most often during the processes of community destruction, as can be witnessed by the many recent examples in Europe and Africa. Stable communities have no reason to exclude individuals or to promote genocide.

From community to affiliation

The fact that geographic communities feed into wider networks of social interaction is a staple of social analysis. Society comprises communities and the individuals within them. As we have noted, the real change in the definitions of community has come in the conceptualizations of time and space. Communities as physical entities have been metamorphosed into the "communities of taste" or "taste cultures" to which Jane Jacobs refers (in Harvey 1990: 67). These "taste cultures" are driven by the market, and as such, change often. So then, according to this reasoning, do communities. What we are left with is a definition of community that is truly driven by the forces of the market, and thus by the needs of capital accumulation.

The space-time compression discussed earlier is reflected in our networks. According to Manual Castells, a Spanish sociologist, new information technologies are "integrating the world in global networks of instrumentality," in what he calls "a vast array of virtual communities"(2000: 21–22). At the same time, as Castells reminds us, there has been an increasingly anxious search for identity, meaning and spirituality. "… why," Castells asks, "do we observe the opposite trend throughout the world, namely, the increasing distance between globalization and identity, between the Net and the self?" (2000: 22). The use of the Internet can increase feelings of loneliness, alienation and depression, as substantial studies have concluded (Wolton, 1998, in Castells, 1997: 387).

As an example, Castells cites the psychoanalyst Raymond Barglow, who reports that his patients are having dreams about their heads being programmed by a computer, to illuminate the paradox that has developed in a society where the self seems lost to itself, isolated and alone (2000: 23).

Our networked society is both a result and a cause of an alienation and aloneness that has pervaded our lives. It has also created a desire for connectedness and affiliation. Although many argue that the Internet has created new communities, the loss of the physical self and physical interactions in these interchanges is real. Even though it can be argued, as Wellman does (Wellman, 1997, Wellman and Wortley, 1990), that virtual communities need not be opposed to physical communities, the increasing dependence of communication by online interaction fosters a sense of the unreal that is very much a part of our daily lives in the twenty-first century, and is reflected in the theory building that is popular in academic circles today.

▲ Anti-globalization protests in Seattle, USA

Class discussion

Do you agree with Castells' description of virtual communities?

As Castells concludes,

So in the end, are virtual communities real communities? Yes and no. They are communities, but not physical ones, and they do not follow the same patterns of communication and interaction as physical communities. But they are not "unreal," they work in a different plane of reality. They are interpersonal social networks, most of them based on weak ties, highly diversified and specialized, still able to generate reciprocity and support by the dynamics of sustained interaction. (1997: 389)

The question remains, of course, of what is represented in this "sustained interaction"? How long does it last? As we see from the protests in Seattle and Washington and from the Zapitistas in Mexico, the use of the Internet can further communication and "communities"of resistance. In these cases, as in most cases of Internet-based communities, their sustainability is limited to the subject at hand: they are not easily maintained or reproduced. They weaken or disappear quickly, sometimes reappearing in different forms or not at all.

Communities and agency

Still, if we acknowledge that communities have been and continue to be the primary sites of resistance to outside domination, then the call for internationalist politics need not contradict this fact. It is not necessary to relegate geographic communities to the past in order to agree that a global system does exist and has transformed social life. As Harvey tells us, the building of new communities though the mechanisms of cultural politics – from the building of Shaker communities to the takeover of the Castro district in San Francisco by a gay community – is still common practice. Thus, he would prefer to see "the differences as oppositions inherent in the condition of both modernity and postmodernity rather than as irreconcilable contradictions..." (1993: 15).

There remains in Harvey's writing, nonetheless, a tension between communities as place-bound, old or new, and other forces, particularly capital, that are not contained by space. For, in his words,

Oppositional movements are generally better at organizing in and dominating space than they are at commanding space. The 'otherness' and 'regional resistances' that postmodern politics emphasize can flourish in a particular place. But they are easily dominated by the power of capital to co-ordinate accumulation across universal fragmented space. Place-bound politics appeals even though such a politics is doomed to failure. (Harvey 1993: 24)

Inherent in this "rule", as Harvey regards it, is the opposition between space and place. Communities operate within place, capital among fragmented space. Resistance to the oppressing forces of capital, then, is doomed because of the free-floating ability of capital to override the constraints of place. The conclusion is therefore a pessimistic evaluation of the possibilities of place-bound politics. But Saskia Sassen (1998), for one, has shown the investment of corporations in the telecommunications infrastructure of global cities is an example of the continued importance of place within the global system and the possibilities that it engenders for collective action. More disturbingly, in putting forth the argument that space dominates place and that the new politics of space is a result of that defeat, there is an assumption that opposition to outside rule has been defeated, and with it, the possibilities for community and class politics (Harvey, 1993: 27). For our present purposes, we know many examples of place-bound resistance. Indeed, the form that place-bound politics takes is not pre-ordained, or necessarily structural. It may be mediated by the possibilities of leadership or by the defeat of attempts to assert place over spatial dominance. Unions, for example, exist over space. Their membership is, however, deeply grounded in the politics of place. If, as Harvey reminds us, place and space are social constructs, then there is reason to be optimistic about the integration of place and space, and the role of communities within that framework.

The (new) civil society

The concept of civil society developed as a way of describing the transition from the feudal household economy to public commodity-based exchange relations, dating back to the early thirteenth century. Civil society came into being as an alternative to the modern coercive State that developed after the fall of feudal relations (that is, the French Revolution). While the State did assume control over the exchange of goods, by the 1800s, the "bourgeois public sphere", as the philosopher Jürgen Habermas (1991: 74) called it, was largely autonomous, separated from the government. Habermas' argument is that during the period of the development of the public sphere, direct control over production was taken out of the hands of the dominating authorities and placed within the public sphere, while the role of the state was to regulate and to administer social controls. It is only when the state interfered with the system of trade, during the latter part of the nineteenth century that we see the destruction of the separation between state and society. Society becomes a state function, and the state assumes public control (to learn more about this change, see Habermas, 1991: 142).

The *new* civil society takes from its older form the separation of State from the public sphere – and by extension its constituent communities – and the struggles to assert agency in societal organization. It was reintroduced both in academic circles and popular culture during the 1980s to explain the phenomenon of independent organizations and affiliations that challenged the mechanisms of the multi-national corporations and the state in controlling public debate and action. Once again, the idea of civil society began to take on a meaning that separated independent forms of communication and organization from institutional structures. The circumstances that have brought civil society back are the same that have caused the differing definition of communities: the increasing fragmentation of society that includes the attempted weakening of geographic social groupings, including the influence of states on the global field. In short, as Jeffery Goldfarb has put it, civil society represents the "use of an old concept for new times"(1998: 91).

For Goldfarb, the "new times" are the events in Eastern Europe that have reshaped the face of politics in the former Soviet bloc. Stemming from opposition to the existent Party-states, new avenues were created to express opposition to state mechanisms of control. Spontaneous protests, newspapers, newsletters, and clandestine radio and TV broadcasts all made demands for a more "humanistic" socialism. They were initiated by intellectuals and other individuals who saw themselves as a loyal opposition to the ruling regimes. Their efforts initially failed, particularly in the late 1950s and 1960s, to gain the reforms they sought, and they were sometimes brutally repressed by the ruling parties, which led to a blossoming of social movements that sought a stable public sphere independent of institutional governance. What evolved, says Goldfarb, was "an extensive alternative cultural system… an alternative system of public life, a free public life" (1998: 88).

Solidarity, as an example, began as a reform-orientated trade union organization that did not challenge institutional control. Lech Wałęsa declined to declare the labour movement a political organization and upheld the organizational base of the Communist Party. "He seemed not to be interested in the state at all," writes Goldfarb. "The image he used was one of the opposition: of society versus the authorities, where the end of social agitation was for society to be left alone, at least a little more than it had been" (Goldfarb, 1998: 88). Adam Michnik, like Wałęsa before him, used the image of society versus the state in his widely cited "A New Evolutionism". What followed was a notion of civil society that presented an alternative to established political norms of social control. The dissidents of Eastern Europe were clear about the diversity that was a component of civil society, the link among social classes and lifestyles across space that comprised a social force in opposition to ruling organization.

It is important to point out, as Goldfarb does, that not all of these developments proved positive. Manipulated xenophobia, as Goldfarb

▲ Members of the Landless Workers' Movement throw corn towards the gates of the US embassy in Brazil, in protest against the Free Trade Area of the Americas (FTAA) and the World Trade Organization (WTO)

calls it, is very much a part of the political landscape (1998: 98). The nationalist response garnered in Eastern Europe has been a very real social alternative to the civil society model. But like civil society, these are integrated parts of the same struggle. Civil society depends on the actions of affiliation across space to counter state domination of the public sphere. Xenophobic nationalism is one negative response to that challenge.

The movements of Eastern Europe have provided a new life for the idea of civil society that has now taken on wider meaning in academic and popular circles. Gellner (1994), in a more general definition, describes it as the place where free associational activity dominates, limiting the possibility of complete state domination. Cohen and Arato add opposition to the dominance of corporate and market entities (Goldfarb, 1998, 84). Similarly, Walzer (1991) delineates civil society as "the space of uncoerced human association and also the set of relational networks – formed for the sake of family, faith, interest, and ideology – that fill this space" (1991: 293). Thus, we are now witnessing the use of the term, in particular, for the widespread growth of indigenous movements around the world, from Christian assertions of identity recognition in Japan and the reassertion of the Welsh language in Great Britain to the Zapitistas in Mexico, Mayas in Guatemala, Brazil's Landless Workers' Movement, Cherokee culture in the United States and the ethnic movements of the Philippines. In all of these developments exists the common cause of autonomy from outside control. For here what drives the maintenance of resistance is the pursuit of community stability.

These accounts are important for our discussion of communities and their continued role in establishing place as an important site of affiliation. Much of the rush to redefine communities is driven by the need to account for the events and social change on a global scale that, on the surface at least, transcend geographic communities. Without engaging arguments around the role of public opinion and the ideologies of power, addressing publics as an analytic tool can clarify the "taste cultures", "abstract communities", and interest groups that are now often defined as communities. The public, as we have discussed, is separate from the institutional structures of power and the coercive ideologies that they represent.

This unit has focused on the many realms of power and governance that exist in global politics today. It is by no means a complete reference manual to what exists in global politics and its rapidly changing circumstances. What is here is a guide for discussions and chances to relate the concepts of global politics to real-world environments. The importance of Unit 1 lies in its discussions and references to power, sovereignty, legitimacy and interdependence that influence the subject of global politics. Each of the following units will have their own focuses and ties to the global environment, but ultimately they all refer back to the basic key concepts that are the subject of this unit.

Research and self-management skills

For more discussion on the role of public opinion on the ideologies of power see Behabib, 1992; Devine, 1992; Fraser, 1992; Lippmann, 1995; Wright, 1993; Speier, 1995.

35

1.5 Exam-style questions

1 Discuss the claim that power in global politics is mostly exercised through the use of force and threats.

Examiner hints

Responses are likely to include a definition of the concept of power; such as the ability to make someone do something – often, but not always, by the use of force or threats – or face consequences; or the ability to achieve a desired outcome through the use of other means, which could involve the use of both coercive (force and threats) and co-optive mechanisms.

Responses may make reference to ideas such as distinctions drawn between hard and soft power. Candidates may also refer to the concept of smart power which in effect combines elements of both hard (coercion and payment) and soft power (persuasion and attraction), sometimes making it difficult to distinguish where coercion starts and ends. Candidates could also highlight the fact that the concept of power is central, yet remains elusive in nature. Better answers may be able to weave relevant theories on power into the arguments.

Arguments for the claim may include:

- the centrality of military and economic power is still accepted by realist thinkers who argue that the possession of superior capabilities is more likely to result in successful outcomes for states

- states aspiring to be more powerful still seek to expand their military capabilities; wealth and economic prosperity – seen as key pre-requisites for building status and power

- the states that exert the most influence globally (for example, agenda setting in UN) also have strong military capabilities and economic resources

- the continued existence of intrastate and transnational wars involving non-state actors requires states to resort to use of force, suggesting that coercion is both effective and essential

- propaganda, censorship and disinformation continue to be used as a means of coercion by state and non-state actors, for example, ISIS using social media to attract fighters.

Arguments against the claim may include:

- aspects of soft power such as political ideals, cultural norms and social policies may be equally if not more influential than force

- the mere possession of resources doesn't always result in a country having the power to achieve desired outcomes: sometimes non-material factors such as changes in strategy and/or leadership can affect outcomes

- diplomacy and economic assistance are useful in furthering goals and interests

- persuasion can be effectively used to achieve goals and preferred outcomes through the use of means such as education and propaganda, for example, through the use of social media

- the acquisition and maintenance of instruments of coercive power – military power, arms procurement, nuclear weapons is increasingly expensive

- incentives such as incorporation into free trade agreements in an era of economic interdependence work more effectively than coercion

- non-coercive means can produce a voluntary response from a given state and lead to a more effective and long-lasting result

- many transnational issues such as climate change, pandemics, cybercrime, drug trafficking and terrorism cannot be mitigated through forceful means.

Responses should contain references to specific examples. These may be taken, for instance, from the continued emphasis on weapons and arms acquisitions by states like China, where rapid military modernization is closely linked to its ambition to become a formidable political and economic power, like the US or Russia. Examples of the increasing use of soft power could be drawn from Japan's pacifist strategic culture and China's so-called charm offensive. Any other valid and relevant examples should be evaluated positively.

2 Examine the claim that increased interactions and interconnectedness in global politics have fundamentally changed the nature of state sovereignty.

Examiner hints

Responses should include an understanding of the concept of sovereignty; for example, they may make reference to features such as territorial control and the principle of non-interference in another state's affairs. The definition may differentiate between internal and external sovereignty. Responses may make reference to ideas such as the equality of states in international law, or may include a brief discussion of Westphalian sovereignty. Responses may discuss interactions and interconnectedness in global politics by drawing on key concepts not mentioned in the question, such as interdependence, globalization, development or sustainability.

Arguments for the claim may include:

- globalization, the rise of non-state actors and the increasing interconnectedness of the world are challenges to state power and sovereignty, as individual states have less control

- states are losing influence through the pooling of some aspects of their sovereignty, such as in the case of the EU

- global issues which are cross-border in nature such as pollution, disease, war or terrorism increasingly require cooperation and action across state boundaries, which may then place limitations on state activity and sovereignty

- increased specialization in the economic organization of the world means that states are no longer self-sufficient in many areas but are dependent on each other for vital supplies and services

- responses to human rights abuses have given rise to the concept of "conditional" sovereignty and to humanitarian intervention.

Arguments against the claim may include:

- the centrality of state sovereignty in the international system has endured despite globalization, as illustrated by the number of states in the international community;

- statehood is still highly desired and most secessionist groups seek to be states and seek full membership of the UN

- no other actors are as powerful as states, as evidenced by the difficulties experienced by non-state actors such as the United Nations in exerting power to influence global issues

- states still rely on and deploy enormous amounts of military power and control and the world is still organized around state-centric security concerns

- states are not necessarily threatened by globalization and may respond to interconnectedness by adapting and competing in other ways for influence (for example, through trade, "cultural imperialism", or the power of agenda setting)

- increased cross- border interactions and interconnectedness have not necessarily changed the nature of state sovereignty: there are other important, often domestically rooted, factors, such as the growth in influence of civil society.

Responses should make reference to specific examples. For instance, candidates could discuss the role of media in war reporting ("the CNN effect") or the phenomenon of the spread of communications technology and the attempted control of social media by states, as in the case of China. They could refer to specific problems that do not respect state boundaries, such as greenhouse gases or refugees, for example, from Syria entering neighbouring countries. Conversely, they could refer to states such as China and Brazil, whose influence has increased in recent years or to the persistence of inter-state conflicts where violation of sovereignty is still the most significant aspect at play, such as in the case of Russia's recent disputed behaviour in Crimea.

Responses should include the candidate's examination of the claim that increased interaction and interconnectedness in global politics have fundamentally changed the nature of state sovereignty.

3 Power is often assumed to be linked to the possession of, or access to, resources. Discuss the validity of this view.

Examiner hints

Responses should include an understanding of the concept of power.

A spectrum of power may be indicated – from influence and capacity through to coercion and force. Candidates may discuss power in the sense of international relations, and/or in the sense of internal control. Responses may make reference to different types of resources (for example, military, economic, or natural resources), or may, equally validly, focus on one particular type of resource such as economic resources.

Arguments in favour of the view that power is linked to the possession of resources may include:

- states that have the most resources do often have the most power on the world stage (for example, the US, China)

- history shows us that those with power often come in and take away resources from resource-rich but less powerful states

- within states, those who possess resources tend to be the powerful actors in the society (for example, the US, Russia).

Arguments against the view that power is linked to the possession of resources may include:

- power can be difficult to measure (for instance, soft power, social power, cultural power) and perceptions of power may matter just as much as having tangible resources

- resources alone are not power; intention and capability (for example, effective leadership and administration) transform resources into power;

- there are states with abundant natural resources that have a relative lack of power on the world stage, as abundant natural resources may go hand in hand with commodity-led, lower value growth (for example, DRC)

- even states which have copious resources still face numerous other challenges that undermine their ability to exercise power or control (for example, the restrictions placed on them by international law, the structure of international institutions, such as the UN Security Council, or the influence of civil society).

Responses should make reference to specific examples. Which examples are included is likely to depend on the selected interpretation of the concept of power and the types of resources discussed.

Responses could distinguish between states that have hard power arising from the possession of military, economic, and/or natural resources (for example, the US, China, Brazil), and states that have soft power that is not based to such a degree on tangible resources and that can be informational, diplomatic, or cultural, and involve agenda setting (for example, UK, Norway).

Candidates could discuss the relationship between power and natural resources in specific countries, for example:

	High natural resources	Low natural resources
Much power	USA, China	Japan
Little power	DRC	Haiti

Responses should include the candidate's evaluation of whether power is linked to the possession of resources.

4 Evaluate the claim that state sovereignty creates obstacles for the realization of justice for individuals and communities.

Examiner hints

Responses are likely to include an explanation of the concept of sovereignty – which implies that the state or government has supreme, unqualified authority. This is reflected in the claim by states to be the sole author of laws within their own territory (internal sovereignty). Internal sovereignty is the location of supreme power within the state. External sovereignty refers to the capacity of the state to act independently and autonomously on the world stage. Candidates should also briefly discuss their understanding of the concept of justice.

Arguments in favour of the claim may include:

- in matters relating to human rights violations and atrocities, states and leaders continue to invoke the concept of sovereignty. They agree to monitoring and judgments by human rights courts and commissions only to the extent that they choose to. Sovereignty has, in that sense resisted human rights agreements

- many human rights agreements have been ratified by states, but with reservations, for example, the UN Convention on Women. For instance, India, Germany and Hungary choose not to be bound by certain sections of the CEDAW

- sovereign states resent the monitoring of perceived injustices to both individuals and communities by NGOs and the media

- sovereignty continues to curb issues related to justice for communities and groups such as women, minorities and gay rights: states set their own limits on the rights given to such communities, and argue that this is within their domestic jurisdiction and is also closely related to cultural and societal practices specific to their jurisdiction

- sovereignty becomes an issue in cases where an individual or group seeks political asylum on the plea that their human rights are being violated in another country. In such situations, the sovereignty of the country in question clashes with issues of justice.

Arguments against the claim may include:

- the emergence of significant international organizations such as the UN, the EU, the WTO and international NGOs has entailed the setting-up of agreed rules, laws and practices, including some enforcement mechanisms

- membership of most of the states in the UN and its institutions involves participating states accepting and allowing other members to intervene in its domestic affairs if it fails in its fundamental duty to protect citizens and communities within its sovereign territory

- the international community has been able to intervene successfully in cases where injustice has been meted out to individuals and groups. Such humanitarian intervention is now increasingly accepted, and is achieved through coalition efforts as well as through international organizations such as the UN.

Reponses should include reference to specific examples to support their evaluation of the claim in the question. Examples that might be used to support the claim that state sovereignty hinders realization of justice to individuals and communities could include the continuation of human rights abuses in North Korea (including enslavement, murder and mass starvation), Somalia, and Sudan, and the fallout of these on the lives of people. They could also cite examples of human rights agreements that have been ratified, but with certain reservations by some states; for example, India, Germany and Hungary chose not to be bound by sections of the CEDAW.

Examples that could be used to illustrate the counterclaim that state sovereignty can no longer obstruct the realization of justice for individuals and groups could cite examples of successful humanitarian interventions such as those in Liberia, East Timor and Sierra Leone. They could also note cases where organizations such as the EC ensure the application of EU treaties and legislation through formal infringement proceedings, or even by referring the member state to the European Court of Justice. These rules dilute state sovereignty.

Responses should include a conclusion on whether or not state sovereignty obstructs the realization of justice for individuals and communities.

5 Examine the claim that the significance of military power is diminishing in contemporary global politics.

Examiner hints

Better answers will demonstrate an excellent grasp of the concept of military power, and are likely to contrast this with other types of power such as economic power. They could include discussion of the various components of power, for example, military, economic (tangible) and leadership (intangible), or of how power has been viewed differently by different schools of thought.

Arguments in favour of the claim that the significance of military power has diminished could include:

- the increasing weight of variables such as economic interdependence, transnational actors and international organizations

- increased globalization leading to less emphasis on individual states and their individual military

- power; economic power being equally, if not more, important than military power, as economic power is required to bolster military power

- the idea that some issues do not lend themselves to military solutions, for example, states may avoid using military action if it could negatively impact future trade agreements etc.

Arguments against the claim that the significance of military power has diminished may include:

- military force remains critical, as shown by the fact that the production of arms continues to increase

- the sale of military weapons has become a major factor in the arming of various contestants for control of resources

- military power is also still important as a deterrent, etc.

Answers should include reference to specific examples. These could include examples such as the anti-military culture in places such as Japan; anti-war movements, such as the protests against the war in Iraq; or the importance of military power in the conflict in Syria.

The responses are likely to end with a conclusion stating to what extent the candidate agrees or disagrees that the significance of military power is diminishing in contemporary global politics.

6 Discuss the impact of NGOs, MNCs, and international organizations on state sovereignty.

Examiner hints

Better answers will demonstrate an excellent understanding of the concept of sovereignty, including reference to sovereignty as characterizing a state's independence, its control over territory and its ability to govern itself. Candidates may talk about the role and functions of the state, and then proceed to explore how and what kind of an impact each of the aforementioned – NGOs, MNCs and international organizations like the United Nations – has had on state sovereignty.

Arguments that these actors have no real impact may include:

- states may control the agenda of many of these organizations
- the strengthening of national security and national interest due to the threat of terrorism and to economic interests
- states sometimes have a choice over whether to align with recommendations/policies etc from these organizations, rather than these being compulsory, etc.

Arguments that these actors have a big impact may include:

- trade agreements
- corporate demands on state laws, for example, environmental or labour laws
- capital flight
- threats to relocate
- the ability of these actors to have significant impact, even bringing down governments or bringing about severe economic consequences for states, etc.

The responses should make reference to specific examples, such as (have no real impact): the EU, the World Bank, and the IMF control the interests of states; states can ban NGO protests such as in Singapore; the US refused to sign the Kyoto agreement; (have a big impact): can bring down governments, for example, Guatemala.

The responses may end with a conclusion/judgment on the impact of NGOs, MNCs and international organizations on state sovereignty.

Arensberg, Conrad. 1961. "Community as object and as sample." *American Anthropologist*, Vol. 63, 241–264.

Behabib, Selya. 1992. "Models of public space: Hanna Arendt, The liberal tradition, and Jersen Habermas", in Craig Calhoun, ed., *Habermas and the public sphere*. Cambridge: MIT Press.

Bourdieu, Pierre. 1982. *Distinction*. Cambridge MA: Harvard University Press.

Castells, Manuel. 1997. *The power of identity*. Malden MA: Blackwell.

Crawford, James R. 2007. *The Creation of States in International Law*, Oxford: Oxford University Press, published to Oxford Scholarship Online: February 2010.

Cummings, Bruce. 2000. "The American ascendancy: imposing a new world order." *The Nation, 8* May, 13–20.

Dalla Costa, Maria. 1996. "Capitalism and reproduction." *Capitalism, Nature, Society*, 7(4), December.

Devine, Fiore. 1992. "Social identities, class identity and political perspective." *The Sociological Review*, 230:252.

Dispatch from Geneva: A treaty on Transnational Corporations? A Declaration of Peasant's Rights? #AIGNETWORK, 15 October, 2014.

Duberman, Martin. 2001. "In defense of identity politics," *In These Times, 9* July.

Eagleton, Terry. 2000. *The idea of culture*. Malden MA: Blackwell Publishers.

Economist Online, "Biggest Transnational Companies". Accessed June 16, 2016.

Eder, Klaus. 1985. "The new social movements: moral crusades, political pressure groups or social movements." *Social Research* 52(4): 28–42.

Farmer, Paul. 2004. "The Anthropology of Structural Violence". *Current Anthropology*, (45)3:305–25.

Fraser, Nancy. 1992. "Rethinking the public sphere: a contribution to the critique of actually existing democracy", in Craig Calhoun, ed., *Habermas and the Public Sphere*. Cambridge: MIT Press.

Geertz, Clifford. 1963. *Old Societies and New States*. New York: Collins McMillan.

Gellner, Ernest. 1994. *Conditions of liberty*. New York: Penguin.

Gillespie, Andrew and Robbins, Kevin. 1989. "Geographical inequalities: the spatial bias of the new communications technologies." *Journal of Communication* 39(3), Summer, 7–18.

Goldfarb, Jeffery. 1998. *Civility and subversion*. Cambridge, UK: Cambridge University Press.

Goody, Jack. 2006, "Globalization and the Domestic Group," in M. Kirsch, *Inclusion and Exclusion in the Global Arena,"* pp. 31–41, London: Routledge.

Gramsci, Antonio. 1971. *Selections from the prison notebooks*. New York: International Publishers.

Gramsci, Antonio. 2011 [1926]. *Prison Notebooks*, Columbia University Press.

Habermas, Jürgen. 1991. *The transformation of the public sphere*. Cambridge MA: MIT Press.

Harvey, David. 1990. *The condition of postmodernity*. Malden MA: Blackwell.

Harvey, David. 1991. *The Condition of Postmodernity*, Boston: Wiley Blackwell.

Harvey, David. 1993. "From space to place and back again: reflections on the conditions of postmodernity", in John Bird et al, eds, *Mapping the futures*. London: Routledge. pp. 3–29.

Kirsch, Max. 1998. *In the wake of the giant: multinational restructuring and uneven development in a New England community*. Albany: State University of New York Press.

Kirsch, Max. 2000. *Queer theory and social change*. London: Routledge.

Kirsch, Max. 2006. *Inclusion and Exclusion in the Global Arena*, New York: Routledge.

Leacock, Eleanor and Lee, Richard. 1982. *Politics and History in Band Societies*, Cambridge: Cambridge University Press.

Leacock, Eleanor. 1982. *Myths of Male Dominance*, New York: Monthly Review Press.

Lippmann, Walter. 1995 (1925). "The phantom public", in Robert Jackall, ed., *Propaganda*. New York: NYU Press.

Mandel, Ernst. 1972. *Late capitalism*. London: New Left Books.

Marx, Karl and Engels, Fredrik. 1952. *The communist manifesto*. Moscow: International Publishers.

Mihalache, A. 2000. The Postmodernity of Cyberspace. http://www.spark-online.com.

Miller, David. 1997. *Capitalism: an ethnographic approach*. Oxford, UK: Berg.

Mintz, Sidney W. 2000. "Sows' ears and silver linings: A backward look at ethnography." *Current Anthropology* 41(2): 169–17.

Nash, June. 1967. "Death as a Way of Life: The Increasing Resort to Homicide in an Indian Maya Community. *American Anthropologist, New Series*, Vol. 69, No. 5 (Oct., 1967), pp. 455–470.

Nash, June. 1981. "Ethnographic aspects of the capitalist world system." *Annual Reviews of Anthropology*. 10: 393–423.

Nash, June. 1981. *Women, Men and the International Division of Labor*, Albany New York: SUNY PRESS.

Nash, June.1990. *From tank town to high tech*. Albany: State University of New York Press.

Nash, June. 2001. *Mayan Visions: the quest for autonomy in an age of globalization*. New York: Routledge.

The New Yorker, 28 March 2016. "Exporting Jihad".

Nibet, Robert A. 1953. *Community and power*. New York: Oxford.

Nisbet, Robert A. 1966. *The sociological tradition*. New York: Basic Books.

Nye, Joseph. 1990. *Bound to Lead: The Changing Nature of American Power*. New York: Basic Books.

Polanyi, Karl. 2011 [1944] *The Great Transformation*, Beacon Press.

Roseberry, William. 1989. *Anthropologies and histories*. New Brunswick, NJ: Rutgers University Press.

Ross, Andrew.1999. *The celebration chronicles*. New York: Ballantine.

Safa, Helen. 1981. "Runaway shops and female employment: the search for cheap labor." *Signs* 7(2): 418–433.

Sassen, Saskia. 1998. *Globalization and its discontents*. New York: The New Press.

Scheper-Hughes, Nancy and Bourgois, Phillipe. 2004. *Violence in War and Peace*. New York: Wiley.

Speier, Hans. 1995, (1980). "The rise of public opinion", in Robert Jackall, ed., *Propaganda*. New York: NYU Press.

Sullivan, Andrew. 2001. "Dot-communist manifesto." *New York Times Magazine* (2000, Section 6: 30–34).

Wallerstein, Immanuel. 1974. *The Modern World System*, Berkeley: University of California Press.

Walzer, Michael. 1991. The idea of civil society. *Dissent*, Spring: 293–304.

Weeks, Jeffery. 1985. *Sexuality and its discontents*. London: Routledge.

Wellman, Barry and Wortley, Scot. 1990. "Different strokes from different folks: community ties and social support." *AJS* 96(3): 558–88.

Wellman, Barry. 1997. "An electronic group is virtually a social network", in Sara Kiesler, ed., *The culture of the internet*. Mahwah, New Jersey: Lawrence Erlbaum Associates.

Williams, Raymond. 1977. *Marxism and literature*. New York: Oxford Publishers.

Wolf, Eric. 1974. *Anthropology*. New York: W.W. Norton and Company.

Wolf, Eric. 1981. *Europe and the People without History*, Berkeley: University of California Press.

Wolf, Eric. 1999. *Envisioning Power: Ideologies of Dominance and Crisis*. University of California Press.

Wright, Eric Olin. 1993. "Class analysis, history and emancipation." *New Left Review*, 2.

2 HUMAN RIGHTS

Key concepts
→ Justice
→ Liberty
→ Equality

Learning outcomes
→ Nature and evolution of human rights
→ Codification, protection and monitoring of human rights
→ Practice of human rights
→ Debates surrounding human rights: differing interpretations of justice, liberty and equality

The concept of human rights and how they have been incorporated into our daily lives has taken on a growing importance in global politics during the twentieth century. This unit will investigate what this means for our understanding of power, politics and social change. We will discuss the evolution of human rights before the United Nations' Universal Declaration of Human Rights in 1948, as well as the assertions and claims of its various definitions.

The key concepts for this topic are *justice, liberty* and *equality*. These components are found on various geographic levels, from the local to the global, and from the arguments surrounding cultural relativity to the debates about whether human rights should be universal.

Human rights are most often understood in terms of rights of the individual and rights of the collective; however, the description and use of human rights as a concept is more complex. In order to go further in our analysis we will look at past examinations of people, power and politics, as well as the aspects of culture and society that some definitions of human rights may fail to include in general usage.

We will also discuss whether the struggle for human rights is always positive, as well as for what political purposes they are used.

The definition of human rights is continually undergoing change, from academic discussions and debates adding complexity to the meaning (such as Karel Vasak's division of human rights into three "generations" or types, which we will explore later in this unit) to the updated covenants and conventions that are often initiated by the United Nations and other non-governmental organizations (NGOs). We will conclude with some questions about what this ongoing change means for the concept and its uses, particularly for politics and power.

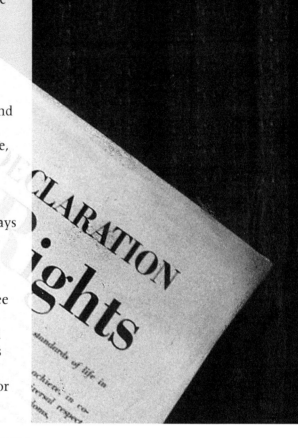

Key questions

1 Are there more significant concepts that may be used to describe our current state of global politics and the interaction of people and power on various levels and for particular purposes?

2 Does the generality of the concept of human rights suffice to offer goals for humanity and a reasonable agenda in this era of rapid globalization and social change?

3 Who would be in charge of that agenda and what problems may it cause?

4 What are some alternatives?

What are human rights?

The most common contemporary definition of human rights is that they are rights held by individuals simply because they are human. These rights are universal, do not have boundaries of sex, gender or nationality, and can be claimed individually or in groups.

Human rights are then those entitlements that are part of the existence of humans, and we may divide these into two categories:

Positive rights refer to rights that are protected by authority, both local and global, and include goods and services that allow people to survive, such as education, protection from harm, places to live and care.

Negative rights are rights that do not require intervention by outside agency. These include the right to live, the absence of torture, community control of the community and the individuals who live within them and self-determination.

Many have noted that in practice the distinction between positive and negative rights is largely circumstantial – based on access to resources and economic, political and social rights. For example, the right to food is a positive right in East Los Angeles, USA, where a lack of local resources means that food must be provided by outside forces, but it is more of a negative right in the wheat fields of Kansas, USA, where the abundant resources can only be taken away through external intervention[1].

This distinction between negative and positive rights is a product of Enlightenment writers and of the French Revolution, where the concepts of liberty, fraternity and equality were taken to apply to all human beings. As the times changed and economic control became a part of contemporary realities, these came to include, for example, the rights of workers and of indigenous people. Today, most definitions of human rights start with the Universal Declaration of Human Rights and the evolution of these rights as they have been debated and amended in the years since.

A brief history of human rights

The term "human rights" as it is applied to contemporary politics and society is relatively recent, coming into common use in the 1940s, after the Second World War and as a result of the United Nations' Universal Declaration of Human Rights (UDHR). Before these events, the term was rarely used and there were no social movements that invoked human rights as their organizing principle. Many people assume that because we now hear about human rights in many forms – for example, the claims by indigenous peoples for their ancestral lands and language, the demands by many around the globe for livable housing and working

▲ A painting depicting the Declaration of the Rights of Man and of the Citizen, an act passed in France on 26 August 1789 with 17 articles that define the rights of citizens and the nation

TOK

Do the human sciences help us to understand the human species as a whole, or just give insight into particular cultural groups?

conditions, the documented lack of medical services and drinkable water for populations in every part of the world and the place of human rights in trade agreements, to name a few – that this concept of human rights is one that is part of a long history involving the relationships within and between countries. However, like globalization (as discussed in Unit 1), the struggle for rights is an integral part of human existence.

For the purposes of this course, our central focus will be on what human rights *are* and who decides which are enforceable and which are not. René Cassin, one of the drafters of the Universal Declaration of Human Rights in 1948, used the declaration of the French Revolution as a starting point. Again, however, the French declaration does not account for specific attempts at delegating human rights to specific populations, and the legislative processes needed to enforce them. Hence our important question: on what level (geographic and political) are human rights enforced and realized within societies, communities and ruling bodies?

▲ Demonstrators protest against Brazilian President Dilma Rousseff and the ruling Workers Party at Paulista Avenue in Sao Paulo, Brazil

The evolution of society and human rights

Statements of intrinsic rights can be found in all of the world's religions. They are held to be the entitlements of human beings as part of our birthright. However, the practice of human rights is contextual, or dependent on time and place. The current concept of human rights is a product of complex society; that is, societies that are multilayered and have a multipart division of labour that incorporates both those who have easy access to resources and those who do not.

The question of when we can identify a beginning for the history of human rights is one that has produced controversy. Micheline Ishay (2004: 6)[2] notes that this is a politically charged question, and one that is difficult to answer. Many accept the commonly held view that ancient Greece and Rome offer early examples of the ethical presentation of human rights, while acknowledging that, for example, the concepts of punishment and justice were present in ancient Babylon, Hindu and Buddhist beliefs. The latter also included a defence of the natural ecosystem, which was recognized as essential to our ability to survive on Earth. Confucianism advocated education for all, and both Christianity and Islam promoted human solidarity (Ishay 2004: 7). These are important developments to include, as a common belief still exists that the West has demonstrated the most advanced incorporation of rights, but as we have seen within the UDHR committee members themselves, there are significant differences among societies around the globe. The existence of written evidence of the consideration of rights within social structures does not automatically provide evidence of a moral superiority. Eric Wolf explains in his classic *Europe and the People Without History*[3] that we often mistake current social conditions as historically universal for all societies. However, human societies have evolved at different speeds and in varying conditions. Some argue that we only begin to see significant similarities among societies that developed in similar natural (ecological) conditions, and later, more significantly, during the massive global changes that came with colonialism and the imposition of outside powers over indigenous social organizations. Wolf says,

> We have been taught, inside the classroom and outside of it, that there exists an entity called the West, and that one can think of this West as a society and civilization independent of and in opposition to other societies and civilizations. Many of us even grew up believing that this West has a genealogy, according to which ancient Greece begat Rome, Rome begat Christian Europe, Christian Europe begat the Renaissance, the Renaissance the Enlightenment, the Enlightenment political democracy and the industrial revolution. Industry, crossed with democracy, in turn yielded the United States, embodying the rights to life, liberty, and the pursuit of happiness.

TOK

To what extent are our perspectives determined by our membership of a particular culture? Is it possible to objectively evaluate the impact of culture on our knowledge and beliefs?

Given the nature of written human rights and its development through Western philosophy, it is fair to conclude that the most popular conception of human rights is European in origin. We have seen how different approaches and views have given Europe, and later the United States, a definitional advantage in the creation of belief systems around human rights, and our general perceptions worldwide have been strongly influenced by current ideas in the most industrialized nations. The assertions of cultural rights, on the other hand, is a more complex topic which concerns the differences in systems on and within different continents, and has provided the material and arguments against accepting the Western version of human rights as the generalized ideal. One assumption that we can safely make is that the development of human rights has always been connected to events and to social movements. Just as the Second World War and the horrors of the Holocaust were the primary trigger for the UN's commission of the United Nations' Universal Declaration of Human Rights, so have indigenous movements, ethnic and gender movements, labour struggles, religious movements and wars over resources and access to those resources been driving forces for the designation of rights for these groups and particularly the "generations" of rights discussed below.

The Greeks and the Romans are the two early civilizations most recognized for having considered the "rights of man", and the Ancient Greek philosophers Plato and Aristotle are often cited for referencing "virtue" as a central characteristic of human life (Ishay 2007: 63).

Ancient Greece and Rome

Many scholars and public policy-makers mention Ancient Greece and Rome as starting points for the discussion of human rights because of the significance they hold in the evolution of complex societies, particularly in the West. They also both hold important reference points for the European Enlightenment, where the idea of universal human rights began to take on form and substance.

The social constructs of Ancient Greece and Rome both relied on the belief that human beings have the capacity to reason. While this belief did not guarantee that there would be equal access to resources by all and that inequalities would not exist, the structure of these ancient civilizations did lead to what we now understand to be universal rights and the common good. It also does not present a complete picture of Greece and Rome, for, as Wolf (1982: 5) also warns, history is not simply an unfolding of moral purpose:

> *What would we learn of ancient Greece, for example, if we interpreted it only as a prehistoric Miss Liberty, holding aloft the torch of moral purpose in the barbarian night?*

Our use of Greece and Rome as precursors to our current analyses of human rights tells us of but one variable in the social relations within these complex societies, and cannot serve as a baseline for the study of these societies on its own.

▲ A depiction of the interior of the Parthenon in Athens, Greece

Greece, Rome and "natural laws"

Both Greece and Rome recognized a distinction between "natural laws" and "custom". The latter would vary from place to place according to the convention, but the former were universal. After the fifteenth century these "natural laws" became associated with "natural rights". While philosophers and clerics of the Middle Ages had recognized the *duties* of humans, they did not specifically identify rights. However, with changes in social structures, specifically with the decline of European feudalism

▲ The swearing of the oath of ratification of the treaty of Munster in 1948, Gerard ter Borch (1617–1681)

The **Magna Carta**, or the "Great Charter" was signed by King John of England on 15 June 1215, in order to soothe the complaints of 40 Barons in the English countryside who felt that they were not getting a fair share of their rights and property from a greedy king. It stated (in part) that "to no one will we sell, to no one will we deny or delay right or justice".

Just 10 weeks after its agreement, Pope Innocent III destroyed the agreement, and England fell into Civil War. King John had hoped that the institution of the Magna Carta would calm the Barons and then fall into obscurity, but the Pope saw it as an attempt to weaken royal rights over the people and, as such, illegal and unjust. The rule over the lives and work of people was important to a feudal system in which the aristocracy owned the land and allowed people to work on it for a price.

The **Charter of the Forest** written in 1217 was sealed by Henry III, and was a reworking of the Magna Carta, assigning the ownership of the forests to the aristocracy. It was put into law in 1225. What was important about the Charter of the Forest was that it stipulated that any land unfairly taken by the king would be given back to the Barons, and that free men would have limited use of the land for special purposes. This was again an attempt to solidify feudal law, through which the aristocracy had control over the English forests and land. Much later the **Petition of Right** (1648) and the **English Bill of Rights** (1689) established rights for individuals, weakening the feudal system.

Research skills

1 What was the relationship between the four documents mentioned above?

2 Did these documents lead to the principles of the French Revolution or not?

3 What was the purpose of the French Revolution?

and the Peace of Westphalia, which was instituted in 1648, labour could be provided to advance a declining feudalism and a growing industrialization. Social changes were taking place all over Europe, and were evidenced by the Magna Carta (1215), the Charter of the Forest (1217), the Petition of Right (1648) and the English Bill of Rights (1689). All of these documents recognized the rights of the individual, culminating in the French Revolution that witnessed the final demise of feudal systems. These rights became more prominent and embedded in social laws during the eighteenth and nineteenth centuries and were presented in documents and charters that revolutionized the social orders of Europe, solidified by the French Revolution and the spread of the catchphrase of "Liberty, Equality and Fraternity".

These social changes and the reorganization of rights and duties which they represented resulted in a more complex labour system and a core reorganization of the division of labour. No longer did individuals and families have land designated by feudal lords on which they could grow their own foodstuffs; instead, mercantile organizations ruled over the production and distribution of goods, for which they needed labour to keep running. Those without land were forced to sell their labour in order to buy those foodstuffs that could feed their families. With this reorganization came a reconsideration of rights and a naming of rights based on this evolution of the division of labour and the control over labour that it presented. The social stratification that became more solidified after the French Revolution was based on the ownership of production and the ability to accumulate goods and the means to trade those goods. This is often recognized as the beginnings of the era of capitalism in which we now live.

Capitalist societies

Capitalist societies have status differences and hierarchies as part of their core organization, and are therefore built on the differences among groups to access the resources needed to live. In contrast, egalitarian societies had no need for "human rights" as such, as all community members were by definition equal. Community labour was for the production of goods that were used in the community and/or traded with other communities that had items not available locally. Status in hunting-and-gathering societies was often a temporary designation and task-oriented (such as building a canoe or organizing a trading expedition), and disappeared once the task was completed.

It is when labour began to be in the control of others, whether through a feudal lord or the selling of one's labour as a commodity to others for survival, that human rights and their *violation* becomes a phenomenon built into the functioning of social organization. This occurs when the labour of the community or individual is no longer for the use or consumption of the producer but for exchange in the market. The individual or group that controls the exchange or product gains power through their control over the materials that are needed to maintain life. The production process changes fundamentally when products are produced for exchange rather than community consumption.

Anthropologists have noted that this change often happened in the nineteenth and twentieth centuries as a result of colonialism, when the autonomous evolution of societies was destroyed and rapidly replaced by the rule of colonial expansion and the reconstruction of societies for the benefit of outside forces. These outside forces easily outpowered indigenous social organization and production; groups of people were given tribal names by outside managers and land was divided into tribal sectors with appointed leaders who worked for colonial administrators. During this period, human rights, both in the way that we know them today and in their most broad definition, were brutally violated. Slaves were shipped off to foreign lands without their kin groups or communities, and forced labour and physical trauma were the earmarks of colonial rule.

With the major changes that occurred during the eighteenth and nineteenth centuries and the evolution of the division of labour, new rights were advocated, most significantly by workers and their families for their own protection. The political realities that were growing among the "haves" and the "have-nots" initiated movements, both peaceful and violent, for the rights to organize trade unions, the protection of child labour, universal suffrage, control over workday hours, the rights to education and the like (see Ishay 2004: 9). From these movements came the recognition of the need for rights that were the precursors of entitlements won by workers and other social movements, and examples for the recognition of rights that led to the Universal Declaration of Human Rights in 1948.

▲ This steel engraving shows slaves being loaded on to a ship in 1881

The Declaration and its initial considerations

While the ideals of the European Enlightenment serve as precursors to what we now refer to as human rights, it is important to remember that they are the precursors of the debates that accompanied the Universal Declaration of Human Rights. The committee that put together the Declaration, started in Eleanor Roosevelt's Greenwich Village apartment, had agreed to disagree on some of the important differences that came to light after the Declaration was adopted by the United Nations. In its development, for example, it had been sent to the then Executive Director of the American Anthropological Association Melville Herskovits, asking for his viewpoints on its claims. Herskovits, who had done his anthropological fieldwork in Africa, wrote to them to say that the American Anthropological Association disagreed with many of its main points, and particularly its orientation towards Western views focused on the rights of the individual.

This focus on Western beliefs and behaviour was commented on in many disciplines at the time, with much disagreement with the Declaration's main audience. Given that the Declaration was a direct result of the Second World War and the horrors of the Holocaust, this is not a surprising outcome.

▲ The logo of a year-long campaign in 2008, marking the 60th anniversary of the Universal Declaration of Human Rights

TOK

The United Nations' Declaration of Human Rights claims to be "universal". Is there anything that is true for all cultures?

The United Nations' Universal Declaration of Human Rights, adopted on 10 December 1948, is the most translated document on the planet, and sets a "common standard" for the achievement for all peoples and all nations. The Declaration was developed largely with the recognition that there had been horrible and barbarous acts carried out by nations during the Second World War, and that these acts could not be allowed to be repeated. The United Nations commissioned a group of scholars and activists from around the world to produce this document, and the Declaration was initiated in the New York apartment of Eleanor Roosevelt, wife of the then US president. However, despite the best of intentions, these leaders and activists – representing both Eastern and Western societies and cultures – were often in disagreement, and Eleanor Roosevelt was forced to concede that there would always be differences that would just have to be accepted. Out of this collaboration came the following document, which outlined basic rights for all citizens of Earth. This document, however, was not the end of the differences on the meaning of human rights, particularly between East and West.

The Universal Declaration of Human Rights

The preamble to the Declaration sets the scope of contemporary human rights:

Whereas recognition of the inherent dignity and of the equal and inalienable rights of all members of the human family is the foundation of freedom, justice and peace in the world,

Whereas disregard and contempt for human rights have resulted in barbarous acts which have outraged the conscience of mankind, and the advent of a world in which human beings shall enjoy freedom of speech and belief and freedom from fear and want has been proclaimed as the highest aspiration of the common people,

Whereas it is essential, if man is not to be compelled to have recourse, as a last resort, to rebellion against tyranny and oppression, that human rights should be protected by the rule of law,

Whereas it is essential to promote the development of friendly relations between nations,

Whereas the peoples of the United Nations have in the Charter reaffirmed their faith in fundamental human rights, in the dignity and worth of the human person and in the equal rights of men and women and have determined to promote social progress and better standards of life in larger freedom,

Whereas Member States have pledged themselves to achieve, in cooperation with the United Nations, the promotion of universal respect for and observance of human rights and fundamental freedoms,

Whereas a common understanding of these rights and freedoms is of the greatest importance for the full realization of this pledge,

Now, therefore, the General Assembly proclaims…

▲ Eleanor Roosevelt holding the Universal Declaration of Human Rights, 1949

Article 1

All human beings are born free and equal in dignity and rights. They are endowed with reason and conscience and should act towards one another in a spirit of brotherhood.

Article 2

Everyone is entitled to all the rights and freedoms set forth in this Declaration, without distinction of any kind, such as race, colour, sex, language, religion, political or other opinion, national or social origin, property, birth or other status. Furthermore, no distinction shall be made on the basis of the political, jurisdictional or international status of the country or territory to which a person belongs, whether it be independent, trust, non-self-governing or under any other limitation of sovereignty.

Article 3

Everyone has the right to life, liberty and security of person.

Article 4

No one shall be held in slavery or servitude; slavery and the slave trade shall be prohibited in all their forms.

Article 5

No one shall be subjected to torture or to cruel, inhuman or degrading treatment or punishment.

Article 6

Everyone has the right to recognition everywhere as a person before the law.

Article 7

All are equal before the law and are entitled without any discrimination to equal protection of the law. All are entitled to equal protection against any discrimination in violation of this Declaration and against any incitement to such discrimination.

Article 8

Everyone has the right to an effective remedy by the competent national tribunals for acts violating the fundamental rights granted him by the constitution or by law.

Article 9

No one shall be subjected to arbitrary arrest, detention or exile.

Article 10

Everyone is entitled in full equality to a fair and public hearing by an independent and impartial tribunal, in the determination of his rights and obligations and of any criminal charge against him.

Article 11

1 Everyone charged with a penal offence has the right to be presumed innocent until proved guilty according to law in a public trial at which he has had all the guarantees necessary for his defense.

2 No one shall be held guilty of any penal offence on account of any act or omission.

Article 12

No one shall be subjected to arbitrary interference with his privacy, family, home or correspondence, nor to attacks upon his honour and reputation. Everyone has the right to the protection of the law against such interference or attacks.

Article 13

1 Everyone has the right to freedom of movement and residence within the borders of each State.

2 Everyone has the right to leave any country, including his own, and to return to his country.

Article 14

1 Everyone has the right to seek and to enjoy in other countries asylum from persecution.

2 This right may not be invoked in the case of prosecutions genuinely arising from non-political crimes or from acts contrary to the purposes and principles of the United Nations.

Article 15

1 Everyone has the right to a nationality.

2 No one shall be arbitrarily deprived of his nationality nor denied the right to change his nationality.

Article 16

1 Men and women of full age, without any limitation due to race, nationality or religion, have the right to marry and to found a family. They are entitled to equal rights as to marriage, during marriage and at its dissolution.

2 Marriage shall be entered into only with the free and full consent of the intending spouses.

3 The family is the natural and fundamental group unit of society and is entitled to protection by society and the State.

Article 17

1 Everyone has the right to own property alone as well as in association with others.

2 No one shall be arbitrarily deprived of his property.

Article 18

Everyone has the right to freedom of thought, conscience and religion; this right includes freedom to change his religion or belief, and freedom, either alone or in community with others and in public or private, to manifest his religion or belief in teaching, practice, worship and observance.

Article 19

Everyone has the right to freedom of opinion and expression; this right includes freedom to hold opinions without interference and to seek, receive and impart information and ideas through any media and regardless of frontiers.

Article 20

1 Everyone has the right to freedom of peaceful assembly and association.

2 No one may be compelled to belong to an association.

Article 21

1 Everyone has the right to take part in the government of his country, directly or through freely chosen representatives.

2 Everyone has the right to equal access to public service in his country.

3 The will of the people shall be the basis of the authority of government; this will shall be expressed in periodic and genuine elections which shall be by universal and equal suffrage and shall be held by secret vote or by equivalent free voting procedures.

Article 22

Everyone, as a member of society, has the right to social security and is entitled to realization, through national effort and international cooperation and in accordance with the organization and resources of each State, of the economic, social and cultural rights indispensable for his dignity and the free development of his personality.

Article 23

1 Everyone has the right to work, to free choice of employment, to just and favourable conditions of work and to protection against unemployment.

2 Everyone, without any discrimination, has the right to equal pay for equal work.

3 Everyone who works has the right to just and favourable remuneration ensuring for himself and his family an existence worthy of human dignity, and supplemented, if necessary, by other means of social protection.

4   Everyone has the right to form and to join trade unions for the protection of his interests.

Article 24

Everyone has the right to rest and leisure, including reasonable limitation of working hours and periodic holidays with pay.

Article 25

1   Everyone has the right to a standard of living adequate for the health and wellbeing of himself and of his family, including food, clothing, housing and medical care and necessary social services, and the right to security in the event of unemployment, sickness, disability, widowhood, old age or other lack of livelihood in circumstances beyond his control.

2   Motherhood and childhood are entitled to special care and assistance. All children, whether born in or out of wedlock, shall enjoy the same social protection.

Article 26

1   Everyone has the right to education. Education shall be free, at least in the elementary and fundamental stages. Elementary education shall be compulsory. Technical and professional education shall be made generally available and higher education shall be equally accessible to all on the basis of merit.

2   Education shall be directed to the full development of the human personality and to the strengthening of respect for human rights and fundamental freedoms. It shall promote understanding, tolerance and friendship among all nations, racial or religious groups, and shall further the activities of the United Nations for the maintenance of peace.

3   Parents have a prior right to choose the kind of education that shall be given to their children.

Article 27

1   Everyone has the right freely to participate in the cultural life of the community, to enjoy the arts and to share in scientific advancement and its benefits.

2   Everyone has the right to the protection of the moral and material interests resulting from any scientific, literary or artistic production of which he is the author.

Article 28

Everyone is entitled to a social and international order in which the rights and freedoms set forth in this Declaration can be fully realized.

Article 29

1   Everyone has duties to the community in which alone the free and full development of his personality is possible.

2   In the exercise of his rights and freedoms, everyone shall be subject only to such limitations as are determined by law solely for the purpose of securing due recognition and respect for the rights and freedoms of others and of meeting the just requirements of morality, public order and the general welfare in a democratic society.

3   These rights and freedoms may in no case be exercised contrary to the purposes and principles of the United Nations.

Article 30

Nothing in this Declaration may be interpreted as implying for any State, group or person any right to engage in any activity or to perform any act aimed at the destruction of any of the rights and freedoms set forth herein.

Research and thinking skills

1   What events led to the establishment of the Universal Declaration?

2   What rights does the UDHR propose and how were they accepted by member nations?

3   Which nations did not agree with these rights and why?

4   How have human rights evolved since the initial declaration?

TOK

Article 19 states that everyone has the right to freedom of opinion and expressions, including the right to hold opinions without interference. What would count as interference in this sense?

▲ French Revolution 1789: Allegorical emblem of the Republic

Our contemporary understanding of human rights relies on the key concepts of human rights, justice, liberty and equality. As the popularity of the UDHR increased outside the confines of the United Nations, various stakeholders and organizations – both government and non-government (NGOs) – saw a need to supplement the document with rights that could relate to all of the world's peoples. Growing social movements, such as the right for equal participation by women in society and the defence of cultural rights for social groups, pushed those participating under the banner of the UDHR to campaign for the inclusion of their ideals in the declaration.

The Czech activist and jurist Karel Vasak first proposed the division of human rights into three categories that corresponded with the three prominent features of the French Revolution: fraternity, liberty and equality. This would produce, Vasak reasoned, a common set of principles that could be applied universally, and that would include all peoples without differences dependent on religion, culture, location, gender or government. This takes us back to the fundamental tenet of rights: that they are part of each individual, cannot be differentiated by access to resources or bought and sold; they are indivisible.

> **First Generation Rights**, or civil and political rights, correspond to the French concept of *liberty*, and are grounded in the freedom of the individual to have opinions, to act politically, to engage in religion and, importantly, to assemble together without interference. These also include freedom from torture and slavery, the violation of which has once again become common in all parts of the world.

> **Second Generation Rights** are economic and social rights that correspond most closely to the French call for *equality*, and include the right to work, access to healthcare, a roof over one's head and food. They are sometimes referred to as "security-oriented rights" as they allow the individual the rights to live, work and to reproduce their families and their communities.

> **Third Generation Rights** are sometimes referred to as cultural rights, corresponding to the French idea of *fraternity*. These include the right to live in a reasonable environment, political rights and economic development. Of all the generations of rights, the Third Generation most clearly includes collective as well as individual rights, especially the formation of political parties and of economic development on all geographic levels.

The generations of rights are more often invoked in political discussions and by activists, rather than widely recognized by the public. Debates around them include the resistance of Second Generation rights by those who deem them socialist and/or long term. More generally, many have argued that these rights are indivisible, and separating them into generations causes contradictions and obligations to States that are unfair or unevenly applied depending on the form of government or stage of industrial development. Instead, rights are argued to be interrelated and interdependent, and thus cannot be separated out according to the situation in which they are applied.

Beyond the Third Generation, the rights as formulated are highly individualistic, and are dependent on the historical processes of the French, English and American revolutions. They are not easily separated given more contemporary circumstances – for example, arguments over the rights surrounding conflict with current debates about climate change and pollution. Many in the developing world insist that they should have the same rights to pollute the atmosphere as the industrialized countries had. The rights promoted by the French Revolution were specifically aimed at existing States and politics that have radically changed since that era. Given the massive shifts that have taken place in the past 50 years, the demarcation of rights into these three categories does not often assist or benefit progress in the implementation of basic rights. While these categories still find a place in the human rights literature and in debates, they are no longer seen as crucial to the human rights discussion.

Class discussion

Can human rights be separated into three types as explained here or are they indivisible?

Universal rights and cultural relativism

The distinction between universal rights and cultural relativism has been a prominent source of conflict since the adoption of the UDHR by the majority of States that make up the United Nations.

Universal rights assume that certain rights are the same for all people, and that even if they contradict local practices and beliefs they are applicable to that locality's people. A good example is the practice and condemnation of genital mutilation. While many countries, mostly in the Middle East, still practice female circumcision and genital cutting on a more or less routine basis, many treaties and covenants have condemned this practice as a violation of human rights that cannot be justified under any circumstances.

Universal suffrage is another example of a universal right agreed upon by the majority of the United Nations' member countries, but this has not guaranteed that women have gained equality with men in many areas of the world.

The distinction between universal rights and cultural relativism is one that stems from the beginnings of the UN's commission that was given the task of drafting the Universal Declaration of Human Rights. As we saw earlier in this unit, as early as Eleanor Roosevelt's meetings in her Washington Square apartment, an agreement had to be reached that there would be differences around these issues and that to get a draft Declaration done, the members of the commission would have to agree to disagree.

▲ The universal suffrage poll in Britain by Gostiaux

The reaction of the American Anthropological Association and other academic organizations to the Declaration because it failed to adequately recognize relativity and the cultural variances among countries still exists today. States and NGOs continue to argue the place of rights in a changing and globalizing world. However, current debates go beyond the complaint that the Declaration is based on Western principles to more contemporary themes that include an awareness of State and regional realities.

While contemporary debates more concretely specify the recognition of cultural differences and the rights of local beliefs, the insistence that the Declaration and its principals and doctrines are Western in origin and therefore of little use in non-Western settings is still the overarching theme. However, the contemporary debates also remind us that human and cultural relativity argue for sovereignty, territorial integrity, national security, economics and the environment.[4]
The excellent and comprehensive entry on human rights in the *Encyclopedia Britannica* puts the division in context by stating the more recent basis of the relativist movement:

> *With the end of the Cold War... the debate took on a more North-South character and was supplemented and intensified by a cultural-relativist critique... The viewpoint underlying this assertion – that the scope of human rights in any given society should be determined fundamentally by local, national, or regional customs and traditions – may seem problematic, especially when one considers that the idea of human rights and many of its precepts are all found in all the great philosophical and religious traditions. Nor is it surprising that it should emerge soon after the end of the Cold War. First prominently expressed in the declaration that emerged from the Bangkok meeting held in preparation to the second UN World Conference on Human Rights convened in Vienna in June 1993 (which qualified a reaffirmation of the universality of human rights by stating that human rights "must be considered in the context of... national and regional particularities and various historical, cultural and religious backgrounds"), the relativist critique reflects the end of a bi-polar system of alliances that had discouraged independent foreign policies and minimized cultural and political differences in favour of undivided Cold War loyalties.[5]*

Both the initial complaints about the Western character of the UN Declaration and the more contemporary debates over access to resources and economic development are reflected in the laws and treaties that have convened stakeholders. This has resulted in documents that reflect the perceived need to emphasize certain kinds of rights – for the environment, for women, for property, as examples – and led to other kinds of discussions of globalization, trade and the recognition of the many differences among industrialized, newly industrializing and underdeveloped areas.

Class discussion

To what extent does the United Nations' Universal Declaration of Human Rights represent Western principles only?

Human rights laws and treaties, human rights and the law

There have been many laws and treaties that emphasize and expand upon parts of the original 1948 Declaration. These have renewed debates among States concerning the implementation of rights and the inalienable entitlements of economic and cultural autonomy. These divisions point to a paradox that Michael Ignatieff has pointed out: we live with the moral universals of human rights with the full awareness that moral universals mean nothing in places like Kosovo and Rwanda. He believes that we have lived with this paradox since the Holocaust.[6] We try to reconcile this paradox with laws and treaties, but like the concept itself, not all are prone to following them. As Ignatieff continues, "The Holocaust laid bare what the world looked like when natural law was abrogated, when pure tyranny could accomplish its unbridled will. Without the Holocaust, then, no Declaration. Because of the Holocaust, no unconditional faith in the Declaration either" (page 5).

There have been treaties, covenants and laws on almost every aspect of human rights one can think of. The problem, however, is that almost none of them are legally enforceable on the international stage. With colonialism coming to an end, many of the foreign powers such as the Dutch and the French had to concede that their foreign colonies had the same rights that they themselves were entitled to; yet these newly independent countries did not initially feel compelled to follow the tenants of the Declaration, and the interests of their own elites often conflicted with the human rights stated there. The Soviet bloc abstained in the vote on the Declaration yet did not actively oppose its principles. Of all the advanced capitalist countries that have participated in the drafting of the Declaration and the meetings that followed, the United States has distinguished itself by voting against or ignoring almost all of the treaties and covenants and laws that have been drafted and passed by the majority of countries in the United Nations. In 1948, however, the divisions between the East and the West were still yet to come, and as Ignatieff (1999: 6) reminds us,

The descent of so many of these newly independent states into dictatorship or civil war had not yet occurred. It was still possible to believe that winning independence and freedom as a state would be enough to guarantee the freedoms of the individuals inside it. The emergence of the Asian Tiger economies and the rebirth of radical Islam were still decades away. The great philosophical conflict between "the West and the Rest" which has called into question the universality of human rights, still lay in the future.

▲ Refugees flee Rwanda in 1994 following the brutal genocide, which estimates say claimed in excess of 800,000 lives

▲ The bombardment of Dubrovnik by the Yugoslav People's Army in 1991, as part of Croatia's War of Independence. In the years that followed, the Balkan Peninsula saw genocide and massacres that shocked the world.

▲ The main gates to the Auschwitz Concentration Camp in Poland. Estimates put the death toll at this network of concentration and extermination camps at 1.25–1.5 million people.

In contemporary times, rights have been intermixed with identity politics, but as Ishay quoting the noted British historian Eric Hobsbawm states "support for rights based on particular identities or cultural allegiance—whether gay, women or ethnic. Promoters of 'identity politics,' [Hobsbawm] explained, 'are about themselves for themselves and nobody else.' Human rights can never be realized by adding the sum total of minorities' interests."[7]

Still, the treaties, covenants and laws that have been adopted by some or most of the United Nations' states do address identity as well as the larger issues of rights, such as education, freedom from fear, rights to housing, climate change, the environment, sexual orientation and the like. The sheer number of these documents begins to confuse the issue of rights as statements of ideals rather than enforceable movements towards promised realities. They are often referred to as instruments of human rights implementation and are monitored by various bodies, both States and NGOs, who regularly report on their violations and those who are violating them. More recent activism has addressed labour and development rights, taking on questions about globalization, contemporary development and the labour that participates in that development, as we shall see in the following unit on development.

Part of the problem with the generalities presented in these instruments is the assumption that they can apply equally to all participants in a given category. Ishay (2007: 390), as an example, tells us,

> With respect to women, American philosopher Martha Nussbaum argued against unqualified cultural rights positions, which she regards as a rationale for repressing women's rights. Drawing her position from a liberal universalist and Aristotelian approach, she maintained in "Women and Cultural Universals" (Sex and Social Justice, 1999) that it is absurd to treat one nation as a single culture. Conversely, it is absurd to treat women's rights, or any individual rights, without an understanding of an individual's capabilities to realize these rights (a concept she draws from Amartya Sen).

Further, the effect of a deepening globalization has made assumptions more difficult as there is a public perception that globalization is making the world a more homogeneous arena. However, others – of special note the anthropologist June Nash in her *Ethnographic Aspects of the World System* – have shown that globalization in fact may be making the world more diverse. This is a result of local cultures incorporating forces and cultural artefacts from the outside into their own existing cultures, changing their everyday practices while maintaining an autonomy that differs from global trade and market standards.[8] This has led, for example, to renewed demands to teach and maintain local languages, as we have seen in Wales, where Welsh has been designated a national language along with English, and all signs must be in both languages. This is a movement that is becoming popular in different geographic areas and symbolizes the claim of peoples to maintain their cultural history. Globalization and globalizing trade has also given rise to questions about the rights of indigenous people, who are often on the world stage as they fight for their own rights, including land and resources, against those who would claim those resources (such as oil and land) for global industries.

▲ A bilingual sign on the Llanberis pass in Wales, UK

The United Nations human rights legal system

Currently, there are three regional human rights systems – Africa, Europe, and the Americas – all responsible for monitoring and reporting on human rights implementation and abuses.

The overarching organization is the United Nations and its 193 member states. The organization of human rights within the United Nations is a growing and multifaceted system that is meant to apply to all United Nations members, but rarely includes all. Human rights laws are not enforceable, and as Human Rights Watch reports[9], the United States rarely ratifies treaties commonly adopted by other nations. In fact, the last international human rights treaties the US ratified were two optional protocols to the Convention on the Rights of the Child (but not the treaty itself) in December 2002. The Convention on the Rights of the Child has since been ratified by every UN member state, with the exception of the US and Somalia. The US has also failed to ratify the Convention on the Elimination of All Forms of Discrimination Against Women (CEDAW), a treaty that has been ratified by all member states except seven: US, Iran, Nauru, Palau, Somalia, Sudan and Tonga.

The problem inherent in human rights enforcement presented by the United States correlates with many nations' refusal to admit to human rights abuses in their own territories. No member of the United Nations Security Council has been brought forward to the International Criminal Court, nor has any powerful industrialized country been formally questioned about human rights violations. As of 2016, 39 individuals have been indicted by the International Criminal Court (ICC).

▲ The logo of the United Nations

The International Criminal Court

The ICC consists of 123 member states that ratified the Rome Statute, the treaty which established the ICC in 1998, and entered into force in 2002. Seven nations voted against the ratification of the ICC, including the United States, China and Israel. A number of nations have signed but not ratified the Rome Statute. The Court's purpose is to prosecute serious international crimes, such as crimes against humanity, war crimes and crimes of aggression. Further action and consequences of prosecution of individuals by the ICC remain to be seen, and are still being contested by some member states. China and India, for example, have openly criticized the existence of the ICC, questioning the legitimacy of an institution that operates beyond national sovereignty.

▲ The logo of the International Criminal Court

TOK

Research how international treaties are ratified.

To what extent are international politics hampered by national sovereignty?

UN human rights mechanisms

The UN promotes, monitors and protects human rights through a variety of mechanisms. Some are composed of independent human rights experts, while others are led by State representatives.

The principal UN human rights bodies are:

> **UN Human Rights Council:** an intergovernmental body composed of 47 States, which discuss and make recommendations on human rights topics. The Council also manages two other human rights mechanisms:
>
> - **Universal Periodic Review:** a peer-review process through which UN Member States' overall human rights records undergo scrutiny every four years.
>
> - **Special Procedures:** independent experts appointed to monitor human rights conditions in specific countries or on particular topics.

> **UN human rights treaty bodies:** ten committees of independent experts that oversee States' implementation of the core UN human rights treaties. Visit http://tbinternet.ohchr.org/_layouts/ TreatyBodyExternal/Treaty.aspx to see which UN human rights treaties and complaints mechanisms each State has joined.

> The UN **Office of the High Commissioner for Human Rights** (OHCHR) coordinates and supports the work of the UN human rights mechanisms, including by distributing useful information and facilitating civil society engagement. The OHCHR also provides assistance to national governments and maintains **country offices** and **regional offices**.

▲ The logo of the Human Rights Council of the United Nations with seat in Geneva

Other UN bodies

In addition to the main UN human rights mechanisms, there are other UN bodies and procedures relevant to the protection of human rights and the development of international human rights law:

> The **International Court of Justice** resolves disputes between States on issues of international law, including on some issues related to human rights.

> The **International Labour Organization** also plays an important role in promotion, protection and standard-setting on topics related to work and employment.

> The **International Law Commission** has the specific mandate, established in the UN Charter, of developing and codifying international law, including in areas pertinent to human rights protection. The Commission is composed of 34 individual members that serve five-year terms.

> The **Economic and Social Council** (ECOSOC) coordinates the work of the UN specialized agencies, with regard to economic and social themes, as well as engaging in its own promotion and protection activities, and formulating policy recommendations within the UN system.

In the area of refugee law, the **UN High Commissioner for Refugees** contributes to legal standard-setting, in addition to providing on-the-ground assistance to refugees.

▲ The logo of the United Nations High Commissioner for Refugees

The **United Nations General Assembly** is the political and policy-making organ of the United Nations, and may make recommendations in the area of human rights. Its **Social, Humanitarian and Cultural Affairs Committee** (referred to as the "Third Committee") provides a forum for discussion of human rights issues, as well.

The **Commission on the Status of Women**, a subsidiary body of ECOSOC composed of 47 States, is the principal forum for advancing gender equality and the rights of women. Its work is supported by **UN Women**.

The Human Rights Office of the High Commissioner lists the primary instruments in the defence of human rights:

Universal human rights instruments

In addition to the International Bill of Rights and the core human rights treaties, there are many other universal instruments relating to human rights. A non-exhaustive selection is listed below.

World Conference on Human Rights and Millennium Assembly

- Vienna Declaration and Programme of Action
- United Nations Millennium Declaration

The right of self-determination

- United Nations Declaration on the Granting of Independence to Colonial Countries and Peoples
- General Assembly resolution 1803 (XVII) of 14 December 1962, "Permanent sovereignty over natural resources"
- International Convention against the Recruitment, Use, Financing and Training of Mercenaries

Rights of indigenous peoples and minorities

- Declaration on the Rights of Indigenous Peoples
- Indigenous and Tribal Peoples Convention, 1989 (No. 169)
- Declaration on the Rights of Persons Belonging to National or Ethnic, Religious and Linguistic Minorities

Prevention of discrimination

- Equal Remuneration Convention, 1951 (No. 100)
- Discrimination (Employment and Occupation) Convention, 1958 (No. 111)
- International Convention on the Elimination of all Forms of Racial Discrimination (ICERD)

- Declaration on Race and Racial Prejudice
- Convention against Discrimination in Education
- Protocol Instituting a Conciliation and Good Offices Commission to be responsible for seeking a settlement of any disputes which may arise between States Parties to the Convention against Discrimination in Education
- Declaration on the Elimination of All Forms of Intolerance and of Discrimination Based on Religion or Belief
- World Conference against Racism, 2001 (Durban Declaration and Programme of Action)

Rights of women

- Convention on the Elimination of All Forms of Discrimination against Women (CEDAW)
- Optional Protocol to the Convention on the Elimination of All Forms of Discrimination against Women (CEDAW-OP)
- Declaration on the Protection of Women and Children in Emergency and Armed Conflict
- Declaration on the Elimination of Violence against Women

Rights of the child

- Convention on the Rights of the Child (CRC)
- Optional Protocol to the Convention on the Rights of the Child on the sale of children, child prostitution and child pornography (CRC-OPSC)
- Optional Protocol to the Convention on the Rights of the Child on the involvement of children in armed conflict (CRC-OPAC)
- Minimum Age Convention, 1973 (No. 138)
- Worst Forms of Child Labour Convention, 1999 (No. 182)

Rights of older persons

- United Nations Principles for Older Persons

Rights of persons with disabilities

- Convention on the Rights of Persons with Disabilities
- Optional Protocol to the Convention on the Rights of Persons with Disabilities
- Declaration on the Rights of Mentally Retarded Persons
- Declaration on the Rights of Disabled Persons
- Principles for the protection of persons with mental illness and the improvement of mental health care
- Standard Rules on the Equalization of Opportunities for Persons with Disabilities

Human rights in the administration of justice: protection of persons subjected to detention or imprisonment

- United Nations Standard Minimum Rules for the Treatment of Prisoners (The Nelson Mandela Rules)
- Basic Principles for the Treatment of Prisoners
- Body of Principles for the Protection of All Persons under Any Form of Detention or Imprisonment
- United Nations Rules for the Protection of Juveniles Deprived of their Liberty
- Declaration on the Protection of All Persons from Being Subjected to Torture and Other Cruel, Inhuman or Degrading Treatment or Punishment
- Convention against Torture and Other Cruel, Inhuman or Degrading Treatment or Punishment (CAT)
- Optional Protocol to the Convention against Torture and Other Cruel, Inhuman or Degrading Treatment or Punishment (OPCAT)
- Principles of Medical Ethics relevant to the Role of Health Personnel, particularly Physicians, in the Protection of Prisoners and Detainees against Torture and Other Cruel, Inhuman or Degrading Treatment or Punishment
- Principles on the Effective Investigation and Documentation of Torture and Other Cruel, Inhuman or Degrading Treatment or Punishment
- Safeguards guaranteeing protection of the rights of those facing the death penalty
- Code of Conduct for Law Enforcement Officials
- Basic Principles on the Use of Force and Firearms by Law Enforcement Officials
- United Nations Standard Minimum Rules for Non-custodial Measures (The Tokyo Rules)
- United Nations Standard Minimum Rules for the Administration of Juvenile Justice (The Beijing Rules)

- Guidelines for Action on Children in the Criminal Justice System
- United Nations Guidelines for the Prevention of Juvenile Delinquency (The Riyadh Guidelines)
- Declaration of Basic Principles of Justice for Victims of Crime and Abuse of Power
- Basic Principles on the Independence of the Judiciary
- Basic Principles on the Role of Lawyers
- Guidelines on the Role of Prosecutors
- Principles on the Effective Prevention and Investigation of Extra-legal, Arbitrary and Summary Executions
- Declaration on the Protection of All Persons from Enforced Disappearance
- Basic Principles and Guidelines on the Right to a Remedy and Reparation
- International Convention for the Protection of All Persons from Enforced Disappearance
- United Nations Rules for the Treatment of Women Prisoners and Non-custodial Measures for Women Offenders (the Bangkok Rules)
- Updated set of principles for the protection and promotion of human rights through action to combat impunity

Social welfare, progress and developments

- Declaration on Social Progress and Development
- Universal Declaration on the Eradication of Hunger and Malnutrition
- Declaration on the Use of Scientific and Technological Progress in the Interests of Peace and for the Benefit of Mankind
- Declaration on the Right of Peoples to Peace
- Declaration on the Right to Development
- Universal Declaration on the Human Genome and Human Rights
- Universal Declaration on Cultural Diversity

Promotion and protection of human rights

- Principles relating to the status of national institutions (The Paris Principles)
- Declaration on the Right and Responsibility of Individuals, Groups and Organs of Society to Promote and Protect Universally Recognized Human Rights and Fundamental Freedoms
- United Nations Declaration on Human Rights Education and Training

Marriage

- Convention on Consent to Marriage, Minimum Age for Marriage and Registration of Marriages
- Recommendation on Consent to Marriage, Minimum Age for Marriage and Registration of Marriages

Right to health

- Declaration of Commitment on HIV/AIDS

Right to work and to fair conditions of employment

- Employment Policy Convention, 1964 (No. 122)

Freedom of association

- Freedom of Association and Protection of the Right to Organise Convention, 1948 (No. 87)
- Right to Organise and Collective Bargaining Convention, 1949 (No. 98)

Slavery, slavery-like practices and forced labour

- Slavery Convention
- Protocol amending the Slavery Convention signed at Geneva on 25 September 1926
- Supplementary Convention on the Abolition of Slavery, the Slave Trade, and Institutions and Practices Similar to Slavery
- Forced Labour Convention, 1930 (No. 29)
- Abolition of Forced Labour Convention, 1957 (No. 105)
- Convention for the Suppression of the Traffic in Persons and of the Exploitation of the Prostitution of Others
- Protocol to Prevent, Suppress and Punish Trafficking in Persons, Especially Women and Children, supplementing the United Nations Convention against Transnational Organized Crime

Rights of migrants

- International Convention on the Protection of the Rights of All Migrant Workers and Members of Their Families (ICPMW)
- Protocol against the Smuggling of Migrants by Land, Sea and Air, supplementing the United Nations Convention against Transnational Organized Crime

Nationality, statelessness, asylum and refugees

- Convention on the Reduction of Statelessness
- Convention relating to the Status of Stateless Persons
- Convention relating to the Status of Refugees
- Protocol relating to the Status of Refugees
- Declaration on the Human Rights of Individuals who are not nationals of the country in which they live

War crimes and crimes against humanity, including genocide

- Convention on the Prevention and Punishment of the Crime of Genocide
- Convention on the Non-Applicability of Statutory Limitations to War Crimes and Crimes against Humanity
- Principles of international co-operation in the detection, arrest, extradition and punishment of persons guilty of war crimes and crimes against humanity
- Statute of the International Tribunal for the Former Yugoslavia
- Statute of the International Tribunal for Rwanda
- Rome Statute of the International Criminal Court

Humanitarian law

- Geneva Convention relative to the Treatment of Prisoners of War
- Geneva Convention relative to the Protection of Civilian Persons in Time of War
- Protocol Additional to the Geneva Conventions of 12 August 1949, and relating to the Protection of Victims of International Armed Conflicts (Protocol I)
- Protocol Additional to the Geneva Conventions of 12 August 1949, and relating to the Protection of Victims of Non-International Armed Conflicts (Protocol II)[10]

Class discussion

Do any of these instruments seem more important than others? Which seem most applicable to contemporary global politics? Why?

Research and thinking skills

Which groups or organizations have been most involved in the inclusion of these human rights instruments?

The practice of human rights

Since the original Declaration, the meaning of human rights has come to mean many things to various peoples, and the *practice* of human rights has become even more varied and complex. In Kenneth Cmiel's Review Essay on "The Recent History of Human Rights", he identifies three waves of activism since the 1940s.

The first was Eleanor Roosevelt and the initial drafting of the Declaration.[11] Before the initial drafting, however, there were many who were working on the rights of humans and the meaning of those rights as a result of the Holocaust, such as Rapheal Lemkin who drafted the UN Convention on Genocide, and fought for keeping the discussion of rights active during the next decade. Winston Churchill promoted the European Convention on Human Rights, and Charles Habib Malik, a Lebanese Diplomat, was a prominent force in the drafting of the Universal Declaration. As Cmiel's review (2004: 129) tells us,

this activism was also designed to build international law, and the new United Nations was at the heart of it... that set of principles was supposed to be quickly turned into binding international law. The Genocide Convention, adopted by the General Assembly the day before it adopted the Universal Declaration, was similarly supposed to matter. Yet the world waited until the 1990s for the next major international tribunal charging someone with crimes against humanity.

The second wave came in the 1970s with what Cmiel calls "an explosion" of interest in human rights. This was represented by the exponential growth of Amnesty International (founded in 1961) and the establishment of Human Rights Watch in New York, the Mothers of the Plaza de Mayo in Buenos Aires, and Helsinki Watch groups in the Soviet Union and Eastern Europe. This wave

▲ Women of the Plaza de Mayo in Argentina protesting against missing children during the 1970s military dictatorship

of activism corresponded with the growth of globalization, and the communication technologies and trade interactions that came with it. NGOs took on the leading role, leaving the United Nations the centre of the promotion of international law and the NGOs more interested in the media distribution of cruel acts against peoples and groups. Cmiel notes that the relationships between these NGOs and the UN steadily worsened during the 1970s, as the promotion of international law became less of a focus for human rights movements.

The third wave, as Cmiel reports (2004, 130) came in the late 1980s and 1990s, when human rights started to actively include women's rights, health rights, economic justice and indigenous people's rights.

The major human rights organizations, Amnesty International in London, Human Rights Watch in New York and the International Commission of Jurists in Geneva, all devoted themselves solely to combating appalling abuses of civil and political rights around the globe.

International law also gained a renewed interest, as the establishment of the International Criminal Court and the International Criminal Tribunal for the Former Yugoslavia attests. There was also a prominent growth of NGOs outside the West, with a wide range of agendas. Cmiel complains that very little research has yet to be done on the explosion in the number of these organizations and the agendas that they promote.

Today it would be difficult to find a college campus without a chapter of Amnesty International and other groups concerned with human rights campaigns. The prominence of these groups signifies another paradox: that the importance of the movements of the 1960s and 1970s that emphasized political economy and status, class and power began to take a back seat to the publicizing of human rights abuses. The full extent of this is a story still to be told, as many have claimed that the headlines of human rights abuses have masked the origin of these abuses in the systemic problems of globalization. These include the growth of multinational corporations, as well as the attack on labour that has been witnessed in the past 20 years and the consolidation of capital into the hands of a few that has made a major difference in the distribution of resources around the world.

This paradox will undoubtedly draw more analyses and discussions in the years to come, as human rights begins to include the uneven distribution of resources that has grown exponentially in the past decade. This growth has also failed to deal with issues such as the United States' "sidestepping" of the UN Convention on Landmines or the ability of other powerful nations to ignore significant issues for future populations.

Other examples needing analysis include the growth of dams that have affected millions of people, particularly in China and India, and the climate change that has caused desertification in villages, communities and regions around the globe.

TOK

How do the meanings of key terms and concepts within disciplines change over time? What might constitute progress in an area of knowledge? How could we know if progress, rather than simply change, has been achieved?

The politicization of human rights

The meaning of human rights and its practice has been highly politicized in recent times, largely as a result of the following:

- The involvement of the United States and other powerful industrialized countries in the enactment of human rights.

- The activist movements that have identified the connection between contemporary industrialization and the deployment of social labour in the effort towards nationalized growth.

- The disputes around universal versus relative rights with regard to cultural differences.

- Most importantly, the effect of globalization of labour practices and the rights of local peoples and communities as they confront powerful outside forces.

ATL

Research and thinking skills

Research the events of the Rwandan genocide. What were the roles of NGOs and the United Nations in this conflict?

Part of the growth of NGOs and the lessening of the role of the UN in human rights discussions revolve around the internal workings of the UN, the hegemony of the Security Council and the UN's agenda of finding agreement rather than differences around issues such as humanitarian intervention. A good example is the case of Rwanda, where the mass killings were not labelled as genocide until the scale of the massacres became widely known and NGOs demanded that these mass killings be recognized. Many NGOs, therefore, began to distrust the United Nations, followed by a general distrust by individual activists and writers familiar with the internal workings of the UN.

The ideals that the Universal Declaration provides correspond with the widest inequality ever seen. In the US alone, between a third and one-half of the population is living on or beneath the poverty line. In China and India, while many developers claim that the recent industrial development has made daily life better for their inhabitants, studies have shown, including those emanating from the UN, that the opposite is the case. Socio-economic inequality, a ceiling between rich and poor, is absent from the Universal Declaration, "as well as the legal regimes and social movements that take it as their polestar".

The contradiction is expressed by the example of Milton Friedman, an ultra-conservative economist, who strategized the takeover of Chile and the Southern Cone of South America in the 1970s, resulting in huge State abuses to life and limb in favour of free market economies. As a result, Friedman won a Nobel Prize in Economics in 1976, while Amnesty International was awarded the Nobel Peace Prize the next year.

Human rights here are closely tied to the wishes of the powerful industrialized States and the free market economics of neo-liberalism. Moyn (2015: 7) says,

> [Naomi Klein] insightfully suggests that when the 'Chicago boys' [Milton Friedman and his followers] of neoliberalism were invited by Pinochet [the then dictator of Chile] to strip down the state (except the military), the earliest human rights movement turned a blind eye to the economic reasons the violence was occurring... and the problem is less the failure of rights movements to offer a better economic theory of the roots of violence – which is someone else's job – than that they had no significant effect in identifying, let alone confronting, inequality.

In other words, human rights movements failed in the socio-economic domain. As Moyn (2015: 7–8) notes,

> *The tragedy of human rights is that they have occupied the global imagination but have so far contributed little of note, merely nipping at the heels of the neo-liberal giant whose path goes unaltered and unresisted... Precisely because the human rights revolution has focused so intently on state abuses and has, at its most ambitious, dedicated itself to establishing a floor for protection, it failed to respond to – or even much recognize – neoliberalism's obliteration of the ceiling on inequality.[12]*

What we have identified here are questions of politics and power. As a result of active NGO human rights networks, Nancy Scheper-Hughes in her "Danger and Endangered Youth" tells us that legal sanctions are being enacted in almost every country in Africa, as they have in many countries around the world. As she tells us,

> *In Africa, the human rights movement has not only permeated the consciousness of elite educated Africans, but given the reach of the transistor radio, the idea of human rights has sometimes touched the lives of ordinary, uneducated people.*

Further, she notes, "human rights could be seen as one of the most globalized political values of our times" (Wilson, 1997: 1, quoted in Moore). The problem is enforcement, and the lack of power wielded by transnational tribunals and United Nations Committees. Again, in her words,

> *The International Criminal Tribunal for Rwanda set up by the U.N. Security Council is such an instance. The ICTR came into being in 1994 to find and prosecute those responsible for the Rwandan genocide in which it is estimated that 800,000 Tutsi and some educated Hutu died. The International Tribunal arrested 59 persons but to date have actually convicted only 8.[13]*

Even human rights NGOs regularly admit that the focus on rights rather than structural change runs the risk of masking the underlying principles that initiated the conditions that lead to the abuse. Legal redress is difficult on both the local and the global levels, and, in some cases, the focus on human rights has even strengthened neo-liberal policies of non-intervention that are backed from economic ideals of free-market economies.

While government agencies resist intervening in the name of neo-liberal principles when it would seem necessary to do so, these same principles do not guarantee the calls for autonomy that are parts of struggles to gain access to or protect resources that have belonged to existing social groups for centuries. Often focusing on individual abuses rather than collective oppression, the discourse around human rights has occupied the space where discussions about collective interest, class consciousness and power were positioned. Further, as human rights NGOs are beginning to show, governmental bodies are experts at expounding the evils of human rights abuses in far-off places, while claiming that their own governments are abuse free. Calls for human rights protections and corrections by governments around the globe serve as definitional acts of their own practices while human rights at home are assumed. There is a geography of human rights, one that assumes abuses in poorly developed economies while ignoring or recasting abuse in the highly capitalized states.[14/15]

▲ The International Criminal Tribunal for Rwanda (ICTR) was housed in Arusha, Tanzania (the farthest white building) until 31 December 2015 when the Tribunal was officially closed

Class discussion

Do all NGOs have a positive influence on human rights?

2.4 Conclusion

▲ A human rights placard held by a participant in the annual Pride London parade, UK

Our discussion of human rights in various contexts, claims, agreements and debates all lead to the grounded enquiry into their implementation, and to the access to resources and protections that the adoption of human rights promises through the Declaration and the many treaties and covenants that have been a result of their adaptation. The critical question here, then, is human rights for whom?

Since the 1940s, there have been many social movements built around the tenets of human rights, and NGOs built around the implementation of human rights for various stakeholders globally. This has led to one author's claim that human rights are now in a "mid-life crisis", with changing stratagems and approaches to gaining access and emphasizing the differences among those successfully using human rights to gain access to resources and those for whom human rights means little in terms of challenging exploitation and enacting social change on a basic level.

Human rights identification, monitoring, social movements and ongoing debates between concepts of the East and West will continue as long as no agreement can be reached as to what human rights consist of, to whom they are directed and what and how they are either put into practice or thwarted. We are in a period where human rights and the analysis of human rights have far outdistanced the arguments and politics around political economy and the place of class, status and place in local, regional, national, international and global geographies. The question then becomes whether this has further confused the idea of human rights or furthered the public awareness of violations and inequality.

TOK

Is it possible for scientists to maintain a detached relationship with the subject matter they are investigating?

Time will only tell if human rights remain the significant and broad concept that has taken over the world stage. Once combined with political economy, for example, it may turn in a new direction that may challenge the elites that dominate the United Nations in favour of those subject to structural power and structural violence. As violence and "people, power and politics" is at the centre of this dialogue in a rapidly globalizing world, the movement of peoples from exclusion to inclusion will require fundamental changes in the way that geographic areas organize social reproduction. The lessons that can be learned from alternate ways of thinking and seeing provide a context for a human rights involvement that can make a difference (cf. Kirsch 2006: 25).

2.5 Exam-style questions

1 Discuss the extent to which cultural relativism can be used to justify different concepts of human rights.

Examiner hints

Responses should include an understanding of cultural relativism and of individual and collective rights, and an indication of how these have been used in discussions on human rights. Responses may also refer to the creation of the Universal Declaration of Human Rights (UDHR) and the controversies that have surrounded it. Responses may also distinguish between cultural relativism and universal rights.

Arguments that cultural relativism can be used as justification may include:

- cultural relativism assumes that the practices of individual cultures represent autonomous rights that should not be compared to those of other cultures and the idea can thus be applied to defend many different practices and concepts of rights

- a cultural relativist approach is more successful than universal approaches, for example, responses may note that individual rights – on which a great emphasis is placed in the UDHR – have been criticized as Western conceptions that have been forced on non-Western cultures through colonialism and other forms of coercion that have often been detrimental to the maintaining of more collective rights around the world

- cultural relativism may be more successful than universal approaches in defending collective human rights, given its emphasis on people's shared experience within a culture.

Arguments that cultural relativism cannot be used as justification may include:

- the notion of cultural relativism has been used to justify controversial cultural practices that infringe particularly on individuals' rights, such as honour killing and female genital mutilation

- cultural relativism does not allow for cultural comparisons and may therefore lead to a misinterpretation of practices within cultures

- universal approaches, in their emphasis on the similarity of all human beings, may be more successful in defending individual human rights, due to their emphasis on the commonality of experience of all human beings.

Responses should make reference to specific examples. They could discuss Asian, African or indigenous conceptions of rights that tend to view human rights in more collective terms. Responses could also mention more recent developments in universal rights, such as covenants and treaties against gender discrimination, for the protection of migrant workers or in favour of hate crime laws, and so on.

Responses should include the candidate's evaluation of the extent to which cultural relativism can been used as an argument to defend alternative concepts of individual and collective human rights.

2 "Human rights covenants and treaties limit development in newly industrializing economies." To what extent do you agree with this claim?

Examiner hints

Responses should include an understanding of the concept of development and of the nature and intention of human rights covenants and treaties. Responses should also show an understanding of what is meant by newly industrializing economies.

Arguments that human rights covenants and treaties do limit the development of newly industrializing economies may include:

- greater monitoring of labour conditions for human rights reasons has reduced flexibility to organize labour in the process of industrialization

- trade agreements, agreements between buyers and suppliers, and self-monitoring by multi-national corporations often specify the ways in which commodities can be produced and distributed, and this places limits on how resources, including labour, can be implemented

- it could be argued that many countries became modern states through a process of industrialization, and that emerging economies should be allowed to follow the same path. The process of industrialization by which many presently developed countries became prosperous was based on practices, such as child labour during the Industrial Revolution, which would nowadays be considered to be violations of human rights,
and would be condemned and/or forbidden by environmental standards and international organizations, such as the World Trade Organization and the International Labour Organization.

Arguments that human rights covenants and treaties do not limit the development of newly industrializing economies may include:

- human rights covenants and treaties are often not enforced, or are not enforceable, and therefore they do not limit development

- it is possible to have development without violating human rights or environmental standards or treaties; for example, in recent years there have been efforts to promote rights-based approaches to development and sustainability

- these sorts of covenants and treaties do not "limit" the process of development, but instead "improve" the process

- although human rights covenants and treaties may place limits on some aspects of development, they also facilitate other aspects, such as education, technology transfer or international cooperation.

Responses should make some reference to specific examples. For instance, candidates could discuss the process of industrialization in a certain country, such as in China or India. They could refer to aspects of specific covenants and treaties, such as to the International Covenant of Economic, Social and Cultural Rights (1966), the Convention on the Protection of Rights of Migrant Workers (1990), the Rome Statute (2002) or the Kyoto Protocol (2005), and evaluate how these aspects have or have not limited development.

Responses should include the candidate's evaluation of whether human rights treaties and covenants limit development in newly industrializing economies.

3 "The Universal Declaration of Human Rights (1948) is no longer relevant for dealing with human rights issues in the twenty-first century." To what extent do you agree with this claim?

Examiner hints

Arguments that the 1948 UDHR is still relevant may include:

- human rights abuses still persist, so it is needed as much as ever: additional covenants and treaties have updated the basic tenets expressed in the UDHR

- it is formulated in non-prescriptive terms so can be adapted to deal with different sorts of rights

- it is the basis for further "generations" of rights including ones that address current concerns such as education and gender equality

- the majority of states are signatories so it is a morally aspirational goal for a great many nations.

Arguments that the 1948 UDHR is no longer relevant may include:

- the UDHR is a historic document limited to the vision of the Western states that created it

- human rights abuses still persist, so has it proved to be ineffectual

- it does not include contemporary issues like same-sex marriage and gender rights

- it does not cater to the differing concepts of rights held in different cultures

- its tenets are not legally enforceable and this has been shown to limit their effectiveness.

Responses should include a conclusion on the extent to which you agree with the claim.

4 Examine the effectiveness of non-state actors in advancing the protection of human rights.

Examiner hints

Arguments that non-state actors are effective may include:

- NGOs like Amnesty International are powerful advocates of human rights in that they can raise awareness of particular cases of abuse through investigations, the organization of social movements, and through the use of social media internationally

- NGOs, because of their independent nature, can address the effects of neglect and other human rights abuses in states

- the structures of NGOs have more flexibility than state structures, which enables them to be quicker in responding to human rights issues

- some IGOs like the United Nations High Commissioner for Refugees (UNHCR) and the International Criminal Court (ICC) can bypass state sovereignty in order to uphold and promote human rights.

Arguments that non-state actors are not effective may include:

- the majority of NGOs are not well supported financially, so this limits their effectiveness

- financial/personal gain motivations of some members of NGOs can be an issue

- large NGOs working with government agencies may be limited in their ability to act independently and to represent local populations

- some international campaigns by non-state actors cannot be effective in all countries because of differing cultural concepts of human rights

- issues of state sovereignty and power prevent IGOs from bringing perpetrators of human rights abuses to international institutions of justice (for example, the United States and China)

- some non-state actors have no interest in promoting human rights, or they may even directly challenge the tenets of the UDHR, and have an agenda that either neglects or doesn't recognize particular rights (for example, the Taliban's renunciation of education for women) – some politically conservative NGOs actively campaign against others' perceptions of human rights (for example, rights to same-sex marriage, or to the use of contraception to protect against unwanted pregnancy and sexually transmitted diseases)

- MNCs – for example, Apple, GE, and organizations like FIFA – make use of lax labour rights in countries as a way of obtaining cheap labour, often perpetuating and/or creating dangerous working environments

- some MNCs are also complicit in the denial of rights such as the land rights of indigenous groups

- well-intentioned campaigns, for example, on social media, may be inaccurate or misleading, for example, #Kony2012, and may sometimes be based on faulty or limited information.

5 Compare and contrast an institutional approach to the ratification and enforcement of human rights (for example, through the Hague Courts) with non-institutional approaches (for example, through human rights NGOs, such as Amnesty International).

Examiner hints

It is not necessary for the response to be equally balanced between similarities and differences to achieve the highest marks.

Better answers will demonstrate an excellent understanding of the concept of human rights; for example they may include references to human rights as often being regarded as universal, inalienable, equal, and indivisible rights which people are entitled to purely by being human.

Answers should explore the similarities and differences between an institutional and non-institutional approach to the ratification and enforcement of human rights.

Similarities may include:

- both try to actively enforce human rights ideals

- both have controversial aspects

- both have become increasingly media centred

- both interact with government bodies and seats of power at various geographic levels.

Differences may include:

- non-institutional organizations such as Human Rights Watch or Amnesty International are often seen to have sufficient influence to have an effect on human rights policies, whereas institutions tend to have more prestige, resources or power;

- institutional approaches tend to be more state centred, whereas non-institutional approaches tend to be more informal or more local

- institutional approaches have to work within systemic frameworks

- there are possible differences in how they are financed.

Candidates may name institutional forums and organizations that consider human rights beyond those mentioned in the question itself. Examples may include the Zapatista rebellion, the International Court of Justice, groups such as Occupy, etc. They may also discuss specific examples of failures of the particular approaches, for example the fact that none of the major powers have been brought to the Hague Courts.

The response may sum up with a conclusion on the similarities and differences between institutional and non-institutional approaches to human rights ratification and enforcement.

6 To what extent do the complex realities and relationships of power in global politics make the concept of human rights an unachievable ideal?

Examiner hints

Better answers will demonstrate an excellent understanding of the concept of human rights and the concept of power. They may then discuss whether the realities of power make the goals utopian rather than realistic.

Arguments that they are unachievable may include:

- inherent differences in resources and opportunities
- they are too idealistic
- they are unrealistic or impractical
- reference to the complex links between political and economic power
- the difficulties posed by entrenched belief systems.

Arguments that human rights are achievable may include:

- there has been progress in gaining recognition of human rights, even in difficult circumstances
- power can be seen to be moving away from the state to grassroots, which links to the importance of the individual rather than the state in human rights.

Answers should make reference to specific examples, such as, for instance, to the fact that 147 countries ratified the Convention against Torture and Other Cruel, Inhuman or Degrading Treatment or Punishment; or they could refer to the success of polio vaccination programmes, or to MNC demands, for example, for free trade zones, etc.

Answers may include a conclusion reflecting on how power and human rights are interlinked, and on the extent to which the complex realities and relationships of power in global politics make the concept of human rights an unachievable ideal. They may, for example, conclude that human rights are aspirational goals, so it does not matter whether they are achievable or not.

2.6 References and further reading

[1] Donnelly, J. 2003. *Universal Human Rights in Theory and Practice.* (Second Edition). New York. Cornell University Press.

[2] Ishay, MR. 2004. *The History of Human Rights.* University of California Press. Ishay, MR. 2007. *The Human Rights Reader.* (Second Edition). London. Routledge.

[3] Wolf, E. 1982. *Europe and the People without History.* University of California Press.

[4/5] From the *Encyclopedia Britannica*, p. 8 of 26.

[6] Ignatieff, M. 1999. "Human rights, the midlife crisis". *New York Review of Books.* Vol 46, number 9, p. 5.

[7] In Ishay, MR. 2007. *The Human Rights Reader.* London. Routledge. Pp 390–391.

[8] Nash, J. 1981. "Ethnographic aspects of the world capitalist system". *Annual Review of Anthropology.* Vol. 10, pp. 393–423.

[9] United States Ratification of Human Rights Treaties, 24 July 2009, *Human Rights Watch*, New York.

[10] From the International Justice Resource Center, New York.

[11] Cmiel, K. 2004. "The recent history of human rights". *The American Historical Review.* February, pp. 117–135.

[12] Moyn, S. 2015. "Do human rights increase inequality?" *The Chronicle of Higher Education, the Chronicle Review.* 26 May, pp.s 1–23.

[13/14] Hughes, NS. 2006. "Dangerous and endangered youth" in Kirsch, M. *Inclusion and Exclusion in the Global Arena.* London. Routledge.

[15] From Kirsch, M. 2006. "Introduction" in *Inclusion and Exclusion in the Global Arena.* London. Routledge.

3 DEVELOPMENT

Key concepts

→ Development

→ Globalization

→ Inequality

→ Sustainability

Learning outcomes

→ Contested meanings of development

→ Factors that may promote or inhibit development

→ Pathways towards development

→ Debates surrounding development: challenges of globalization, inequality and sustainability

There are many definitions of development, imparted by the beliefs and goals of those defining it. In an advanced capitalist society, such as the United States or Western Europe, the mainstream definitions of development generally reflect the way, and include the social conditions, in which those capitalist economies grew. If you are a mother living in an indigenous community concerned about the fate of the land and culture that your community and your ancestors have based their lives on, then development can have a very different set of goals. If a country is newly industrializing, for example, China and India, and the main goal is to become like the advanced capitalist countries with strong capitalist economies, then the goals and actions, embedded in the policies and politics of the government and industries, will be different.

Definitions of development reflect the social systems that they represent. The differing definitions of development are generated by interest groups, and often present conflicts and disagreements among and within countries and communities. A good example of the causes of internal strife are the dams of India, some of the largest in the world, which have been created by government policy to provide water for the agricultural industry but in the meantime are literally submerging thousands of indigenous villages that have depended on the rivers for centuries. The political power of the villagers cannot compare with the halls of government, yet they have been able to mount a significant resistance to the powers that threaten their very ability to survive. They have mounted an international defence, taking the government to court and arguing their position in the centres of power located in New Delhi, Paris and New York.

For our purposes, we will be using the broader, more encompassing definition of development, which includes the "people, power and politics" focus of the course. This is in line with a broader perspective that is becoming more popular, and includes the human and environmental dimensions, as seen in measuring indexes such as the Happy Planet Index (HPI) and Genuine Progress Indicator (GPI).

At a very basic level, development can be defined as a continuous rise in the living standards and well-being of a social organization. At the global level, the universality of the quest for development is shown by the fact that all societies, states and communities aim to best promote their well-being. The means to pursue this goal includes everything from the elimination of poverty to the provision of healthcare, education and food.

This unit examines what development means, how it can be analysed and what may stand in the way of the comprehensive well-being of people, communities and countries. The debates surrounding development will be examined, noting the differences in definitions and what those differences represent. Each may have their own goals for individuals, communities, states and global geographies, just as each may come from differing interests and biases.

Key questions

1 What do we mean by "development"?

2 Who defines "development"?

3 How do we define "development" for contemporary global politics?

▲ The logo of the International Monetary Fund (IMF)

Introduction

Capitalism is the dominant social/economic system in the world today. Because of this position and the power that it generates, capitalism's functioning and development provide the most influential definitions of development in common use. The advocates of capitalism have obtained the power to promote their vision and ideas for the definition of development.

From classrooms to the institutes of public policy-making (that is, the World Bank (WB), the US Agency for International Development (USAID), the International Monetary Fund (IMF) and many other agencies – both government and non-government – based around the world), development is primarily defined as the growth and the accumulation of capital, and many of the theories that we now find in textbooks about development reflect this goal.

Unlike other ideas of development that may emphasize the well-being of communities, the health of peoples or the stability of cultures, capitalism requires its own growth to survive, regardless of the effects or the results of its needs on communities, nations and whole populations. This results in some confusing contradictions: while, for example, the United States is one of the most capitalist-intensive countries in the world, it is ranked 37th in the provision of healthcare for its citizens and 28th in the number of 4 year olds in early childhood education – and 14th among the 37 countries that form the Organization for Economic Co-operation and Development (OECD). The percentage of the children of parents without higher education experience who will attend college in the US is only 29 per cent, among the lowest of OECD countries; Korea, followed by Japan, Canada and the Russian Federation are the top countries whose populations have attained tertiary education, as of 2010. Iceland spends the most on education per gross national product (GNP), while Luxembourg, Switzerland, Germany and the Netherlands top the charts for expenditures on teachers' salaries.[1] Cuba, one of the poorest nations on earth, has been ranked by the United Nations Organization for Education, Science and Culture (UNESCO) as first on international mathematics and reading tests.[2]

These rankings mean that there are profound global differences in development goals, such as education, and these differences are prominent in the definitions of development that are employed by governments and policy-makers.

This does not mean that all development goals in capitalist societies are directed only at the growth of capital. There are many different stakeholders and spheres within any complex society, and they may have their own goals for development within the context of capitalism. For example, many non-governmental organizations (NGOs) promote the well-being of people in their definitions of development.

The Millennium Development Goals, established by the United Nations Millennium Summit in 2000, emphasized eight worldwide objectives, from the eradication of extreme poverty and hunger, to the combating of HIV/AIDS, to the establishing of a global partnership for development. These objectives, however, were criticized for not taking into account inclusive social goals for development, and they heavily depended on the World Bank, the IMF and the African Development Bank Group (AfDB), among others, all of which are organizations with goals derived from capitalist development.

The most cited definitions of development are therefore focused on the growth of capitalist societies, and the goals of development are the expansion of capital. Without these goals, as David Harvey, a prominent anthropologist and economist tells us, and many of the most well-known economists agree, the capitalist system would collapse. Because of the requirements of its economic system, capitalist economic systems require a growth rate of at least 3 per cent per year for it to function without generating crises.[3]

Also, populations necessarily need to be able to reproduce, and to remain healthy. Education may be more important in one era of capitalism than another (a good example is the period after Sputnik, when the US was competing with the Soviet Union on science-related issues, and money available for education was plentiful). The National Institutes of Health (NIH) in the United States provide billions of dollars in health research, and the pharmaceutical industry is an important part of capitalist development. As we are witnessing today, however, when capitalist enterprises find it cheaper to find labour overseas than to train domestic workforces, the provision of money drops for public education and healthcare, which is viewed by policy-makers as an unnecessary burden on capital expenditure.

Development in global politics: Links with other units

Each of the four units in this course has an impact on all of us as individuals and communities, and also on states and global politics at large. They affect the way that complex political, social, economic and cultural issues evolve – both within the confines of state borders and in the increasingly interconnected world. While each of these units is a complete field of study in itself, it is interesting to note that a thread of connectivity links them together in one way or another.

A closer look at the comprehensive and humanistic understanding of development (encompassing economic growth, along with human development and sustainable development) in a globalized world makes two facts evident:

1 Development is a universal and basic aim for individuals, communities, states and the world. Although the term may hold different meanings for different people, all have a common interest in promoting its advancement.

2 Our definition of development is related to many other key concepts, such as security, peace, conflict, human rights and even gender equality. This overlap is evident in the words of Helen Clark (former

Thinking and social skills

View the film *Drowned Out*, where villagers in India have vowed to drown with their village as the dams redirect water over their land and living spaces. Have a class discussion on the differences in the definitions of development portrayed by its major characters. Is there a right and a wrong here? What of the communities that are being submerged in the name of development and of the industries that are benefiting from the redirection of water?

▲ Helen Clark served three terms as the Prime Minister of New Zealand, from December 1999 to November 2008

Prime Minister of New Zealand and Administrator of the United Nations (UN) Development Program (UNDP)):

[A] more peaceful world would not be possible without stable societies, more prosperous communities, and universal respect for the human rights of all people... Ever since 1945, the UN has linked the three pillars of its mandate – peace, human rights, and development. That has helped to broaden the focus on development... the common understanding of development [has shifted] from a narrow economic concept to one which is broad, people-centred, and multidisciplinary. Pioneering UN Conferences... were successful in making human rights, conflict resolution, environmental stability, gender equality and peace and peace-building integral to what the UNDP considers today to be sustainable human development.[4]

Clark rightly notes that in order to have peace and security, it is imperative to have a stable and prosperous society and universal respect for human rights, based on the tenets of sustainable human development. Peace, human rights and sustainable human development are interlinked and have an impact on one another. For instance, respect for gender equality can help foster development. An interesting example of this is Japan – a developed country, with a low ranking in the Global Gender Index. It has often been mentioned that the increased inclusion of Japanese women into the workforce would help boost productivity and Japan's economic revival. In contrast, the absence of one variable is also likely to have an impact on another. For example, poverty, rising inequality, hunger and other issues related to underdevelopment can prove to be perfect breeding grounds for conflict, thereby marring peace.

Power, sovereignty and development

Power is often linked with the possession of resources – military, natural, human or economic – and most of the powerful, resource-rich countries such as the US and China are either developed or firmly set on the path of development. These powerful countries also have the capacity to take away the resources they may need for their own development from other resource-rich countries. China's inroads into Africa for resources, for example, are well known and documented. Beijing's use of soft power or "charm offensive" has also been successful in aiding its development goals. Similarly, the Iraq war has been called a resource war by many analysts, fought not really to find weapons of mass destruction, but for energy security needed by the advanced capitalist countries.[5]

The changing nature of state sovereignty can also be found to be related to development. In an era of globalization, the significance of international and regional organizations cannot be understated or underestimated. While these organizations are known to have an eroding effect on the traditional conceptualization of state sovereignty, there is also a clear realization that membership in such groupings aids and assists development. Free trade agreements, treaties, and investment opportunities supported by these organizations are all examples of how countries can spur their own development through pooling their sovereignty. Similarly, transnational issues such as terrorism, climate change, pollution and disease cannot be managed by states

independently and thus restrict state sovereignty. At the same time, these cross-border problems need to be tackled in order to pursue the goals of development.

Development and peace and conflict

In considering the twin concepts of *development* and *peace and conflict*, for instance, it can be noted that most ongoing conflicts in today's world are taking place in underdeveloped or developing parts of the world.

The Global Peace Index 2014 survey results showed that Europe remained the most peaceful region and Denmark, Austria, New Zealand and Switzerland ranked among the most peaceful countries. At the bottom of the index were Syria, South Sudan, Afghanistan, Iraq and Somalia. All these are struggling with the ills of underdevelopment and are ridden with hunger, poverty, income inequalities and lack of basic amenities. This snapshot is enough proof that poorer and underdeveloped countries are more prone to conflict.

The index also reveals some more interesting points, citing a recent OECD report that states that economic growth in the 1980s has not benefited everyone equally. As much as 40 per cent of people have not seen any fruits of this development. This in turn has led to a weakening of the social fabric and a waning trust in institutions.[6]

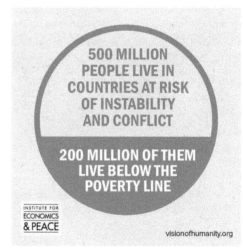

▲ The Institute for Economics and Peace (IEP)

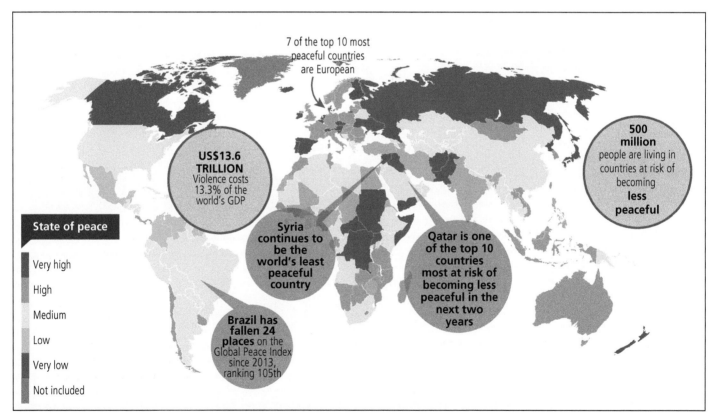

▲ The Global Peace Index 2016: A snapshot of the global state of peace

Development and human rights

Another significant link exists between *development* and *human rights*. Sustainable development requires a continuous care for human rights.

The European Commission (EC) notes:

> *They have the same ultimate objective to improve human well-being and freedom, based on the inherent dignity and equality of all people. Human rights and development policies and strategies are mutually reinforcing and complementary. Whereas development will focus on social welfare and on economic growth, human rights established a universally accepted legal regime that conceptualizes rights in terms of "duty bearers" and "rights holders."* [7]

There could be several examples establishing this connection. Countries associated with human rights abuses are likely to suffer setbacks in the process of development. This is in keeping with the view that economic sanctions can be an effective tool in reducing human rights violations. Many aid donor countries use the carrot-and-stick policy and base their assistance on the condition that the recipient country has a good human rights and rule of law record. Human rights abuses in countries such as North Korea, Somalia, Sierra Leone and Sudan have led the international community to impose economic sanctions, reduce or cut off aid and take similar measures that hamper development. [8] Similarly, a favourable record in human rights is an important requirement in order to receive foreign direct investment or establish trade connections.

Development and key concepts

Before we begin our discussion of the multifaceted and fascinating field of development and its many forms, it is prudent to first understand each of the major concepts set out to form a base for this unit and their relationship with the subject of development. These key concepts are: globalization, inequality and sustainability.

The term *development* was conventionally used in the context of economic growth or technological advancement. Today, it is a more multidimensional and dynamic concept involving social, economic, political and cultural changes, as well as the remodelling of society. For development to occur, it is important that economic growth also translates into an improved quality of life for people in every area of society, bringing in a human dimension to its understanding. At the same time, it also has to be sustainable – that is, planned well enough to ensure that the needs of the future generations are taken care of as well.

Globalization

Globalization can best be described as the interconnectedness and process "by which the peoples of the world are incorporated into a single world society". [9] In simpler terms, globalization can be defined as the increasing interdependence among countries, regions and peoples due to the integration of trade, culture, finance, people and ideas in one global marketplace.

It is no surprise that any development in one part of the world has repercussions on another. For example, a financial crisis in Asia has an adverse impact not just on Asian economies, but also beyond. Similarly, human rights violations in one state could have repercussions on neighbouring states, for example, an influx of refugees. The impact of the reach of social media and Internet incorporates ideas and goods across borders and creates a kind of cultural globalization.

▲ Members of the United Nations Security Council vote on sanctions against North Korea, 2016

TOK

To what extent do the concepts that we use shape the conclusions that we reach?

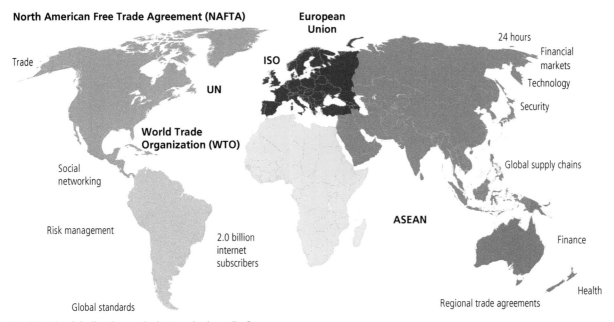

North American Free Trade Agreement (NAFTA)

European Union

Trade

ISO

UN

24 hours

Financial markets

Technology

Security

World Trade Organization (WTO)

Social networking

Global supply chains

Risk management

2.0 billion internet subscribers

ASEAN

Finance

Health

Global standards

Regional trade agreements

▲ What is globalization and what are its benefits?

If globalization does connect the world closely, it is bound to have an impact on all facets of development. The effect is both positive and negative.

On the positive side, transnational problems, such as environmental pollution, climate change and the threat of terrorism, all of which are impediments to the goal of sustainable human development, can be managed and handled more effectively. Globalization sometimes provides a wider market, more jobs and higher profits for countries, bolstering development.

At the same time, there are several disadvantages. It can mean loss of jobs for people in countries with a high cost of living as factories and manufacturing units are shifted to underdeveloped countries that provide cheaper labour and materials. At the same time, while this may mean more employment opportunities in underdeveloped countries, there is a great likelihood of the exploitation of local labour, including working conditions that present a threat to life.

Inequality

Reduction in *inequality* is a major challenge for the international community. According to a report prepared by the UNDP entitled "Humanity Divided: Confronting Inequality in Developing Countries", income inequality increased on average by 11 per cent in developing countries from 1990 to 2010, taking into account the population size. More than 75 per cent of the population lives in societies where income is more unequally distributed than it was in the 1990s. The report states that beyond a certain threshold, inequality harms growth, poverty reduction, the quality of relations in the public and political spheres of life and an individual's sense of fulfilment and self-worth. In a global survey conducted for this report, policy-makers acknowledged that inequalities in their countries are a threat to long-term social and economic development.[10]

There are a wide range of views on how inequality affects the process of development. According to one, the process of globalization will ultimately benefit the underdeveloped or developing countries. Changes such as free trade and open markets, along with the culture of liberal democracy will only add to the prosperity, progress, growth and well-being of less fortunate people.[11] A few others have an opposite point of view, according to which development does not necessarily translate into inequalities in societies or between states. The rich continue to get richer at the expense of the poor, and large organizations, such as multi-nationals, are the real winners as whole populations become losers in the global scheme.

Sustainability

The term *sustainability* simply means ensuring that present actions to improve the lives of human beings and the environment should endure for future generations. This involves a prudent and optimal use of limited resources to ensure that the needs of growing populations are met. This would include meeting a number of challenges, such as the provision of clean energy for all without damaging the environment, the provision of food, nutrition, health, clothing and shelter for all, the inclusive and equitable quality of education, gender equality, energy security, productive employment for everyone or the eradication of poverty.[12] The United Nations' Sustainable Development Knowledge Platform recommends that

> *poverty eradication, changing unsustainable and promoting sustainable patterns of consumption and production and protecting and managing the natural resource base of economic and social development are the overarching objectives of and essential requirements for sustainable development.*

United Nations Department of Economic and Social Affairs

A brief history of development

The history of discussions and debates around contemporary development does not go back too far in time. The beginnings can be traced back to the time after the Second World War – around the 1950s – which marked the end of colonization and the beginning of the Cold War. The world was divided into two camps led by the former Soviet Union and the United States. The concept of development at that time was simply understood to be equivalent to Western modernization and industrialization. Prominence was given to economic growth (in terms of gross national product (GNP)), industrialization and science and technology in the process of achieving and reaching the status of a developed country. The widespread belief was that developing countries could imitate and emulate the West and gradually transition towards development. Most importantly, the human angle involving an improvement in human welfare and conditions was unaccounted for completely.

Discussions over development in the 1950s and 1960s were conducted largely on the basis of two theories – modernization theory and dependency theory. The question of how an underdeveloped country could make a shift to becoming a developed and modern society was addressed by prominent American economic historian Walt W. Rostow.

Rostow's stages of growth

Rostow propounded a five-step linear process leading to economic growth in his treatise *The Stages of Economic Growth: A Non-Communist Manifesto* published in 1960. According to Rostow, there are five stages of economic growth:

- The first stage of "traditional" society is characterized by a primarily agrarian society, a low level of technology and a rigid and hierarchical social structure.[13]

- The second stage is marked by emergence of the positive conditions required before development can take place. This could be stimulated by the influence of external actors through improved trade and communication.

- The third and most important take-off stage is said to have been reached when investment and industrial output rise, along with the restructuring of supporting social and political institutions.

- The last two stages involve an establishment and consolidation of development.

The traditional society
Based on subsistence; farming, fishing, forestry and some mining.

Pre-conditions for take off
Building infrastructure that is needed before development can take place; for example, transport network, money from farming, power supplies and communications.

Take-off
Introduction and rapid growth (industrial revolution) of manufacturing industries, better infrastructure, financial investment and culture change.

Drive to maturity
New ideas and technology improve and replace older industries and economic growth spreads throughout the country.

High mass consumption
People have more wealth and so buy services and goods (consumer society), welfare systems are fully developed and trade expands.

▲ The Rostow model of development

It was argued that the developed countries had all surpassed the take-off stage, while the developing ones continued to be either in stage one or stage two. According to the modernization theory, obstacles to development such as corruption, distrust, political instability, gender discrimination and civil war are all internally present impediments to development.[14]

The benefits and ideas of development were expected to filter down to the less-developed areas. Capitalism and a liberal democracy were considered to be prerequisites of the modern system that these developing countries would aim to reach for and achieve. The state had a critical role to play in ensuring development by formulating appropriate policies. By the time a state arrived at the fourth stage, it had to turn its attention towards consolidating development. Rostow's model of development has been widely critiqued and is no longer used in most contemporary discussions and debates around development. The problem with his model is that it is circular: if a country succeeds in economic development, it is because the model works; if a country fails, it is not the model that is at fault but the governments and people who failed to implement it properly. The model cannot be faulted. It was widely used for policy purposes, and the deforestation of Vietnam with Agent Orange is one example of how academic theory (Rostow's in this case) works its way into policy and action. Because the model assumes that you need a large labour force in cities to work in factories to advance the production of goods and therefore enable development, policies were established to get people out of the countryside in Vietnam and into populated areas, and deforestation was the method that was used to accomplish this plan.

▲ A US Air Force jet spraying Agent Orange over an area near Saigon (modern-day Ho Chi Minh City)

Another example of this kind was the application of the ideas of Milton Friedman and his colleagues at the University of Chicago, who, collectively, were known as "the Chicago Boys". Friedman's theories emphasized that capitalism had to have a free reign of labour practices and independence from governmental sovereignty for a country to develop quickly and successfully. In the 1970s they proposed that the overthrow of democratically elected Salvador Allende in Chile was necessary to establish the power to develop without interference. With that came the support of dictatorships throughout the Southern Cone of Latin America, and necessitated the violence that became part of that strategy. With the admitted help of the CIA, Allende was violently overthrown and Pinochet was put into power in Chile, in charge of the junta and the military that enforced the United States-backed dictatorship. Many other dictatorships were established in this region, and many people went missing or were killed.

The consequences of these events are still being felt today. Pinochet was indicted and charged with human rights violations. He was placed under house arrest in 2004, but died before he was formally brought to trial. It is now estimated that at least 30,000 people went missing and in the region of 80,000 were tortured in Chile alone, while similar numbers were killed or went missing in the 1970s and 1980s in Argentina. To this day, the mothers of the missing gather each week in the Plaza de Mayo in Buenos Aires with pictures of their children, demanding to know what happened to them. Contemporary economists and development theorists now see the harm that this era created for the peoples of this region, and question the goal of an unfettered capitalism over the well-being and human rights of the region's population. Development can be a bloody business.

The dependency theory

The 1960s marked the development of another noteworthy theory on development – the dependency theory. Prominent proponents of this theory were Andre Gunder Frank and Celso Furtado. These theorists were reacting to modernization theory and the work of the Chicago School, and started with the common premise that development of the West was only due to its pursuit of capitalism. This capitalism in turn is nothing but a mechanism to exploit the underdeveloped and restrain them from developing. The dominant countries are imperialist developed countries such as the US and Europe. The exploited countries include those in Latin America, Asia and Africa, which have been exploited through methods such as colonization.[15] These poor countries provide cheap labour and raw materials to the developed countries. As a result, while the rich become richer, poor countries find themselves being drained.

The dependency theorists called on the underdeveloped nations to break strong unequal ties with developed countries and pursue internal growth in order to attain a level of development. The state was advised to step in to promote the nationalization of key industries and begin the process of import substitution (replacing foreign imports with domestic production).

The Structural Adjustment Programmes

The 1980s was a period during which the outlook on development changed yet again. There was a call for scaling down state intervention and allowing free markets to encourage development. The role of private capital, multi-nationals and banks had a greater role to play in this model of development. However, due to rising oil prices and the resultant debts incurred by developing countries, international financial institutions such as the World Bank and IMF decided to shift focus to structural adjustment and a stabilization process. They created plans and programmes aimed at reducing inflation and bringing about economic growth. The Structural Adjustment Programmes, or SAPs as they came to be known, were economic policies for developing countries promoted by the international financial institutions. Any countries that chose to follow the SAPs were entitled to receive loans from the IMF and the World Bank. The main idea behind the programme was decreased state controls replaced by free market mechanisms.[16] In the process, however, the human and environmental aspects of development receded into the

TOK

What is the difference between facts, data and theories? Do these terms mean the same thing in all areas of knowledge?

background. This resulted in what has been termed as the "lost decade" for countries of sub-Saharan Africa and Latin America.

The SAPs and the related policies came to be known as the Washington Consensus – a term coined by John Williamson in 1989 to encapsulate a set of about 10 policy recommendations that had the support and backing of US and international financial institutions. Some of these suggested reforms included trade liberalization, privatization, and liberalization of foreign direct investment (FDI) inflows.[17] It also recommended the protection of property rights.

The Millennium Development Goals

The year 1990 was a landmark with the publication of the first ever Human Development Report (HDR) by the United Nations Development Program. This report was a shift away from the Washington Consensus. The HDR moved focus from people-centred development by "enlarging people's choices and strengthening human capabilities", an idea proposed by Nobel Prize winner Amartya Sen and Mahbub ul Haq.

Millennium Development Goals

1 ERADICATE EXTREME POVERTY AND HUNGER

2 ACHIEVE UNIVERSAL PRIMARY EDUCATION

3 PROMOTE GENDER EQUALITY AND EMPOWER WOMEN

4 REDUCE CHILD MORTALITY

5 IMPROVE MATERNAL HEALTH

6 COMBAT HIV/AIDS, MALARIA AND OTHER DISEASES

7 ENSURE ENVIRONMENTAL SUSTAINABILITY

8 A GLOBAL PARTNERSHIP FOR DEVELOPMENT

ATL Research skills

In 2015, the United Nations replaced the Millennium Development Goals with a set of seventeen aspirational "global" goals, called the Sustainable Development Goals. Research how these differ from the MDGs. Select one SDG as a case study and examine how progress has been made in this area since 2015.

There were still strong currents of concern over the apparent failure of development policies to improve living conditions. Poverty, lack of education, poor health and lack of food and water security continued to plague a huge section of the world's population. In response to this quandary, the United Nations announced a set of eight Millennium Development Goals to be achieved by the year 2015. Most of the MDGs found a place in the national development strategies of member states and a number of reviews have been carried out on their effectiveness. It is now time to set out on another path towards the goal of development and build further on achievements thus far.

Levels of analyses

Development in its broadest sense – encompassing economic, human and sustainable aspects – has a bearing on all levels of society, ranging from the individual to the global. For example, matters related to poverty and inequalities have a direct impact on people at an individual and community level: poverty leads to problems such as lack of purchasing power, malnutrition, lack of education and shelter, and the very survival of communities.

These problems also have repercussions: a malnourished and uneducated population cannot prove to be a good human resource or contribute to nation building and development. On the contrary, an increase in income would mean that people acquire the power to purchase more goods or invest in education and acquiring skills. This in turn would mean a skilled, healthy workforce that is an asset to any country's development.

Similarly, environmental protection and sustainable development at the global level cannot be ensured without combined efforts. At the grassroots level involvement of individuals and communities is important, and has to be supplemented and supported by efforts at the regional and international level. Individuals and communities could help ensure sustainable development and environmental protection through making simple alterations and additions to their daily lives – such as using solar and wind energy, rainwater harvesting and energy-efficient electrical fittings.

At the same time, countries have to formulate policies and laws to support sustainable development in synchronization with international and global efforts. According to the Environmental Protection Index, countries such as Switzerland, Singapore and Australia have emerged as front runners in this field. To cite an example, Singapore has emerged as a leader in reducing its carbon footprint. The 2009 Sustainable Singapore Blueprint set forth targets such as certifying 80 per cent of buildings as energy efficient by 2030. The government does not provide for any energy production or consumption subsidies. In terms of water management, it is one of the few countries to harvest urban storm water for boosting water supply.[18] All these could also be effectively supplemented by regional-level efforts such as those made by the Southeast Asian countries under the Association of Southeast Asian Nations (ASEAN) Declaration on Environmental Sustainability signed in 2007 and the MDGs at a global level.

▲ Levels of development

ATL

Thinking and communication skills

Divide the class into three or four groups. Within your group assign themes/subjects for case studies to another group for them to discuss how development has an impact at more than one level – individual, community, national, regional, international and global – and how each of these in turn can contribute to the process of development. Present your findings to the class and try to identify the factors that comprise your initial understanding of the term "development".

Contested meanings of development

Some economists believe that a mere rise in GNP can be considered synonymous with development. As we have seen, conventionally "development" was simply used in the context of economic growth or perceptible and quantifiable economic and technological advancement. In other words, economic growth could simply be described as growth of national product. This would ordinarily mean an increase in a country's GDP, GNP, the investment–income ratio, the labour force in the industrial sector, the availability of goods and services and a measurement of the overall standard of living of people. An increase in the GDP per capita or per person (an approximation of income per person derived by dividing the GDP by the size of population) leads to a reduction in poverty and a consequent improvement in the lives of people.[19]

▲ Skyline of Business Bay in Dubai, United Arab Emirates

> **Gross Domestic Product (GDP)** is the total market value of goods and services produced within a country in one year. This includes income, wages, profits and consumption.

> **Gross National Product (GNP)** is the total economic output including earnings from foreign investments as well as final goods produced by a country's firms within and outside the country.

The connection between GDP and income

A country produces and sells $1 million worth of goods in a year. When goods are sold, firms that produced goods and services earn $1 million. This is income for all contributors – workers, owners, suppliers and so forth. Thus, production becomes sale and finally income.

A worker produces $100 worth of goods daily, which when sold brings in revenue, part of which is used to pay wages to the worker. More production will lead to more income and increase in wage – rise in GDP or output per person means more income per person.

Source: Secondi, Giorgio. 2008. *The Development Economics Reader*. London. Routledge, pp. 2–3.

Some determinants of development

- Value of goods and services produced
- Savings and investments
- Natural resources
- Good quality of human resource
- Good governance
- Good infrastructure
- Favourable political and economic climate fostering growth, such as democracy and free market
- Modernization and industrialization

However, this understanding is rather limited and does not do justice to the much wider connotation of the concept as it is understood and discussed today. Central to understanding the current debate on "development" is the fact that it is no longer measured purely in terms of changes in economic indicators (at the individual, national or international level). It is an increasingly multidimensional and dynamic concept involving social, economic, political and cultural changes, and remodelling of society. For development to occur, it is important that economic growth also translates into an improved quality of life for people in every area of society, bringing in a *human* dimension to its understanding. At the same time, it also has to be *sustainable* – that is, endure for future generations.

The very challenge of defining the concept of development reasserts the belief that it is a contested, ambiguous and complex term, tied to the interest of those defining it. As noted by Ravi Kanbur, "Since [development] depend[s] on values and on alternative conceptions on the good life, there is no uniform or unique answer."[20] The term has diverse meanings and forms for different stakeholders, ranging from international organizations, governments and non-governmental organizations to families and individuals. It has different benchmarks unique to the society or country being studied. While development for all sections of society necessarily includes the basics of food, clothing and shelter, the significance of what else has to be considered varies considerably.

Poverty reduction and equitable distribution of wealth

We will begin with the most obvious and commonly understood subtexts in the literature on economic growth and development – eradication of poverty and an equitable and just distribution of wealth. It is a well-known fact that the twin problems of poverty and income inequality are fundamental to all development-related policies, and a solution to both the causes and indicators of poverty coupled with equitable distribution of wealth are essential prerequisites to any progress. In view of the enormity and magnitude of the problem, reduction of extreme poverty formed one of the most significant MDGs set out by world leaders in the year 2000 as part of a blueprint for the future. The first target of the MDGs was to halve the proportion of people with an income of less than US$1 per day between the years 1990 and 2015, while ensuring employment for all. It also envisaged halving the number of people suffering from hunger. The table below summarizes the 2013 review of the progress made for MGD 1.

Thinking and communication skills

1 Note down a set of 8–10 words or phrases that you associate with the word "development". Discuss with a partner how the term invokes different ideas for different people.

2 Divide into groups of three or four and discuss what sets a developing and developed country apart from each other.

3 In your groups, prepare a presentation on what the term "development" would mean for different stakeholders *at various levels* – individual, community, national/ state level, regional, international, global. Share your findings with the rest of the class.

Millennium Development Goals: 2013 Progress Chart										
MDG GOAL 1: ERADICATE EXTREME POVERTY AND HUNGER										
GOALS AND TARGETS	AFRICA		ASIA					OCEANIA	LATIN AMERICA AND CARIBBEAN	CAUCASUS AND CENTRAL ASIA
		Sub-Saharan	Eastern	South Eastern	Southern	Western				
Reduce extreme poverty by ½	Low Poverty	Very high poverty	Moderate poverty*	Moderate poverty	Very high poverty	Low poverty	Very high poverty	Low poverty	Low poverty	
Productive and decent employment	Large deficit in decent work	Very high deficit in decent work	Large deficit in decent work	Large deficit in decent work	Very large deficit in decent work	Large deficit in decent work	Very large deficit in decent work	Moderate deficit in decent work	Moderate deficit in decent work	
Reduce hunger by ½	Low hunger	Very high hunger	Moderate hunger	Moderate hunger	High hunger	Moderate hunger	Moderate hunger	Moderate hunger	Moderate hunger	
Target already met or expected to be met by 2015										
Progress insufficient to meet the target if prevailing trends persist										
No progress or deterioration										

Note: The progress chart operates at two levels. The words in the box indicate the present degree of compliance with the target. The shades of colour show progress towards the target according to the legend above. *Poverty progress for eastern Asia is assessed based on China's progress only.

Source: http://www.un.org/millenniumgoals/pdf/report-2013/2013_progress_english.pdf

▲ A crowded favela sits next to modern apartment buildings in Sao Paulo, Brazil

Defining poverty

Before taking the discussion any further, let us go back to the rather simple sounding question – what is poverty and how can it be measured? The answer is both complicated and challenging. Poverty has been simply defined as the absence of minimum resources necessary to meet basic human needs of food, clothing and shelter. However, probing further, it becomes clear that the reality stretches beyond the purely economic aspect of low income. This outlook on poverty from a human development perspective is encapsulated in the Human Development Report 1997 as a "denial of choices and opportunities for a tolerable life".[21] These kinds of human deprivations could include ill health, malnutrition, lack of involvement in decision-making and homelessness in developing or underdeveloped countries and social exclusion and unemployment in developed countries.

Views about poverty vary among people based on differences of age, gender or nationality and other social, cultural and psychological variables. A report by the World Bank entitled *Voices of the Poor* encapsulates the broad range of perspectives on what poverty means for different people. For instance, the report found that men in Ghana perceived poverty as a lack of material needs. Similarly, a poor man from Kenya described poverty as the lack of basic necessities – housing conditions, utensils and clothes. For a poor person in Latvia, poverty is the feeling of dependency – "humiliation, the sense of being dependent... and of being forced to accept rudeness, insults, and indifference when we seek help".[22] For a Brazilian, it is "the cost of living, low salaries and lack of jobs... not having medicines, food and clothes". Many of these perceptions and definitions could be grouped into the following subheadings: material needs, economic circumstances and social circumstances.

Indicators of poverty

- Lack of resources to meet basic needs of life
- Health issues
- Lack of education and literacy
- Poor living conditions
- Perilous and unfulfilling jobs
- Lack of respect
- Alienation from community

Source: *The World Bank*

Material needs

Specific needs – when people lack certain things essential to them, they are deprived, for example, lack of food or housing.

Pattern of deprivation – not just lacking something, but general conditions in which people are in need over an extended period of time, for example, not just living in bad housing, but not being able to get out of it.

Low standard of living – low income and consumption over a period of time. Managing with less than others.

Economic circumstances

Lack of resources – inability for people to obtain their wants (a lack of resources is a definition of poverty, need is a result).

Economic distance – people with less resources cannot afford things that others can. In competition for scarce resources, such as land and housing, they cannot afford them even if their income is higher than other people's elsewhere. Economic distance means people cannot afford to live where they are.

Economic class – "class" in economic terms is determined by people's relationship with the system of production. The economic position of elderly or disabled people, for instance, means that they are not able to command resources in many societies and are thus poor.

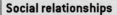

> **Social relationships**
>
> Social class – social position depends on economic position, education, and social status. Poverty, for many, is a position of lowest class in which people lack the power, status, and opportunities that others possess.
>
> Dependency – on social assistance or "welfare" – a link between benefits and poverty is assumed. No distinction made in press between receiving gifts and being poor.
>
> Social exclusion – a term used in the EU to refer to people excluded from society due to poverty, vulnerable people (asylum seekers, disabled) or socially rejected people (AIDS sufferers, disabled people).
>
> Lack of entitlement – Amartya Sen argues that poverty is not a lack of goods but a lack of entitlement or legal, social, and political arrangements.

Source: Spicker, Paul. *The Idea of Poverty.* Pp. 4–5.

Poverty can be caused by a number of factors. These range from a history of colonization, overpopulation, unequal distribution of wealth, war and ethnic conflicts, and lack of employment opportunities to problems such as natural disasters, lack of education and improper governance. In order for development to occur at a sustained level, it is imperative to cut off the roots of these problems by devising and implementing effective strategies to tackle them.

Eradication of poverty has to be effectively combined with ensuring an equitable distribution of wealth – often termed as "sharing the fruits of development". Unequal distribution of wealth or a wide gap in incomes exists in society not just among the rich and poor, but also among certain ethnic or gender groups, as well as between geographical regions within a country, for example, villages, towns and cities.

Increased poverty and inequality can cause harm and obstruct development in a great number of ways. They can lead to festering discontent among the poor and eventually to disorder in economic activities through reactions such as strikes, conflicts or civil unrest. Such situations also impact peace in society and cause political disruption. Moreover, inequalities increase the possibility of migration and the outflow of skilled and educated people. The impact on developing countries proves to be more negative due to the fact that the government institutions are often not efficient or able enough to assist the poor effectively.

ATL Research and communication skills

Divide the class into groups of four. Each group chooses one developed and one underdeveloped country. Research data on the level of existing poverty and inequality in each of these countries. What has been the impact of poverty and inequality on these countries? Discuss whether economic growth has had a positive impact on all sections of society or not in each case.

Economic growth

TOK

Is having more data available always helpful in the production of knowledge?

Self-management and research skills

Prepare a case study of a country that has shown robust economic growth, but continues to suffer from human and sustainable growth issues. Compile data and supporting arguments for the same. This case study could be built upon as this unit progresses and we delve deeper into the nuances of human and sustainable development, including measures of development such as the Global Peace Index (GPI), Inclusive Wealth Index (IWI) and House Price Index (HPI).

A contemporary understanding and discourse on development is incomplete without a discussion of human and sustainable development. This alternative and broadened conceptualization of development raises questions on whether progress in purely economic terms would suffice to take care of overall development or if this development filters down to all areas of society. Concerns have also been raised over the side effects of development and industrialization, such as the environmental damage it has been leading to. While economic growth is ideally able to provide the basis for development in other social and environmental areas as well, there is an increasing realization that this has not necessarily been the case. Persistence of problems such as disparities in income, erosion of democratic institutions and environmental damage despite robust economic growth continue to be a cause for worry.[23] Consequently, these so-called gaps in the understanding of development began to be plugged with a more wholesome definition and understanding, incorporating both the human and environmental aspects.

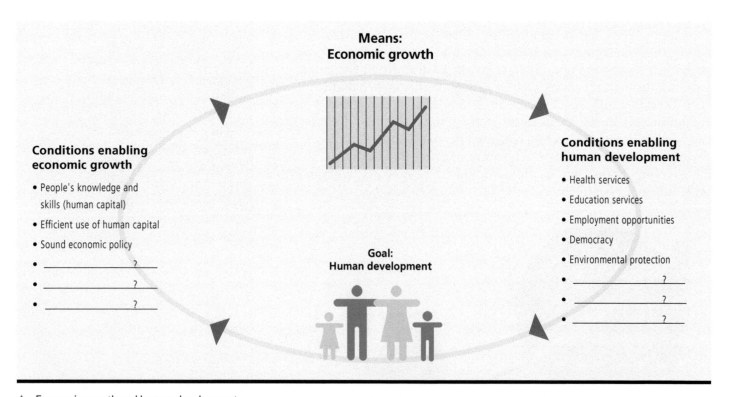

▲ Economic growth and human development

Human development

People are the real wealth of a nation. The basic objective of development is to create an enabling environment for people to live long, healthy and creative lives. This may appear to be a simple truth. But it is often forgotten in the immediate concern with the accumulation of commodities and financial wealth.

Human Development Report, 1990

The above excerpt from the first ever Human Development Report effectively sums up what forms the core of human development: people. The concept of human development was advanced by noted economists such as Mahbub ul Haq and Amartya Sen and found expression in the Human Development Reports brought out by the United Nations Development Programme. Human development has been defined as enlarging people's choices in a way that enables them to

- lead longer, healthier lives
- gain knowledge
- have a comfortable standard of living.

It also encompasses other factors, such as the ability to be gainfully employed, breathe fresh air and possess political freedom, guaranteed human rights and personal self-respect.[24] This approach is based on the premise that human beings are the real end of all activities. Therefore, it is imperative that the process of development focuses on two things:

1 the process of widening people's choices through formation of human capabilities – through improved knowledge, skills and health

2 the level of their achieved well-being and the use people make of these capabilities – for leisure, productive purposes or being active in political, social or cultural affairs.[25]

The proponents of this concept of human development do not discount the significance of incomes, wealth or commodities, but argue that economic growth does not necessarily mean an improvement in people's standard of living.[26] This growth has to be evenly distributed, needs to improve human lives and should be sustainable in the long run. This school of thought favours an expansion in social, cultural, economic and political choices as a significant factor in human development. For instance, an increase in a country's GNP does not mean that the inhabitants will have an improvement in their standard of living. A number of reasons could be attributed to this anomaly. The poor may not be able to enjoy the benefits of this increase in income due to their income disparities. Besides, weak governance, an absence of a government or leader inclined to assist the poor or just a high level of corruption with power in the hands of a few may not allow everyone to enjoy the fruits of a higher GNP.

In this sense, human development, as noted by an analyst, is:[27]

- *of* the people – that is, focuses on development of human resources through securing their health and education
- *for* the people – stressing the fact that economic growth has to fuel the quality of human lives
- *by* the people – meaning that people themselves should be in a position to influence this process of development.

> *Living sustainably depends on accepting a duty to seek harmony with other people and with nature. The guiding rules are that people must share with each other and care for the Earth. Humanity must take no more from nature than it can replenish. This in turn means adopting life-styles and development paths that respect and work within nature's limits. It can be done without rejecting the many benefits that modern technology has brought, provided that technology also works within those limits.*
>
> *Caring for the Earth: A Strategy for Sustainable Living,* IUCN, UNEP, WWF, 1991

Human development, therefore, cannot be achieved in a vacuum and requires a lot of changes in the economic, social and political systems of a country. Some of these could include easy credit for the poor, progressive tax systems and good healthcare facilities for all.

The process of human development works at two levels – firstly, building and improving human capabilities through ensuring good nutrition, education and sharpening skills, and secondly, as a follow-up, making sure that these honed skills and improved human capital are used to acquire better employment or participate actively in political decision-making and so forth. It is important that the underprivileged sections of society are provided with adequate "social safety nets".[28]

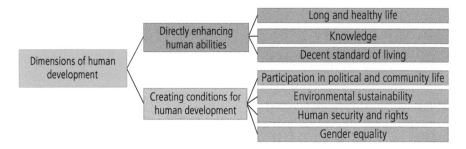

The Human Development Index is used to quantify development and has been reviewed by the UNDP every year since 1990.

▲ The United Nations Sustainability Summit at the United Nations General Assembly

Sustainable development is "development that meets the needs of the present without compromising the ability of future generations to meet their own needs".

Our Common Future by The World Commission on Environment and Development, 1990

Sustainable development

"Sustainable development" is a widely discussed term today. A number of definitions, explanations and interpretations have been offered to sum up the concept. One of the most well-articulated and circulated definitions of sustainable development can be found in the report entitled "Our Common Future" (or the Brundtland Report) of 1987. It highlighted the term "sustainable development" and placed it firmly on the global agenda as a matter of urgent concern. Thereafter, it has been the subject of discussion at a number of international fora. The UN Rio Conference on Environment and Development held in 1992 unanimously adopted the "Agenda 21: A Blueprint for Sustainable Development".

It was also promoted as one of the MDGs adopted at the 2000 UN Millennium Summit where environmental sustainability and reduction of poverty were envisaged as one of the major areas of focus. The aim set out was to reduce environmental damage and loss of biodiversity and halve the number of people without access to clean drinking water and sanitation, and reduce poverty. The World Summit on Sustainable Development held in 2002 took yet another significant step in this regard.

But what does sustainable development mean? In simple terms, the concept of sustainable development stresses the need to balance the three

interlinked areas – social, economic and environmental. The idea is to foster social and economic development while ensuring environmental protection for future generations. This is due to the fact that resources are finite and have to be used with caution and care. The concept also stresses the need to eliminate poverty, alter consumption patterns and protect natural resources in the process of economic and social development.

The concept of sustainable development rests on the three pillars below. The following table then contextualizes the objectives and necessary conditions for sustainable development as envisioned by the World Commission on Environment and Development (WCED).

SUSTAINABLE DEVELOPMENT

SOCIAL DEVELOPMENT
- Needs like medical care, housing, food and sanitation must be met equally for all.
- The pursuit of a higher standard of living should not harm/exploit others.
- Social development promotes equality, education and participation in local communities to address these needs.

ECONOMIC DEVELOPMENT
- Improvement in standard of living requires the generation of wealth through economic activity.
- Sustainable economies have to be competitive in the world market.

ENVIRONMENTAL PROTECTION
- There are limited resources and a need for clean water, air and land, and adequate food.
- Sustainable activities seek to protect the environment for the future and curb problems such as global warming and deforestation.

Source: Adapted from **United Nations** Environment Programme, *What is Sustainable Development?*

Critical objectives and necessary conditions for sustainable development identified by the World Commission on Environment and Development	
Critical objectives	**Necessary conditions**
Revival of growth	Political system – secures effective citizen participation in decision-making
Changing quality of growth	Economic system – provides for solution of tensions arising from disharmonious development
Meeting important needs for jobs, food, energy, water and sanitation	Production system – respects obligation to preserve ecological base for development
Ensuring sustainable level of population	Technological system – fosters sustainable patterns of trade and finance
Conserving and enhancing resource base	International system – fosters sustainable patterns of trade and finance
Reorienting technology and managing risk	Administrative system – flexible and capacity for self-correction
Merging environment and economics in decision-making	

Source: UN Documents, *Our Common Future*, 1987

Thinking and social skills

Note down a set of five developmental needs of a community and a country and compare them with a partner's list. Do some of the needs conflict with one another? How?

Thinking and communication skills

For most of the last century, economic growth was fuelled by what seemed to be a certain truth: the abundance of natural resources. We mined our way to growth. We burned our way to prosperity. We believed in consumption without consequences. Those days are gone… Over time that model is a… global suicide pact. So what do we do in this current challenging situation? How do we create growth in a resource constrained environment? How do we lift people out of poverty while protecting the planet and ecosystems that support economic growth? How do we regain the balance?… It is easy to mouth the words "sustainable development", but to make it happen we have to be prepared to make major changes – in our lifestyles, our economic models, our social organization, and our political life… We are running out of time… Time to ensure sustainable, climate resilient green growth… The sustainable growth agenda is the growth agenda of the 21st century.

UN Secretary General Ban Ki-moon, Davos, 2011

In the speech quoted above, UN Secretary General Ban Ki-moon has very succinctly outlined and highlighted the compelling need to follow the path of development, while ensuring that this is done in a sustainable and effective way. In the light of the above statement, form a group with two or three other students and answer the following questions.

1   Is sustainable development urgently the need of the hour?

2   How can each one of us contribute to promoting sustainable development at the individual, community and national level?

3   Suggest five ways in which development can go hand-in-hand with sustainable development.

Measuring development

The discussion over meanings of development makes it very clear that it is indeed a complex term. This makes the task of measuring development equally difficult. The section below will introduce and briefly discuss some old and some relatively new measures of development as it is understood today.

Gross National Product

Gross National Product is the value of all final goods and services produced in a country in a year (including all incomes – wages, interest, profits, rent and expenditures – consumption, investment, government purchases, net exports [that is, exports minus imports]) along with any income that a country's residents have received from abroad, minus income claimed by non-residents.[29]

Gross Domestic Product, on the other hand, is the value of all final goods and services produced in a country in one year. It can be calculated by adding the incomes of an economy – wages, interest, profits, rents – or by calculating the sum of the final uses of goods and services, that is, expenditures through consumption, investment, government purchases and net imports (exports minus imports). [30]

Human Development Index

The Human Development Index has been a feature of the Human Development Reports since 1990. The HDI was developed by Amartya Sen and Meghnad Desai along with Haq, who saw it as a measure which would draw attention to issues of primary concern to people; one "that is not blind to social aspects of human lives, as the GNP is".[31] The index addresses three dimensions of human development, which are shown in the figure below – that is, life expectancy at birth, average years of schooling of people 25 years old and above, expected years of schooling of a child along with PPP GNI per capita to calculate the HDI for each country. The ultimate aim clearly is the well-being of the people.

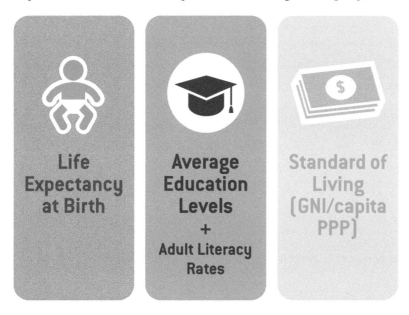

Life Expectancy at Birth

Average Education Levels
+
Adult Literacy Rates

Standard of Living (GNI/capita PPP)

According to Haq, the Human Development Index reveals the following:[32]

- National priorities in terms of which countries are effectively combining economic progress with social development. The rankings also reflect on which sector – education, health or income – has been successfully built on or is lagging behind.

- Potential growth – if a country has built up human capital, it can boost its GNP growth by choosing good economic policies. If there has been investment in education and health, it is very likely that people will have access to market opportunities, resulting in equitable economic growth.

- Disparities between people – the report has breakdowns of data on the basis of gender, income, geographical region and ethnicity.

There are four levels of human development in the HDI – Very high, High, Medium, and Low.

2014 Human Development Index

Very high human development	High human development	Medium human development	Low human development
1. Norway	50. Uruguay	103. Maldives	145. Nepal
2. Australia	51. Bahamas	103. Mongolia	146. Pakistan
3. Switzerland	52. Montenegro	103. Turkmenistan	147. Kenya
4. Netherlands	53. Belarus	106. Samoa	148. Swaziland
5. United States	54. Romania	107. Palestine, State of	149. Angola
6. Germany	55. Libya	108. Indonesia	150. Myanmar
7. New Zealand	56. Oman	109. Botswana	151. Rwanda
8. Canada	57. Russian Federation	110. Egypt	152. Cameroon
9. Singapore	58. Bulgaria	111. Paraguay	152. Nigeria
10. Denmark	59. Barbados	112. Gabon	154. Yemen
11. Ireland	60. Palau	113. Bolivia (Plurinational State of)	155. Madagascar
12. Sweden	61. Antigua and Barbuda	114. Moldova (Republic of)	156. Zimbabwe
13. Iceland	62. Malaysia	115. El Salvador	157. Papua New Guinea
14. United Kingdom	63. Mauritius	116. Uzbekistan	157. Solomon Islands
15. Hong Kong. China (SAR)	64. Trinidad and Tobago	117. Philippines	159. Comoros
16. Korea (Republic of)	65. Lebanon	118. South Africa	159. Tanzania (United Republic of)
17. Japan	65. Panama	118. Syrian Arab Republic	161. Mauritania
18. Liechtenstein	67. Venezuela (Bolivarian Republic of)	120. Iraq	162. Lesotho
19. Israel	68. Costa Rica	121. Guyana	163. Senegal

1 Choose one country from the table above.

2 Collect data on all variables related to the HDI. Compare the HDI with the GNP of that country. If there are differences, what reasons would you attribute them to?

3 Choose any two countries with similar GNP and see how you would compare them with their HDI scores. Do you find countries with low GNP having a high HDI score?

Genuine Progress Indicator

The "Genuine Progress Indicator (GPI): A Tool for Sustainable Development" is yet another attempt at moving beyond the confines of GDP in measuring development. As mentioned earlier, the GDP is "a gross tally of products and services bought and sold".[33] The GPI has been formulated to overcome the pitfalls associated with using GDP as a measure of welfare, progress or well-being of a country.

But what are some of the weaknesses of using the GDP as a measure of development? Firstly, the GDP is based on the assumption that any monetary or financial transaction means that the country is progressing and developing, thereby adding to the welfare of the society. This is not necessarily true. There are a number of other intangible and tangible variables (such as level of education, health facilities, income distribution) which have an important role to play in the process of development. Secondly, GDP does not take into account non-economic activities which are critical for development such as volunteer work, childcare and parenting. Such activities are critical to the well-being and progress of society, but are completely ignored when computing GDP. This point of view was expressed very aptly by American politician Robert F. Kennedy in a speech to the University of Kansas in 1868, when he said,

> *Our Gross National Product (or GDP)… counts special locks for our doors and the jails for the people who break them. It counts the destruction of the redwood and the loss of our natural wonder in chaotic sprawl… Yet the gross national product does not allow for the health of our children, the quality of their education or the joy of their play… It measures neither our wit nor our courage, neither our wisdom nor our learning…, it measures everything, in short, except that which makes life worthwhile.*[34]

In order to fill in these gaps, the Genuine Progress Indicator uses a set of 26 indicators including social, environmental and economic factors which are used to measure the quality of life. Beginning with the GDP, the GPI factors in all the intangible and unaccounted positives such as parenting, volunteer work and higher education and then lessens the costs of social and environmental setbacks such as deforestation, crime and air, water and noise pollution.[35] Some of these indicators can be seen in the figure below.

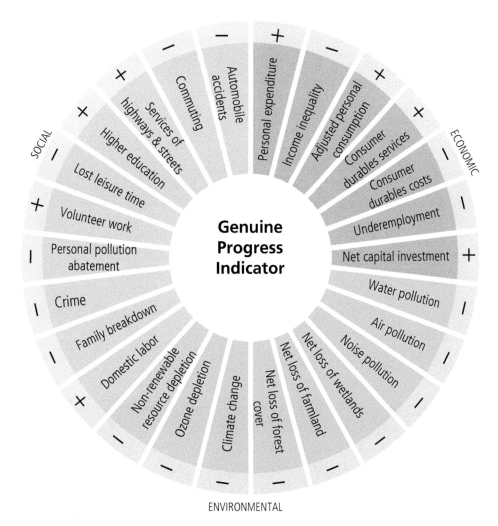

Source: *http://www.donellameadows.org/genuine-talk-progress-and-the-gpi/*

Inclusive Wealth Index

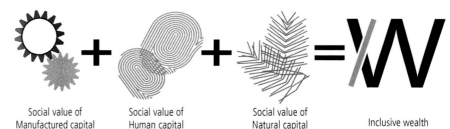

Social value of Manufactured capital + Social value of Human capital + Social value of Natural capital = Inclusive wealth

The Inclusive Wealth Index is another measure of development that seeks to offset the problems related to the social, economic and environmental aspects of development. These include imbalances in the distribution of resources despite higher riches, currencies remaining in a state of collapse and human beings destroying the very ecosystem and environment so crucial for their existence. The index measures a country's wealth using three parameters – progress, well-being and long-term sustainability. It defines sustainability as a positive change in the well-being of people and inclusive wealth as a sum of the social value of all assets – natural, human and produced capital – from which human welfare could be ensured.[36] The table below shows the components of each of the three kinds of capital that are used in calculating this index. By examining the stock of these capitals, the index gathers how much wealth a country can possibly create not just in the present but in the future as well.

Capital types		
Manufactured capital	**Natural capital**	**Human capital**
Investment	Fossil fuels	Population by age/gender
Depreciation rate	Minerals	Mortality probability by age/gender
Lifetime of assets	Forest resources	Discount rate
Output growth	Agricultural land	Employment
Population	Fisheries	Educational attainment
Productivity		Employment compensation
		Labour force by age/gender

By using the aforementioned indicators, the index aims at plugging the loopholes found in using the GDP or the HDI as a measure of development – considering that they do not cover the level of human welfare or the environmental sustainability of a country. For example, the index is able to indicate the value of natural resources being lost in the process of economic growth. At the same time, the results are also able to indicate whether the growth is sustainable or not. The Inclusive Wealth Report (IWR) released in 2012 carried a study of 20 countries that together accounted for almost three quarter of the global GDP from 1990 to 2008. Out of these, as many as 19 saw a fall in their natural capital. Among other things, the report recommended that countries with depleting natural resources should turn towards renewable resources to raise their Inclusive Wealth Index, and include the index in their planning in order to work towards sustainable development.[37]

Inclusive wealth approach		
Country's wealth: Progress, well-being and long-term sustainability		
In inclusive wealth sustainability is defined as a positive change in human well-being	Inclusive wealth is social value (not dollar price) of all capital assets – human, natural and produced	If inclusive wealth is positive, well-being across generations is positive

Source: http://inclusivewealthindex.org/#our-approach

Happy Planet Index

The Happy Planet Index initiated by the New Economics Foundation (a British think tank) measures the extent to which countries are able to provide a happy, long and sustainable life for their citizens and inhabitants. In order to compute the HPI, the index uses three indicators:

- Life expectancy (drawn from UN Development Report)

- Experienced well-being (computed using a question called "Ladder of Life" in which respondents can rank their lives on a scale of 0 to 10 representing the worst to best possible life)

- Ecological footprint (measure of consumption of resources – a per capita measure of the amount of land needed to sustain the consumption patterns of a country)

Countries are ranked on the basis of how many happy and long lives are produced for every unit of environmental output.

The HPI 2012 is not very positive or encouraging in terms of its results, with no country being able to attain sustainable or high well-being. Only nine countries are close to doing so, of which the top five are Costa Rica, Vietnam, Colombia, Belize and El Salvador, and the bottom three are Qatar, Chad and Botswana. In sum, the report suggests that we are not living on a happy planet. It also reveals that most of the high-income countries ranked low on the index due to their use of the environment. For example, if everyone lived like the Americans did in 2008, we would need four planets to maintain our consumption.[38]

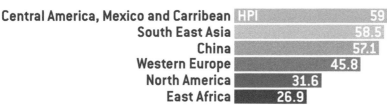

	HPI
Central America, Mexico and Carribean	59
South East Asia	58.5
China	57.1
Western Europe	45.8
North America	31.6
East Africa	26.9

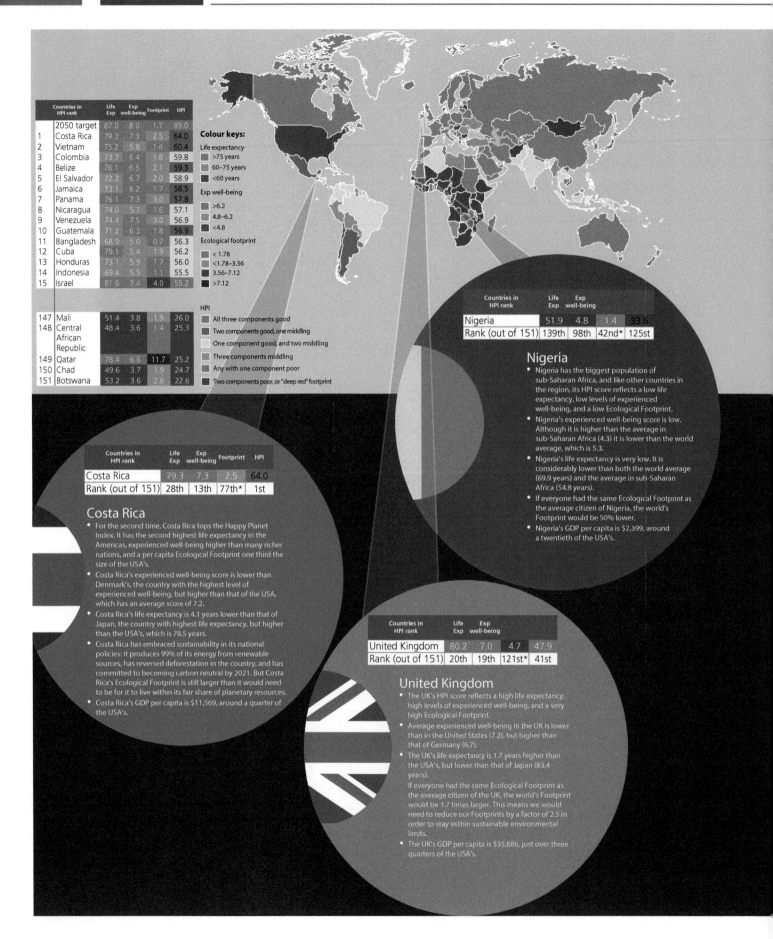

Countries in HPI rank	Life Exp	Exp well-being	Footprint	HPI
2050 target	87.0	8.0	1.7	89.0
1 Costa Rica	79.3	7.3	2.5	64.0
2 Vietnam	75.2	5.8	1.4	60.4
3 Colombia	73.7	6.4	1.8	59.8
4 Belize	76.1	6.5	2.1	59.3
5 El Salvador	72.2	6.7	2.0	58.9
6 Jamaica	73.1	6.2	1.7	58.5
7 Panama	76.1	7.3	3.0	57.8
8 Nicaragua	74.0	5.7	1.6	57.1
9 Venezuela	74.4	7.5	3.0	56.9
10 Guatemala	71.2	6.3	1.8	56.9
11 Bangladesh	68.9	5.0	0.7	56.3
12 Cuba	79.1	5.4	1.9	56.2
13 Honduras	73.1	5.9	1.7	56.0
14 Indonesia	69.4	5.5	1.1	55.5
15 Israel	81.6	7.4	4.0	55.2

Countries in HPI rank	Life Exp	Exp well-being	Footprint	HPI
147 Mali	51.4	3.8	1.9	26.0
148 Central African Republic	48.4	3.6	1.4	25.3
149 Qatar	78.4	6.6	11.7	25.2
150 Chad	49.6	3.7	1.9	24.7
151 Botswana	53.2	3.6	2.8	22.6

Colour keys:

Life expectancy
- >75 years
- 60–75 years
- <60 years

Exp well-being
- >6.2
- 4.8–6.2
- <4.8

Ecological footprint
- < 1.78
- <1.78–3.56
- 3.56–7.12
- >7.12

HPI
- All three components good
- Two components good, one middling
- One component good, and two middling
- Three components middling
- Any with one component poor
- Two components poor, or "deep red" footprint

Countries in HPI rank	Life Exp	Exp well-being	Footprint	HPI
Costa Rica	79.3	7.3	2.5	64.0
Rank (out of 151)	28th	13th	77th*	1st

Costa Rica

- For the second time, Costa Rica tops the Happy Planet Index. It has the second highest life expectancy in the Americas, experienced well-being higher than many richer nations, and a per capita Ecological Footprint one third the size of the USA's.
- Costa Rica's experienced well-being score is lower than Denmark's, the country with the highest level of experienced well-being, but higher than that of the USA, which has an average score of 7.2.
- Costa Rica's life expectancy is 4.1 years lower than that of Japan, the country with highest life expectancy, but higher than the USA's, which is 78.5 years.
- Costa Rica has embraced sustainability in its national policies: it produces 99% of its energy from renewable sources, has reversed deforestation in the country, and has committed to becoming carbon neutral by 2021. But Costa Rica's Ecological Footprint is still larger than it would need to be for it to live within its fair share of planetary resources.
- Costa Rica's GDP per capita is $11,569, around a quarter of the USA's.

Countries in HPI rank	Life Exp	Exp well-being	Footprint	HPI
Nigeria	51.9	4.8	1.4	33.6
Rank (out of 151)	139th	98th	42nd*	125st

Nigeria

- Nigeria has the biggest population of sub-Saharan Africa, and like other countries in the region, its HPI score reflects a low life expectancy, low levels of experienced well-being, and a low Ecological Footprint.
- Nigeria's experienced well-being score is low. Although it is higher than the average in sub-Saharan Africa (4.3) it is lower than the world average, which is 5.3.
- Nigeria's life expectancy is very low. It is considerably lower than both the world average (69.9 years) and the average in sub-Saharan Africa (54.8 years).
- If everyone had the same Ecological Footprint as the average citizen of Nigeria, the world's Footprint would be 50% lower.
- Nigeria's GDP per capita is $2,399, around a twentieth of the USA's.

Countries in HPI rank	Life Exp	Exp well-being	Footprint	HPI
United Kingdom	80.2	7.0	4.7	47.9
Rank (out of 151)	20th	19th	121st*	41st

United Kingdom

- The UK's HPI score reflects a high life expectancy, high levels of experienced well-being, and a very high Ecological Footprint.
- Average experienced well-being in the UK is lower than in the United States (7.2), but higher than that of Germany (6.7).
- The UK's life expectancy is 1.7 years higher than the USA's, but lower than that of Japan (83.4 years).
  If everyone had the same Ecological Footprint as the average citizen of the UK, the world's Footprint would be 1.7 times larger. This means we would need to reduce our Footprints by a factor of 2.5 in order to stay within sustainable environmental limits.
- The UK's GDP per capita is $35,686, just over three quarters of the USA's.

The Happy Planet Index (HPI)

The Happy Planet Index (HPI) is the leading global measure of sustainable well-being. It integrates environmental limits into the measurement of development and puts current and future well-being centre stage. It does this by using global data on life expectancy, experienced well-being and Ecological Footprint.

How is the HPI calculated?

The HPI blends subjective and objective data to build a picture of progress within a country. The Index uses global data on life expectancy, experienced well-being and Ecological Footprint to rank countries. It asks the question: "how much well-being is achieved per unit of resource consumption?"

$$HPI \approx \frac{\text{Experienced well-being} \times \text{Life expectancy}}{\text{Ecological Footprint}}$$

- Well-being. If you want to know how well someone's life is going, your best bet is to ask them directly. In this year's HPI, experienced well-being is assessed using a question called the 'Ladder of Life' from the Gallup World Poll. This asks respondents to imagine a ladder, where 0 represents the worst possible life and 10 the best possible life, and report the step of the ladder they feel they currently stand on. Evidence indicates that this is an effective measure of overall well-being.

- Life expectancy. Alongside experienced well-being, the HPI includes a universally important measure of health – life expectancy. We used life expectancy data from the 2011 UNDP Human Development Report.

- Ecological Footprint. A society that achieves high well-being now, but consumes so much that the same resources are not available for future generations can hardly be considered successful. The HPI uses the Ecological Footprint by the environment NGO WWF as a measure of resource consumption. It is a per capita measure of the amount of land required to sustain a country's consumption patterns, measured in terms of global hectares (g ha) which represent a hectare of land with average productive bio-capacity.

The Happy Planet Charter

We need new measures of human progress.

The Happy Planet Index offers us an excellent example of how such measures work in practice. It shows that while the challenges faced by rich resource-intensive nations and those with high levels of poverty and deprivation may be very different, the end goal is the same: long and happy lives that don't cost the earth.

We must balance the prominence currently given to GDP with those measures that take seriously the challenges we face in the 21st century: creating economies that deliver sustainable well-being for all.

By signing this charter we:

- Call on governments to adopt new measures of human progress that put the goal of delivering sustainable well-being for all at the heart of societal and economic decision-making

- Resolve to build the political will needed across society to fully establish these better measures of human progress by working with partner organizations

- Call on the United Nations to develop an indicator as part of the post-2015 framework that measures progress towards the key goal for a better future: sustainable well being for all.

The HPI Report points out that although it does help to measure significant indicators on the state of the planet, it does have caveats. The index is not able to factor in issues such as human rights abuses or deforestation and other ecological issues that have an impact on the well-being of people and the environment respectively.

Source: http://www.happyplanetindex.org/assets/happy-planet-index-poster.pdf

▲ Refugees from war. The Second Congo War is the deadliest conflict the world has seen since the Second World War. By 2008, in the region of 5.4 million people had died, principally due to starvation and disease, and approximately another 2 million were displaced.

A rounded conception of development encompassing both the human and sustainable dimensions requires the interplay of a medley of factors. These may range from political, economic and social to institutional and environmental. While some of these promote development, others inhibit or obstruct it. This chapter will make an attempt to identify and briefly touch upon some of the factors that either further or hinder development.

Political factors

Conflict and development

The presence of a conflict does not bode well for any society considering that development depends on the bedrock of peace, security and respect for human rights. Inter- and intra-state conflicts ranging from civil wars and crime-related violence to ethnic and communal strife have in fact been termed as being a condition of "development in reverse".[39] Violence and conflict eats away at the level of economic progress already achieved. The centrality of peace and stability as a foundation for development has been aptly reiterated and stressed upon by the UN High-Level Panel report on post-2015 development.

How do conflicts hamper development? To begin with, conflicts destroy the social, economic, political and cultural fabric of society through a trail of ill effects such as loss of life, disease, forced migration, damage to infrastructure and refugee crisis. It erodes trust and the attractiveness of conflict-ridden areas as investment destinations and trade partners – both of which are an intrinsic part of the process of economic growth. It has also been proven that poverty continues to persist in countries plagued by violence, while the rest of the world has taken strides towards a reduction in poverty.

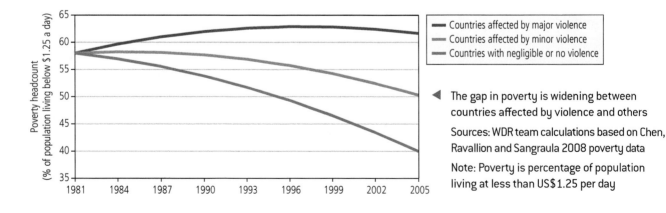

Countries affected by major violence
Countries affected by minor violence
Countries with negligible or no violence

◀ The gap in poverty is widening between countries affected by violence and others

Sources: WDR team calculations based on Chen, Ravallion and Sangraula 2008 poverty data

Note: Poverty is percentage of population living at less than US$1.25 per day

The World Development Report (2011) states that:

New poverty data reveal that poverty is declining for much of the world, but countries affected by violence are lagging behind. For every three years a country is affected by major violence (battle deaths or excess deaths from homicides equivalent to a major war), poverty reduction lags behind by 2.7 percentage points.

A lack of economic growth can in turn result in civil and political unrest as interest groups dispute their rights to available resources. Besides which, a state's decreased ability and capacity to govern a conflict-stricken area is marred and could mean an increased chance of the conflict relapsing, as has been seen, for example, in Somalia and Congo. A number of further conflict-related problems include the following:

- The risk of a conflict impacting neighbouring countries due to the high possibility of forced migration and refugees.

- In an attempt to hinder violence and conflict, governments are forced to redirect their funds from development, including social welfare and poverty alleviation, towards other sectors such as maintaining the military or managing these conflicts.

- War-torn countries become easy bases for terror group networks.

- Conflicts also have an impact on the environment and therefore on sustainable development. For example, due to the destruction of Liberia's hydropower infrastructure there has been an increased use of charcoal and wood fuel for energy needs leading to deforestation and atmospheric pollution.

▲ Congolese soldiers, Democratic Republic of Congo

Conflict and fragility

Growth and wealth
- International barriers to export
- Post-conflict economic growth and aid
- Economic and financial liberalization

Violence and security
- Trans-national organized crime
- Markets for military and security goods and services
- International engagement with non-state armed groups

Meaning and movement
- Radical ideas and modern technology
- Migration from/to fragile states

▲ Conflict, stability and development

Communication and research skills

Divide into two groups. In your group choose one conflict occurring in any part of the world (you could choose an example or case study that you are working on for the unit on Peace and Conflict) and note down the impact it is having in terms of economic growth, human and sustainable development. Present your findings to the other group and compare notes on how similar or different the impact of both of these conflicts has been in terms of development on the area or country in question.

TOK

Given that they have access to the same facts, how is it possible that there can be disagreement between experts in a particular area of knowledge?

Ideology and political systems

For governments around the world, development is one of the primary stated national goals. Of course, there are different paths they can take to achieve this ambition based on the ideology they believe in. Liberals hold that economic growth can be pursued with economic expansion, which in turn fuels increased incomes, raising demand for goods, jobs and overall growth. They encourage privatization and a free market economy to spur development. Socialism, on the other hand, is inclined towards a centrally planned economy and state-ownership of property. Authoritarian regimes involve the possession of power by a leader or a small group of elites.

Every ideology – whether liberal, socialist, authoritarian or capitalist – has had its supporters and opponents, yet there is no unanimity or consensus on what could be the best possible option to boost development. While liberal democracies have often been hailed as the key to growth and development, there are a number of examples of the successes and failures of each of these models. Despite the much touted failures of socialism, such as in the former USSR, there have been success stories as well. One such example has been of the socialist regime of Bolivia under Evo Morales. According to a report, Bolivia has seen a decline in extreme poverty and income inequality, and a rise in real minimum wages and social spending.[40]

Governance: accountability and transparency

Much of a country's development is related to matters concerning governance, such as stability, accountability, transparency, legal frameworks, political culture and bureaucracy. Governments and leaders who have a positive approach towards an accountable and transparent system with a strong and efficient bureaucracy are known to have an accelerated growth rate. It is worth reiterating here that development is not only to be considered in the material sense, but would also encompass what noted economist Amartya Sen terms as "expansion of freedoms".

Thinking skills

Divide into two groups to work on the following question:

Has the growing GNP in China and India helped all sections of society?

The discussion should be based on the fact that poverty is still rampant and most people still suffer from a lack of access to basic needs.

Corruption indices

The Corruptions Perceptions Index and Global Corruption Barometer are surveys on corruption conducted by Transparency International. According to the 2014 results, of the 175 countries surveyed, public sectors in Denmark, New Zealand, Sweden, Norway and Singapore feature among the least corrupt, while Somalia, North Korea, Sudan, Afghanistan and Iraq are ranked as among the highly corrupt. Survey results reveal that more than two-thirds of the countries score a 50 on a scale of 0 (highly corrupt) to 100 (very clean). Moreover, no country scores a perfect 100. The countries with low rankings suffer from problems such as bribery, lack of punishment for corruption and public institutions that do not respond to the needs of citizens.

The World Bank also brings out a similar index called the Criminal Procedure and Investigations Act 1996 (CPIA) Transparency, Accountability and Corruption in Public Sector Rating (see map below). The index reflects these three eponymous variables in the public sector and assesses variables such as accountability of those in power and access of civil society to public affairs information.

5

1 = low to 6 = high

1

▲ CPIA Transparency, Accountability and Corruption in the Public Sector Rating

In sum, poor governance marked by corruption, lack of rule of law, governmental interference in the market, lack of transparency and accountability, and ill-planned allocation of resources all have a negative impact on development.

Economic factors

Access to capital, credit and aid

Access to capital and credit can assist the process of development. Capital could be defined as a stock of wealth used to produce goods and services and could be either in the form of produced goods, natural or human capital.[41] On the other hand, credit is an agreement under which a borrower receives something of value in the present and has to repay the same with interest in the future.[42] Capital in all forms can be used as building blocks to foster growth. Similarly, institutes providing microfinance can play a critical role in assisting small-scale industries and small entrepreneurs to begin and sustain their work, which in turn helps them to get out of poverty. The Grameen Bank of Bangladesh is one such institution that has made a difference to so many lives.

Foreign aid could have a dual effect on development in terms of either supporting or hindering it. Aid can prop up the process of development in a number of ways. External assistance in areas critical to human development, such as food, education and health, are directly related to the basics of human development. For a country that has been suffering, or is in the process of recovering from natural disasters or conflicts

▲ Foreign aid cartoon

of any kind, aid is required to ensure relief and stability. Similarly, aid in areas such as the establishment of sound infrastructure facilities can help establish a solid foundation for industrialization and growth. The Japanese Official Development Assistance (ODA) can be an example in this regard.

However, aid can also obstruct development. First, it could promote the tendency for states and governments to develop a pattern of reliance, even as it expunges the spirit of self-help, hard work and entrepreneurship. Moreover, aid can prove to be harmful when combined with poor governance – corruption and a lack of transparency. A corrupt government could swindle aid for private gains and become even stronger at the cost of the poor population. Lack of transparency on how aid has been spent only aggravates the problem.

Social factors

The overall social milieu of a country has a very subtle, but powerful, impact on its development. Intangible variables such as values, cultures, traditions, gender and migration could have both positive and negative effects.

Values, cultures and traditions

The term "culture" includes a society's or community's value systems and beliefs. It can be used to provide an impetus to growth and development. To begin with, since culture and traditions help shape and condition the values and ethics of society, they also have an impact on the social and economic aspects of their lives. For instance, a study by two Harvard economists, Robert Barro and Rachel McCleary, partly based on the World Values Survey, found that economic growth responds positively to religious beliefs in heaven, hell and an afterlife (apart from other factors such as education). The study suggested that religious beliefs help growth because they influence individual behaviour to improve productivity.[43] Culture and values also determine how resource allocation is carried out within society. It could be clearly noticed that some ethnic groups, communities and even nations achieve far more than others, despite having a sound economic base to build upon. Values such as hard work, respect, honesty, trust and discipline add to the quality of a workforce and their output, and finally have a bearing on economic growth and development.

Second, culture creates an impression for the economic performance as well as attractiveness of a country. A culture clear of corrupt practices and with an ethos conducive to innovation, entrepreneurship, gender equality and racial harmony augments the attractiveness of a country as a destination for investments as well as a favourable location for setting up operations for companies, institutions and organizations. In today's global politics, how often this is actively the case is a matter of some debate.

Third, culture could also be used as a tool of "soft power" to further economic growth. The example of China's so-called "charm offensive" is the subject of much discussion. Several analysts have commented that Beijing uses soft power tools to assure the world of its peaceful intentions and to continue to procure a steady supply of resources in order to pursue its growth.

TOK

This chapter claims that culture helps to shape our values and beliefs. To what extent are we aware of the impact of our culture on what we believe or know?

For given religious beliefs, increases in church attendance tend to reduce economic growth. In contrast, for given church attendance, increases in some religious beliefs – notably heaven, hell, and an afterlife – tend to increase economic growth.

Barro and McCleary. "Religion and Economic Growth". *NBER Working Paper No. 9682.*

▲ China–Africa trade grows

The cultural sector, if developed, could add to the probability of providing income and employment opportunities. For instance, according to statistics released by the United Nations Educational, Scientific and Cultural Organization (UNESCO), 5.72 per cent of Bosnia and Herzegovina's GDP came from cultural activities in 2011, while 2.1 per cent of the employed people in Colombia had jobs in the cultural sector in 2012.[44] Culture could also be used to attract tourism – a major revenue earner for many countries, providing jobs and income to many (although it is generally noted that this is most often low-paying service employment). UNESCO has also initiated a programme known as Culture: A Bridge to Development, under which it aims to bring artists, teachers and intellectuals on a platform to exchange ideas and visions to create a cohesive network among politicians, professionals and civil society in order to enable them to be involved in development projects.

In contrast, trade union culture, strikes, loss of labour hours and a lack of discipline are all cultural attributes that deter both interest and investment in societies, communities or a country. For example, Tata Motors moved their factory out of the state of West Bengal in India following violent protests by farmers in 2008. The farmers were protesting against what they called a "forcible snatching" of their land without adequate compensation.[45]

3 DEVELOPMENT

Gender and sustainable development

Women have a vital role in environmental management and development. Their full participation is therefore essential to achieve sustainable development.

Rio Declaration, 1992

Integrate gender concerns and perspectives in policies and programmes for sustainable development.

Beijing Declaration

We recognize that gender equality and women's empowerment are important for sustainable development and our common future. We reaffirm our commitments to ensure women's equal rights, access and opportunities for participation and leadership in the economy, society and political decision making.

Rio+20

Factors driving migration

- Inequalities in education, human rights, jobs, resources
- Demand for and supply of labour
- Relatively cheap international transport
- Easy electronic communication
- Transnational family networks

Gender matters

Gender and development have a close-knit relationship and examples clearly show that the favourable position of women in society acts as a boost to development and growth. A society in which women have rights and access to opportunities provides an environment for the expansion of capabilities (the ability to read and write, have a long and healthy life, earn a respectable living and also take part in decision-making) and the freedom of social, political, cultural and economic choices, and thus has an edge above others. There are different facets to existing gender discrimination – education, property, employment opportunities, economic freedom and empowerment.

In purely economic terms, provision of education, business opportunities and support can help empower women, generate additional income and productivity, and create employment. Healthy and educated women would have healthier children, adding directly to a good quality of human resource. Enhanced reproductive health and low infant mortality would also help uplift development. Studies have shown that there is a link between literacy and reduction of fertility rates. Fewer and healthier children will keep population in check and also slow down environmental degradation. Besides, women have a big hand in the production, storage and distribution of food and are central to food security of the family and community. An additional involvement of the female workforce in the agricultural sector will increase food production.

The contribution of the myriad roles that women can play in development cannot be disputed. This has been acknowledged and documented in many reports on development (see left). We will discuss a few of these matters in the section on the capabilities approach later in this unit.

Migration

Migration is generally defined as the "crossing of the boundary of a political or administrative unit for a certain minimum period of time".[46] This includes movement of refugees and uprooted and displaced people as well as economic migrants. Migration is one of the variables encompassing the phenomenon of globalization. It has both positive and negative impacts on development.

Migration can provide an impetus to the economic growth and the development of a recipient country simply due to the fact that it involves the transfer of skilled workforce as well as labour force, both of which are required to increase productivity and GDP in purely economic terms. Countries that lack a young workforce can open the doors to facilitate its inflow and fill in any gaps, thereby increasing productivity. Additionally, the immigrants often send money back to their families, paving the way for them to come out of poverty and have the resources to spend on food, education and housing – all of which are considered to be basic human needs. They also add to the GDP and add to the foreign exchange of the recipient country. This also gives the returning migrants or their family members opportunity to set up entrepreneurial ventures in their home towns with the capital raised, leading to further employment.

The positive impact of migration contrasts with the negative effect on the economic growth and development of a country. The most obvious being the loss of human resource – both skilled and unskilled labour. The oft-discussed "brain drain" takes away from the valuable human resources a country can exploit to its advantage. The presence of a large number of immigrants sometimes leads to social unrest in the host country. Refugees that form a section of the migrant population become an added burden on limited resources.

FOR EVERY **$1** DEVELOPING COUNTRIES **GAIN**

Other official flows **3¢**
Charitable **3¢**
Portfolio equity (stocks & shares) **6¢**
Aid **10¢**
Remittances from migrant workers **34¢**
Foreign direct investment **44¢**

Interest repayments on foreign debt **14¢**
Profits taken out by foreign investors **42¢**
Lending to rich countries **59¢**
Illicit financial flows **93¢**

THEY LOSE MORE THAN $2

Efficacy of national and local institutions

Local and national institutions are significant stakeholders, actors and contributors in the process of growth and development. They are a critical link in the process of development by virtue of the fact that they are a part of the multi-tier governance system planning, coordinating and executing activities, resources and their distribution into the wider society.

What makes these institutions relevant and critical is also the fact that almost all aspects of development, ranging from food, housing, education, healthcare, protection of the environment and equitable distribution of income, require efficient planning and implementation at the grassroots level. Considering that they are closest to the ground and well connected and adapted to local conditions, they can play a very important role in accelerating the process of development in tandem with the indigenous culture, values and traditions.

An example of how the national – and local – level institutions could join hands to further development may be seen in one of the poorest countries, Mali, Africa, where a Community Development Programme was initiated in the year 2000 by a national non-governmental organization (NGO), Jeunesse et Developpement. The NGO began its work with a focus on areas such as health and literacy and gradually expanded its area of work. It involves community development workers, village committees and facilitators from the community itself. The programme has made a difference. There are learning spaces earmarked for reading, writing and arithmetic, community health centres, hygiene committees in villages and programmes involving women and making them independent.[47]

If local and national institutions can be effective in bolstering development, they can have a potentially harmful impact as well. In communities, societies and countries where these institutions are prone to corruption, fragmented or suffer from problems such as lack

Indigenous people and their communities and other local communities have a vital role in environmental management and development because of their knowledge and traditional practices. States should recognize and duly support their identity, culture and interests and enable their effective participation in the achievement of sustainable development.

Rio Declaration on Environment and Development, 1992

of experience, skills or lack of literacy, the same process of development could be derailed. In keeping with the fact that these are significant actors in sourcing, usage and distribution of resources among society, any kind of inefficiency or omissions on their part would have a negative impact.

Environmental factors

Safeguarding the environment and sustainable development are critical aspects of the discourse and practice of development goals in today's world. The environment is directly related to the daily lives of all individuals. It is no surprise, therefore, that environmental sustainability is one of the most significant MDGs set out by world leaders.

In considering the impact of geography on development, a few things could be noted. One, the location of a country, which in turn affects weather and climate, has an impact. At a macro level, countries with coastal lines and access to other countries have easier chances of development. This not just makes it easier to transport material and labour, but also decreases the costs of doing so. Similarly, climate and weather have an impact on the overall health and well-being of people. Climates that have a greater chance of fostering diseases and ill-health have a negative bearing on the human capital of that region and therefore on their output and contribution to development. A good climate that supports agricultural production is also helpful in furthering development.

Impact of climate change

Climate change directly opposes sustainable development. Communities and countries are harming and destroying the very resources on which they depend for survival. Climate change and global warming are having a direct impact on weather and rainfall patterns. This in turn results in floods, droughts, rising seawater levels, higher temperatures and other natural disasters that affect agricultural production, hitting poor farmers and fishermen the most. Disease, hunger and malnutrition are additional problems that the poor are likely to face, bringing about added cost to healthcare and a fall in productivity of human resource. A report by the Intergovernmental Panel on Climate Change released in 2007

> The notion of "development versus environment" has given way to a new view in which… better environmental stewardship is essential to sustain development.
>
> World Bank, *World Bank Atlas*, 1997

TOK

Is it possible to have knowledge of future events? Are some areas of knowledge better equipped than others to make predictions about the future?

Bangladesh is situated on the Ganges delta and so is prone to severe flooding. In the catastrophic 1998 floods, in the region of 30 million people were made homeless and approximately 4.5 million tons of crops were damaged.

highlighted the fact that developing countries – more specifically, the poorest – will bear the brunt of climate change. The report earmarked four vulnerable areas: sub-Saharan Africa (due to drying), Asian mega deltas (flooding), small islands and the Arctic region.[48]

The problem gets aggravated because of the fact that while these countries are hit hard, they have not contributed as much towards the reality of climate change as it stands today. They also do not have the resources or the expertise to face this challenge as they try to move ahead on the path to growth. This is important keeping in mind the fact that any development now has to be in tandem with the sustainability factor.

The following chapter will dwell upon the pathways towards development, including the models of development and approaches to developing society and the economy.

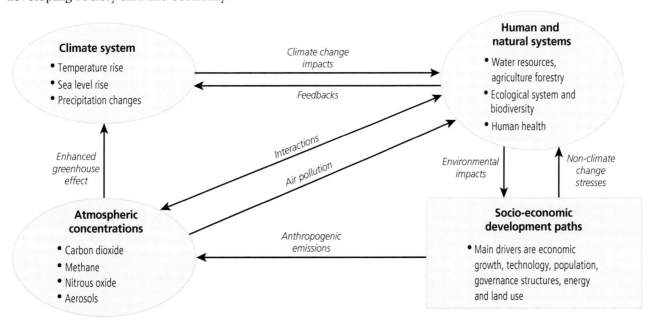

▲ Climate change is a sustainable development issue

Models of development – neoliberalism, state capitalism and capability theories

Neoliberal theories (Washington Consensus)

Neoliberal theories of development form a very significant contemporary aspect of development theories. The neoliberal model of development that emerged during the 1970s endorsed the belief that for the well-being of people and the economic growth and development of a country it was best for the state to minimize its intervention and leave the market free to function on its own, setting wages and prices. This in many ways reinforced classical theorist Adam Smith's concept of the "invisible hand" under which the market regulates itself towards the goal of economic growth.

Neoliberal thinkers believe that the market is the "optimal space for the production and distribution of wealth and… the optimal vehicle for social mobility".[49] It is, according to them, counterproductive for the state to pursue protectionist policies for domestic industry. These theorists stress the need to follow a policy of the expansion of exports. This has to be supported by deregulation and the removal of tariffs and barriers. They also emphasize the need for privatization and development based on the theory of comparative advantage, first put forward by David Ricardo in his 1817 book on the principles of political economy in which he argues that countries should specialize in the production of goods that they can produce at a lower cost than others, thereby gaining an advantage in trade relationships. Furthermore, the neoliberal path requires that countries permit and welcome foreign investment.

Trade liberalization

Trade liberalization is any act that would make the trade regime more neutral, nearer to a trade system free of government intervention.

The Washington Consensus was a term coined by the English economist John Williamson in 1989 to capture a few policy reforms unanimously advocated by the US government and international financial institutions in order for countries to pull out of the mire of economic instability. It was formulated as a set of 10 policy reforms targeted at Latin America to help it out of a debt crisis that had begun in 1982. Some of these included tax reform, trade liberalization, deregulation and privatization and encouraging inward foreign direct investment.[50]

Deregulation involves removal of barriers to competition, legislations and laws in the market by the government

Privatization: Transfer of ownership of assets to the private sector.

Mary M. Shirley, *The What, Why and How of Privatization*

Thinking and social skills

With a partner, discuss the neoliberal model of development. Afterwards write a critique or note down the drawbacks of this model.

This neoliberal way of development found support in policies set forth by the IMF and World Bank. These institutions supported similar policy prescriptions for those developing countries that were facing problems while following the path of import substitution in the 1980s. The World Bank introduced the Structural Adjustment Programme (SAP), a set of policy prescriptions that had to be applied by countries to recover from their economic woes. These included cuts in government expenditure and real wages, elimination of subsidies, trade liberalization and raising agricultural prices.[51] The implementation of the SAP was also put forth as a precondition for the receipt of any lending from the Bank. The SAP came under criticism for not eliminating poverty and creating more dependency.

State capitalism (China, Russia)

State capitalism can be described as a political system in which the state has the supreme control over both production and the usage of capital and thereby utilizes the market for political advantages, protected from the ups and downs of a market system. It involves a "widespread influence of the government in the economy, either by owning majority or minority equity positions in companies or by providing subsidized credit and/or privileges to private companies".[52] Governments could use different methods and tools to exercise their control over the economic sphere. These include sovereign wealth funds (SWFs), state-owned enterprises and national champion firms. Many national oil companies are owned by states. The strong nexus between politics and economics could show both pros and cons. The success story of countries such as China that have exhibited a consistent growth rate in the past few years has been touted as a success story of state capitalism.[53] The dangers, on the other hand, include the possibility that political ends may have a negative impact on decisions taken on the economic front. Also, those in power who ultimately will take significant economic decisions may not have the necessary expertise to do so.

> [W]ith the injection of politics into economic decision-making, an entirely different set of winners and losers is emerging. [S]tate officials in… Beijing… Moscow, and New Delhi make economic decisions – about strategic investments, state ownership, regulation – that resonate across global markets.
>
> Ian Bremmer, *State Capitalism Comes of Age,*
> *Foreign Affairs, 2009.*

China and Russia are two major examples of countries following the state capitalist system. The saga of state capitalism as it has evolved in China has been a success story. China's GDP has been consistently growing for the past few years. The Chinese government is a primary stakeholder in the top 12 companies that are state owned. The central government exercises control over these companies through major decisions on investments and through appointments to the top posts. They are protected from competition by the state mechanism.[54]

Russia has been following a similar system. All large businesses have to maintain a cordial relationship with the government. The political leadership is known to exercise control over state enterprises. A group of people called "oligarchs" wield power and money. Some of them are known to be helping powerful politicians. For instance, Arkady Rotenberg whose company earned profits while doing business with state-owned Gazprom is alleged to have helped fund Vladimir Putin's 2012 election.[55]

Sovereign wealth funds

A sovereign wealth fund (SWF) is a state-owned investment fund or entity commonly created from balance of payment surpluses, fiscal surpluses and so forth.

Research skills

Research countries that are following the state capitalism model and measure the pros and cons of the system to decipher whether it has been a success or failure.

Self-management and research skills

Watch the following online video on state capitalism in China:
https://www.youtube.com/watch?v=7T302G5wAS4

Capability theory (Sen, Nussbaum)

▲ Amartya Sen and Martha Nussbaum

Functioning – achievement of a person, what he/she manages to do or be. For example:

- Escaping mortality
- Working, resting
- Literacy and health
- Adequate nourishment
- Achieving self-respect
- Taking part in community living

Capability – combinations of functionings a person can achieve and reflects an individual's freedom to choose between different ways of living

Research and thinking skills

Listen to Martha Nussbaum speaking on the capability approach to development at http://www-personal. umd.umich.edu/~delittle/ nussbaum.htm

Research further about the two theorists' conceptualization of capability theory and spot similarities and differences.

The capability theory was propounded by famous economist and Nobel Prize winner Amartya Sen and has been built upon and furthered by scholars such as Martha Nussbaum. The approach is based on the premise that economic development in terms of a rise in GNP does not necessarily guarantee a good quality of life for people. According to Sen, a human being's life is a set of "doings and beings" – termed together as "functionings".[56] The quality of life can be evaluated and assessed in terms of the capability to function – that is, the opportunities to perform actions they wish to and be what they want to be.[57] In sum, according to this school of thought, the focus of policy should be to ensure a person's well-being and development, and to provide the freedom to live the kind of life they choose or find valuable. The capability approach covers a full spectrum of variables defining well-being, for instance, health, education and political freedom. All of these require different kinds of inputs – some may need economic resources, others political freedoms or even social institutions and structures.[58]

Sen's conceptualization of the capability approach was elaborated further by Martha Nussbaum. Nussbaum's contribution to the capability approach has been particularly noteworthy in the field of gender issues. She has argued that people across a cross-section of cultures and societies have a few basic capabilities required for a good life. These capabilities, according to her, should be followed as a guideline in the formulation of development policy. Some of the central human capabilities as listed by Nussbaum include:

- ability to live a life of normal length
- good health, nutrition, shelter
- ability to use senses, imagine, think, reason and have the education to realize all of these
- ability to live for others and show concern for other human beings
- ability to laugh and enjoy recreation.[59]

Approaches for developing the economy

Trade liberalization and export orientation

Trade liberalization and export orientation became buzzwords in the face of failure of the import substitution model of the economy. Liberalization, or the opening up of the economy to trade and investment with the outside world, has thus become one of the salient features of many countries on their road to development. Countries have adopted export orientation – increase in the production and export of goods in which they possess comparative advantage – in order to raise the level of the economy. In the process, they also open their markets for inflow of foreign goods or promote free trade.

A number of advantages have been attributed to trade liberalization and export-oriented economic growth. First, in developing countries it is expected to enhance product development and enable firms to compete globally. Second, opening up of the economy and focusing on exports encourages innovation and facilitates transfer of skills and technology enhancement.[60] The East Asian economies of Japan, Hong Kong, Taiwan, Singapore and South Korea came to be known as the Asian Tigers in the light of their rapid economic development based on export-led growth and liberalization of the economy. They increased their share of world trade by exporting manufactured goods, including telecommunication equipment, computers and robotics.[61] These countries were followed by other Southeast Asian countries, Thailand, Indonesia and Malaysia. More recently, India and China have also become success stories in the economic arena while following a similar economic plan.

Tourism and entrepreneurship

Promotion of tourism and entrepreneurship are two other approaches that can be used for developing the economy. Tourism involves the movement of people from one place to another within or across borders. People travel for the purpose of leisure, business, health or just visiting relatives and friends. This kind of travel has grown rapidly in an increasingly globalized world, where transportation is relatively cheap, and where borders are becoming blurred. In many countries and continents the rapid growth of tourism has made a significant contribution to the growth of the economy. Currency spent by visitors also brings foreign exchange into the host country, helps in firming up infrastructure and provides added revenues for industries such as airlines and telecommunications. Moreover, money spent by cross-border visitors is counted as exports for the destination country and imports for the visitor's country of residence.[62] The local small-scale and handicraft sales receive a boost with increased demands for their goods. The data in the diagram below speaks volumes about how each of these can contribute to the growth of the economy.

The long-term forecast for tourism in 2030 is promising, making it one of the key sectors to be kept under a watchful eye as an important contributor to the development of the economy. It should be remembered, however, that tourism creates primarily low-paying jobs, so

Trade Liberalization is defined as any act that would make the trade regime more neutral – trade system free of government intervention.

S.M. Shafeddin, *Trade Liberalization and Economic Reforms in Developing Countries*

ATL Communication and thinking skills

Pick a case study of any country that has followed the path of liberalization and export-oriented growth. Present your findings to the class. Discuss whether the fruits of growth and development have trickled down to all parts of society and sum up your findings by discussing whether liberalization and export-oriented growth ends up as a success story in every case. If not, what other factors are needed to make it a success?

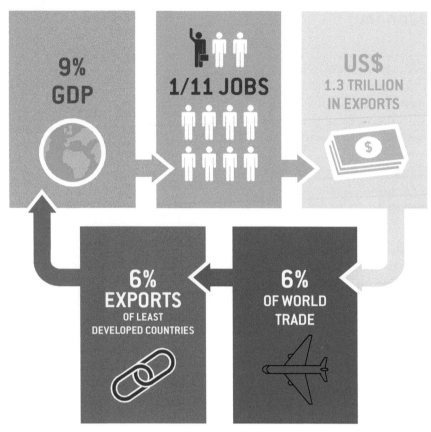

9% GDP

1/11 JOBS

US$ 1.3 TRILLION IN EXPORTS

6% EXPORTS OF LEAST DEVELOPED COUNTRIES

6% OF WORLD TRADE

▲ Why tourism matters

the winners in the growth of tourism are the owners of tourist establishments rather than the workers who keep the tourist industry functioning.

Promotion and development of entrepreneurship is considered an essential and integral component of the process of economic growth. But what is entrepreneurship? Economist Joseph Schumpeter defined entrepreneurship as the "assumption of risk and responsibility in designing and implementing a business strategy or starting a business".[63] In other words, it is a process by which an individual or a group of people make an attempt to convert an idea into a business or economic activity. Entrepreneurship can help spur the economy by creating jobs and making good use of capital from investors. Besides, a successful entrepreneur able to create products and services adds to the GNP of the country. If these are exported to an overseas market, they would also help bring in foreign currency. Apart from the purely economic advantages, entrepreneurs can also lead to innovation.

In order to facilitate entrepreneurship a few significant conditions have to be present. As shown in the diagram below, a good entrepreneurial spirit has to be supported by the presence of a sound infrastructure, a promising market, governmental policies free of "red tape" and procedural barriers, funding and financing systems and stable institutions. All these factors can coalesce to create and support viable, stable and strong entrepreneurial ventures, which in turn can boost economic development. At the educational level, it can also help to encourage, train and educate people to set up enterprises in a planned manner.

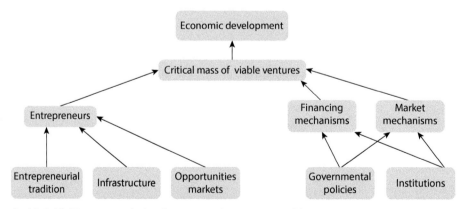

▲ Model linking economic development and entrepreneurship

Knowledge economy

We have discussed the significance of various drivers of development – ranging from natural resources and capital to a large labour force. The term "knowledge economy" has been gaining prominence in recent years and refers to knowledge and intellectual capabilities. It is based on "the production, distribution and use of knowledge and information".[64] Considering the fact that it involves "production and services based on knowledge-intensive activities that contribute to an accelerated pace of technical and scientific advance", it is also likely to face the peril of becoming obsolete very quickly.[65] Thus, according to the World Bank, there are four basic requirements for a country to have a knowledge economy (see right) – an educated and trained workforce capable of participating in such an economy; a sound infrastructure, including Internet access to enable the dissemination and communication of information; an environment conducive to the dispersal of knowledge, entrepreneurship, investment in information and communication technology; along with a set of think tanks, research centres and human resource that is able to understand, create and suitably use knowledge. Inherent in this set of credentials is the presence of a workforce that is able to adapt to rapid changes in technology. This requires an educational system that enables students to learn how to adapt, not only in technological fields, but in ways that teach the art of "critical thinking".[66]

The knowledge economy thus thrives on an educated and knowledgeable human resource with the capability to use their expertise and intellect to create and innovate consistently through the process of research and development. It includes advance in higher education, technology and innovation. This kind of an economy forms a significant portion of the economic pie of developed countries.

The World Bank has a Knowledge Assessment Methodology that measures countries on the basis of the variables mentioned in the diagram below. According to the Knowledge Index 2012, the top five countries include Sweden, Finland, Denmark, the Netherlands and Norway. They are high performers in areas such as innovation, information and communication technology (ICT) and education.[67]

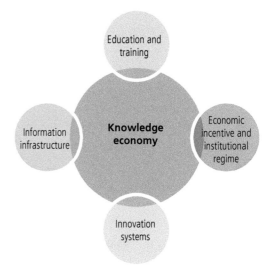

▲ The four basic requirements of a knowledge economy

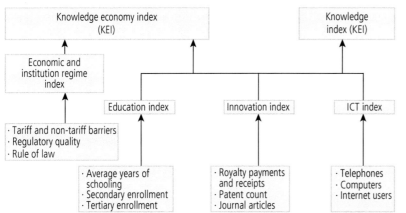

▲ The knowledge indices

Research and self-management skills

Watch the following videos on knowledge economy:

https://www.youtube.com/watch?v=2EzOLhYNd84

https://www.youtube.com/watch?v=_-8uhMBl6vI

Circular economy

Consider the following:

- Mobile phone production could be reduced by half if the phones manufactured could be dismantled, improved upon and recycled and if there were incentives on returning devices.

- All clothing disposed of in the UK could be recycled and generate gross profits. They could be reused in a variety of ways – used by new owners, recycled into yarn to make cloth or even used as stuffing for upholstery.

A typical industrial economy relies on usage and consumption of primary energy resources for the purpose of manufacturing while aiming for growth and development. In such a set-up, resources are used to manufacture goods that are then disposed of after usage. This process, as discussed earlier, has a negative impact on the environment and tends to drain resources. A circular economy is a system devised to ensure that the production process allows for the recycling of material and products.

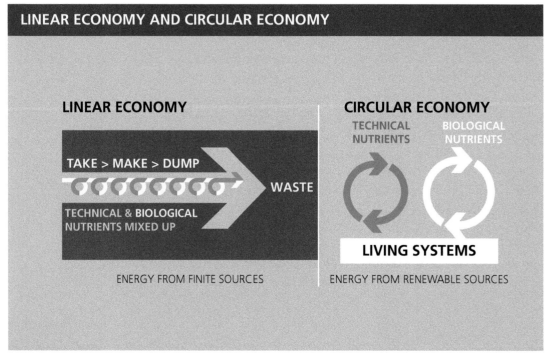

▲ The linear and circular economies, Ellen MacArthur Foundation

In a circular economy, all kinds of material are divided into primarily two groups:[68]

- Biological material that is non-toxic and can pass through the biosphere without harming the environment.

- Technical material that cannot be processed through the biosphere. These thus need to be kept in the best possible condition to be purposed for other products.

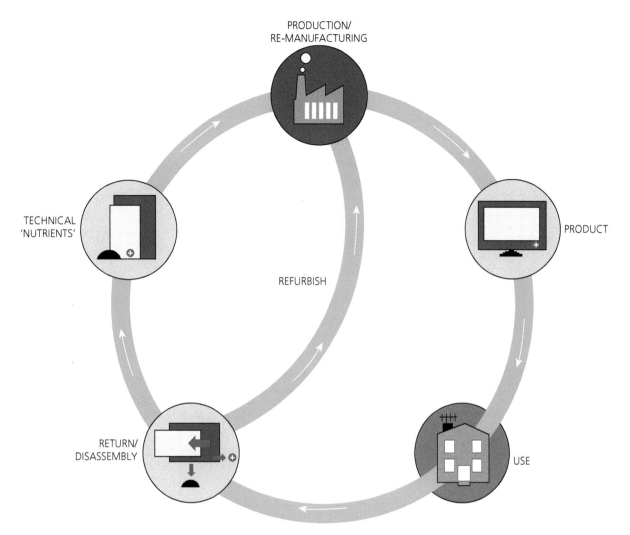

PRODUCTION/
RE-MANUFACTURING

TECHNICAL
'NUTRIENTS'

PRODUCT

REFURBISH

RETURN/
DISASSEMBLY

USE

▲ Technical circular economy, Ellen MacArthur Foundation

Such an economy attempts to make products out of secondary raw materials and use waste purposefully.[69] This model is expected to spur development, create employment, encourage innovation in eco-friendly industries and also safeguard the environment. In order for the circular economy to be set in motion, there is a need to make changes both in the system of production and also the consumption behaviour of people to ensure that all materials are reused. This places the concept of circular economy in harmony with the concept of sustainable development.

Self-management skills

See the interactive diagram on circular economy here:

https://www.ellenmacarthurfoundation.org/circular-economy/interactive-diagram

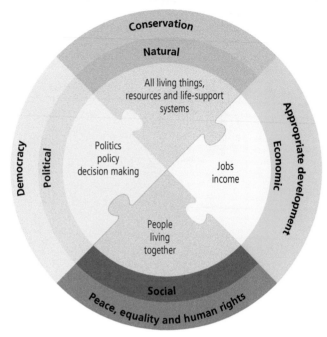

Conservation

Natural

All living things, resources and life-support systems

Democracy

Political

Politics policy decision making

Appropriate development

Economic

Jobs income

People living together

Social

Peace, equality and human rights

▲ Four dimensions of sustainable development

Concern for citizenship skills and engagement

Human beings make a society and it naturally follows that each member of society as an individual, in a family set-up or a community needs to remain engaged and involved in order to ensure steady progress and development of society. It is also evident that in order for development to be sustainable, citizens need to be imbued with a few basic skill sets to ensure they are actively contributing to and are involved in the process of development at the societal, national and global levels. An open interaction and system of inputs and feedback from people is critical both for adding value in the form of ideas as well as the ability to acquire support for the decisions taken by the government. This ensures that the voice of the people has an impact on policies and actions taken by the government.

Building citizenship skills would primarily include being aware and informed (the ability to scrutinize problems at the local and community levels), solving problems and taking decisions (the ability to recognize the social, economic, ecological and political dimensions of issues needed to solve those problems) and taking appropriate action (the ability to participate in steps taken towards a sustainable future).[70] Building citizenship skills and engagement are thus an intrinsic part of the quest for sustainable development and also encourage accountability and transparency of the government.

We, the Ministers of Education (of the world) strive resolutely to pay special attention... to educating caring and responsible citizens committed to peace, human rights, democracy and sustainable development, open to other cultures, able to appreciate the value of freedom, respectful of human dignity and differences, and able to prevent conflicts or resolve them by non-violent means.

[I]t is necessary to introduce, at all levels, true education for citizenship which includes an international dimension.

UNESCO *Declaration and Integrated Framework of Action on Education for Peace, Human Rights and Democracy,* 1995

Member states should promote, at every stage of education, an active civic training which will enable every person to gain a knowledge of the method of operation and the work of public institutions, whether local, national or international; and to participate in the cultural life of the community and in public affairs.

UNESCO *Recommendation concerning Education for International Understanding, Co-operation and Peace and Education relating to Human Rights and Fundamental Freedoms,* 1974

Citizenship skills could include a broad range of attributes such as the ability to critically think and enquire about issues while keeping in mind different perspectives, institutions and policies, making informed decisions, actively participating in activities, tolerance towards all and communication. These will encapsulate a few skills, attitudes and knowledge required to mould people into citizens capable of steering the community, nation and world towards a peaceful, just and sustainable society. To cultivate some of these, information could be gathered through the optimum usage of the media, public resources and government documents. Similarly, citizens could participate in community service, help to raise funds for worthy causes and be good citizens by showing respect for the law of the land and other cultures as well as living in harmony. The foundation of this would lie in the promotion of character building, which in turn impacts the way people behave. Education and training has been recognized as an effective tool towards achieving this end. The idea, however, has to be to not just target children, but adults too.

Different countries have their own ways and methods to ensure that citizenship skills and engagement are developed. Education, of course, forms the crux of the method to ensure this. The box below provides an insight into one such effort being undertaken in South Africa. Similarly, Singapore has a well-articulated and documented framework on character and citizenship education to empower and train citizens to be engaged in the process of development. Keeping character building at the heart of the endeavour, it also highlights social and emotional growth in terms of skills, knowledge, disposition and citizenship literacy.[71]

> **Class discussion**
>
> Are the most advanced capitalist countries actively investing in education to create an informed citizenship capable of contributions to economic growth? What are the factors that contribute to or work against this development goal?

> **Example of youth-led initiative: Activate! Change drivers, South Africa**
>
> Activate! is a network of young leaders equipped to drive change for the public good across South Africa. It connects young people who have the skills, sense of self and spark to address tough challenges and initiate innovative and creative solutions that can reshape society. It is a three-year programme for young people aged 20–30, identified as "activators", or mobilizers, innovators, connectors, trendsetters and change drivers.
>
> Year 1 includes a residential learning module that promotes self-discovery, collective self-reflection, leadership, project management and social and political navigation. The year's programme culminates in a two-day gathering of participants of all types and levels.
>
> Year 2 connects activators to one another, deepens their resources and offers opportunities for exchanges and networking.
>
> In year 3, seminars, workshops and online learning platforms enrich activators' leadership for public innovation.
>
> Activate! "aims to move beyond episodic events. Many have done episodic events! We want to move to developmental and then transformational, individual, organizational, societal", explained Injairu Kulundu, Practitioner with Activate! "If we can articulate it and take it forward, the power could go much broader than we imagine. What are the spaces for us to speak about an agenda for social change? Not just to 'tolerate each other' but really looking at each other and creating change."
>
> For more information on Activate! see also: http://www.activateleadership.co.za

ATL Research skills

Go to the link below and create a report by ticking on citizen engagement. You will find a number of case studies such as those mentioned here. Choose one or two of those and work on them in detail.

How effective have they been in achieving the aim of citizen engagement?

http://www.opengovguide.com/report-builder/

In terms of citizen engagement, a number of examples can be cited. Croatia has a system of public consultation on laws. Similarly, Denmark has developed an innovation unit called Mindlab, including business representatives and citizens in order to assist the government in problem-solving.

In a globalized and interconnected world, there is also a need for people to identify and perceive themselves as not just mere citizens of a country or community, but as citizens of the world. There is thus a responsibility attached to this realization, considering the fact that any actions or changes in an individual's life have an impact on the family, nation and at an international level and vice versa. Validating and reasserting the need for these efforts, UNESCO has initiated a Global Citizenship Education plan with a few aims in mind, such as inspiring people to analyse problems and identify feasible solutions and involving people individually and collectively to bring about required changes.[72] A task force is in place to recommend a set of core values and competencies that cut across borders for measuring global citizenship as well as recommend innovative ways of imparting these values and abilities to governments and teachers. Some of the suggested questions that can be addressed can be found in the box below.

Examples of variables and questions related to Global Citizenship Education

Knowledge and skills:

- Knowledge about global challenges and problems (for example, "To what extent do global environmental challenges require you to change your own behaviour?")

- Knowledge of languages

- Use of the Internet and modern ways of communications (for example, "How often, if ever, do you use a personal computer or mobile phone?")

Attitudes and values:

- Global identity and openness (for example, level of agreement with the statement "A benefit of the Internet is that it makes information available to more and more people worldwide")

- Willingness to help others

- Acceptance of universal human rights, equality

- Sustainable development

- Anti-fatalistic attitudes (for example, level of agreement with the statement "People can do little to change life")

Behaviours:

- Involvement in civic activities (for example, "Are you an active member of an NGO?")

- Pro-environmental behaviours (for example, "How often do you make a special effort to sort glass, tins, plastic or newspapers for recycling?")

Source: Skirbekk, V, Potančoková, M, Stonawski, M. 2013. "Measurement of Global Citizenship Education: Background Paper on Global Citizenship Education." *Paper commissioned by UNESCO for the global citizenship education programme.* Paris, UNESCO.

Class discussion

1 Can the goals on the right be successfully implemented globally to create a successful and involved citizenry?

2 What are the factors that help or inhibit in the creation of such a citizenry, and where has it been successful or failed, and why?

Improving education and healthcare

An improvement in the education system both in terms of quality and quantity (number of people) will have a direct and positive bearing on the development of society.

- Firstly, education opens the doors for economic gains by enabling individuals to find employment and earn income. This facilitates their ability to provide the basic needs of food, clothing and shelter to their families. Of those educated, people with a higher level of education have more chances of earning higher incomes, which in turn adds to national income.

- Secondly, education also enables people to be in better health. Statistics and studies prove that education of girls has many positive effects – decreased fertility and thus fewer but healthier children, more job opportunities and their elevated status in the family along with increased decision-making powers.

- Thirdly, an educated and aware citizenry takes informed and better decisions on all matters – political, economic, environmental, social and cultural. It sharpens the skills and attitudes of people, thus improving the quality of human resource of a country.

Apart from human and economic dividends of education for development, it also helps promote sustainable development. UNESCO has stressed the need for education to achieve sustainable development through education under a programme known as Education for Sustainable Development that attempts to use education to "empower people to assume responsibility to create a sustainable future".[73] This has to be done by ensuring more people get a basic level of education, increasing awareness and skills among people to help them pursue sustainable education as well as revising and formulating the curriculum to help achieve this aim.

Besides education, good healthcare and wellness are critical to the development of individuals, societies and countries as a whole. First, people in good health and also those with access to good healthcare would be better workers, ensuring optimum productivity in their own field of work. This increases efficiency as well as enhances the chances of more income with better performance at work. Besides, children can reap the benefits of education if they are in good health. Such children when grown up will prove to be a good human resource. Improved health and healthcare also means augmented savings for individuals and families. Resources that are spent on incurring expenditure on curing diseases could be utilized for other purposes, such as education, more nutritious food or even savings. Lastly, a healthy, skilled, educated and productive workforce acts as a significant positive factor when countries are looking at investment destinations or even setting up factories and manufacturing hubs. Such investments could in turn add to the development of society and the country at large.

Interesting facts

- No country has achieved rapid and continuous economic growth without at least a 40 per cent literacy rate.

- A single year of primary school increases a boy's future earning potential by 5 to 15 per cent and a girl's even more.

- A child born to a literate mother is 50 per cent more likely to survive past the age of 5.

- Doubling primary school attendance among impoverished rural children can cut food insecurity by up to 25 per cent.

Source: http://www. canadianfeedthechildren.ca/ what/education

▲ Schoolchildren in Kathmandu, Nepal

Links between health and GDP

Poor health reduces GDP per capita by reducing both labour productivity and the relative size of the labour force.

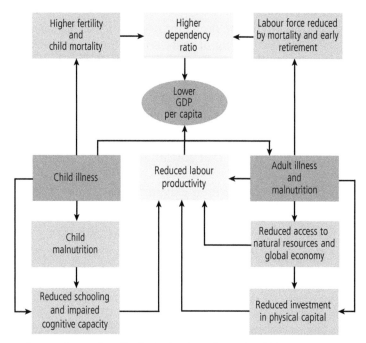

Source: Ruger, Jennifer Prah, Jamison, Dean T and Bloom, David E, 2001

Changing roles of women

On women

- Two-thirds of the 774 million adult illiterates worldwide are women (same proportion for the past 20 years across most regions).

- The vast majority of more than half a million material deaths in 2005 occurred in developing countries.

- Globally, women's participation in the labour market remained steady between 1990 and 2010; gender gap in labour force participation was considerable at all ages except early adult years.

- Occupational segregation and gender wage gaps continue to persist in all regions. International Labour Organization (ILO) statistics clearly prove that women's average wages are from 4 to 36 per cent less than men.

- Becoming heads of state or government was elusive – there are very few countries where women comprise critical mass (more than 30 per cent) in national parliaments, with a worldwide average of one woman in six cabinet ministers.

- Women underrepresented in private sector – only 13 out of 500 largest corporations in the world have a female CEO.

- Fewer women than men participate in high-level decision-making related to the environment.

Source: United Nations, The World's Women 2010, Trends and Statistics

The unequal status and role of women in society has long been a subject of intense debate. Although there is enough evidence to support the fact that women are vital and critical actors supporting development, they have suffered neglect and discrimination all over the world for a variety of social, cultural or religious reasons. The empowerment of women can accelerate the pace of economic and social growth as well as environmental protection and sustainable development. In fact, the nature, form and extent of their participation often forms the backbone of development. There has been a conscious effort to gradually alter the role of women in many fields and bring about a change in gender-related attitudes. The MDGs, Beijing Declaration and Platform for Action have been focusing on many aspects of their well-being. Positive changes are happening in terms of widening the role of women, improving their lives and bridging the gender gap. There have been some overt results – greater life expectancy, more education and laws favouring equal rights for women – yet, there is still a long road to be traveled. There is still a pressing need to reduce gender disparities in all arenas, such as access to resources, education, healthcare, decision-making power, political participation and rights. They are also exposed to a greater risk of poverty and dependence.

Research and communication skills

Divide the class into three groups and each research one example of how steps taken to close the gender gap have brought about economic, social and political benefits. Present your findings to the other groups.

Women have a special place in the development process of society. It is, therefore, imperative that they are empowered. Women need to be educated and integrated into the workforce in order for them to contribute to the family, community and country's income. Higher education opens more doors and introduces possibilities of more income as well as providing better decision-making powers within the family. There is also a need for women to have an equal access to ownership of economic resources (such as capital and land) to enable them to utilize it not just for monetary gains, but also their social emancipation. Educated women are known to have fewer and healthier children. They are also more likely to be able to teach proper usage of natural resources to the next generation. Being primary caretakers of the family, women also naturally have a great deal of control over the use of resources. They can thus be powerful and effective agents of positive change in terms of using natural resources such as trees, water and fuels optimally and efficiently. There is thus a need to enable women, and indeed all citizens, to participate in the development process, solve any problems that may arise in the process and also enjoy the fruits of development.

Thinking skills

For further questions, see the list of suggested activities by UNESCO on women and sustainable development at http://www.unesco.org/education/tlsf/mods/theme_c/mod12.html

1 Evaluate the view that globalization harms rather than benefits the poorest people in countries with the lowest incomes.

Examiner hints

Responses should include an understanding of the concept of globalization, for example, the idea that societies and cultures are becoming increasingly integrated and connected, and that goods, services and ideas are flowing more freely as barriers and borders are reduced. They may also consider the meaning of the phrases "countries with the lowest incomes", or "the poorest people", for example, referring to definitions such as the World Bank definition (2013) of a low income country as being a country with a per capita income of less than US$1035 per year and a poor person as being someone living on less than US$1.25 per day. Responses may also include a discussion of what is meant by "harm", for example, making reference to concepts such as structural violence, and by "benefit", for example, economic benefits, technological benefits, social benefits, and so on.

Arguments that support the view may include:

- even though the process of globalization has accelerated in recent years there has been an increase in economic and social inequality within many countries

- the richest countries have gained most from globalization through their multi-national corporations, their ability to finance and build up large scale operations anywhere in the world and the predictability of their political environments and legal frameworks

- globalization leads to many different forms of harm, including the exploitation of cheap labour, erosion of local cultures and large scale environmental damage.

Arguments against the view may include:

- globalization fosters employment possibilities that previously did not exist

- globalization offers new opportunities to the poorest people: it is national structures and policies that may not allow people to benefit from these

- globalization brings with it developments that benefit entire populations, including the poorest people, such as an improved knowledge of nutrition and health and the building up of communications infrastructure.

Responses should contain references to specific examples. Candidates could, for example, give examples of multi-national corporations that exploit child labour, or that use suppliers who tolerate dangerous working conditions, or operate in poorly regulated countries to avoid health and safety legislation, for example, the well-reported collapse of the Rana Plaza factory building in Bangladesh, killing or maiming many workers, where garments for several global clothing chains were manufactured.

Examples of globalization working in favour of the poorest people in the poorest countries could include the setting-up of microfinance organizations such as the Grameen bank that syndicate loans to entrepreneurs in developing countries, or the rising importance of mobile phone technology in facilitating economic activity in sub-Saharan Africa.

Responses should include the candidate's evaluation of the validity of the view put forward in the question.

2 Discuss the view that sustainable development will never be achieved until state and non-state actors can be persuaded or forced to act in the common interest.

Examiner hints

Responses should include an understanding of the concepts of sustainable development, as well as of state and non-state actors, and an attempt to explain the phrase "act in the common interest". This may be defined in different ways, for example, as the common interest of people within a particular region or country, or as the common interest of humanity in general. Integral to the question is the idea that "the common interest" may mean different things to state and non-state actors now and in the future. Non-state actors such as NGOs and multi-national corporations may envisage sustainable development in very different ways.

"Acting in the common interest" implies a discussion of whether or not state and non-state actors will need to be persuaded, or forced, to act together in the common interest to achieve sustainable development, and this need for cooperation is the most fruitful line of inquiry. However, some candidates may interpret the phrase differently, and discuss whether each group will need to be persuaded, or forced, to act individually in the common interest. This interpretation should also be accepted and valid points rewarded.

Arguments may follow an environmental, sociopolitical or economic perspective, and responses may also consider the timeframe given ("never").

Arguments in favour of the view may include:

- development so far has not been sustainable, so persuasion or force is likely to be necessary to produce action for the common good – the failure of the climate change agenda to achieve significant change so far, despite growing evidence of increasing environmental damage, indicates this

- state and non-state actors need to work together, otherwise sustainable development is unlikely to grow, but each group is likely to need persuasion or force to encourage it to do this, given their differing agendas. Non-state actors on their own cannot force action in the common interest: they may, for example, lack the political and/or other power needed to enforce change; conversely, states acting on their own may not be able to bring about changes as effectively as when acting in concert with non-state actors, who often have a greater potential for bringing about practical changes (for example, MNCs), and for mobilizing popular support for policies (for example, NGOs).

Arguments against the view may include:

- many state actors are proactive and take action themselves to promote sustainable development, no persuasion or coercion from outside is needed

- outside attempts at "interference" are not always welcome – states need to be seen to make decisions for themselves, and undue external attempts at persuasion may in fact have the opposite effect to that anticipated

- many NGOs and other non-state actors already promote sustainable development, and need no persuasion of its benefits. This willingness is not just limited to NGOs: businesses, who traditionally were seen as opposing sustainable development, but have been increasingly cooperating with efforts towards attaining sustainable development, where they have found easy ways to do this

- finally, on a pessimistic note, it could be argued that force or persuasion are futile, because sustainable development is an impossible ideal. The whole area is so complex and highly contested that greed, self-interest and/or national priorities will always be given precedence over, or be interpreted as, the common interest, so getting state and non-state actors to cooperate with each other is an unachievable ideal.

Responses should contain references to specific examples. For example, activities such as logging in Sumatra, and felling in the Amazonian rainforest are seen by the global community as militating against the common interest, but the governments of Indonesia and Brazil, and local and international business interests, often seem unwilling to respond to these concerns. The fishing industry provides further examples, for example, the failure to address the problem of overfishing, and the failure of arguments for the necessity of doing this.

Examples of successful cooperation between state and non-state actors to work for sustainable development could include, for example, cases where governments are financing development initiatives that are managed by NGOs.

Responses should include the candidate's discussion of the validity of the view put forward in the question.

3 Discuss the view that social factors such as gender relations or migration can both help and hinder development.

Examiner hints

Responses are likely to vary in focus depending on how development is conceived of, for instance, if it is conceived of in material terms then social factors will be viewed from a material perspective only. Better responses will define development as incorporating all aspects of a whole population's well-being, and so discuss a wider range of social factors, and whether or not these help and/or hinder development. Gender relations or migration are suggested as examples in the question, but candidates are free to discuss one of these, both of these, or any other social factor/factors of their choice.

Arguments in favour of the view that social factors can help development may include:

- inward migration: migrant populations are likely to be primarily young and male so add to the existing labour force – unskilled and skilled – in the receiving countries; migrants abroad may remit funds to families back home to support education and healthcare

- gender relations: women's empowerment, for example, through education, political participation or take up of economic opportunities (for example, the receipt of microloans), increases the likelihood of development for families and communities

- values: honesty, commitment to human rights, upholding of the rule of law are all helpful in promoting development

- cultural aspects: immigrants may bring cultural diversity, energy and innovation

- traditions may stimulate tourism, and traditional values often inspire craft/artisanal industries.

Arguments suggesting that social factors can hinder development may include:

- outward migration – emigration can lead to brain drain, gender imbalance, greater pressure on gender relations, loss of working age population, loss of educated people who are most mobile; immigration can lead to lower wages

- where discouraged, inward migration may go underground, leading to people-smuggling, slavery, and the diverting of state resources to police these. Inward migration may lead to greater income inequality, visible in areas of deprivation and impoverishment, and estranging of local people

- values: corruption hinders development, rights of migrants are not protected leading to exploitation, lack of belief in the rule of law

- cultural aspects: language difficulties, poor race relations leading to social tensions, pressure on housing and community services, diversity not always leading to social cohesion, causing integration difficulties

- traditions and traditional decision-making may inhibit changes needed for development.

Responses should contain references to specific examples to support the "help" and "hinder" aspects of the question. Examples could include: countries which have suffered "brain drains" and the loss of skilled workers through migration, leading to lower than expected rates of development might include the Philippines and Bulgaria; countries in which female participation in the workforce is low or limited by cultural factors, leading to lower rates of development might include Saudi Arabia, Iran, Pakistan; countries in which perceptions of corruption might inhibit business initiative and international trade, leading to lower rates of development might include Zimbabwe, Myanmar or Venezuela; or corruption and political instability (Afghanistan). Candidates may also cite countries that have not been able to develop due to international isolation (for example, North Korea), and argue that this isolation is due to social factors.

Responses should include the candidate's evaluation of the validity of the view put forward in the question.

4 Examine the view that successful development cannot be achieved without addressing political inequality.

Examiner hints

Responses are likely to include an explanation of political inequality. This might be phrased as the extent to which groups are unequal in their influence over the decisions made in governance structures, noting in a development context that political inequality is often associated with economic inequality and rigid social hierarchies.

Arguments that support the view that successful development cannot be achieved without addressing political inequality may include:

- if development is broadly conceived to incorporate all aspects of the whole population's well-being, not just economic growth, this by definition requires a commitment to equality, including political equality

- a more democratic government is more likely to engage with development efforts because it is held accountable by the whole population including by the most needy

- people and communities with low levels of development may be unable to make their voices heard due to a lack of access to education and healthcare, and so do not have the power to influence decisions about their own concerns

- the granting of political rights to groups such as subsistence farmers, refugee communities, women, or indigenous groups not participating in the formal economy is a prerequisite for development

- there is evidence that in unequal societies resources are often diverted away from development.

Arguments against the view may include:

- if development is narrowly conceived to mean measurable, aggregate, economic growth, it could be argued that a country is developing even though political inequalities persist

- it can be argued that tolerating inequality through supporting political elites will benefit everyone in the long run through the trickle-down effect and because these elites are best-placed to make decisions for the rest of the population

- the advancement of development for groups such as subsistence farmers, refugee communities or indigenous groups not participating in the formal economy is a prerequisite for the granting of greater political equality

- international organizations such as the World Bank liaise and delegate the power to political elites to address development needs

- MNCs and NGOs are more powerful in affecting development outcomes than political actors.

Responses should contain references to specific examples. Candidates could, for example, give examples of countries where political inequality has been high and development low due to the rule of long-running autocrats or cliques such as in North Korea, Congo, or Sudan.

Responses should include the candidate's evaluation of the validity of the view put forward in the question.

5 Evaluate the claim that development through aid relies heavily on a stable government and a lack of corruption.

Examiner hints

Better answers will demonstrate an excellent understanding of the concept of development and the concept of aid. They may also distinguish between different types of development, such as human and sustainable development, and different types of aid. Answers may also contain an explanation of the meaning of the terms "stable government" and "lack of corruption", and may contrast development through aid to development through other methods. The focus of the question is on the factors that enable development, rather than on the removal of obstacles to development (emphasized at the time of the MDGs).

Arguments supporting the claim may include:

- that development depends on the removal of barriers such as corruption

- that corruption can lead to a misallocation of resources, and to resources not being used for their intended purpose

- that development relies on stable governance and infrastructure.

Arguments against the claim may include:

- that often the countries that need aid are exactly those that have unstable governments and issues with corruption

- that the success of development relies far more on factors other than the two mentioned, such as financial stability

- that bureaucracy can actually stifle economic activity whereas corruption and bribes can stimulate/facilitate economic activity.

Answers should make reference to specific examples such as Transparency International, worldaudit.org, the Corruption Perception Index, UNDP, the UN Convention against Corruption, etc. They may also make reference to specific examples of countries where instability and corruption have postponed development, such as in Sudan, and to countries where a relative stability and lack of corruption have promoted it, such as in Chile. Responses may end with a conclusion/judgment on whether development through aid depends on stable government and lack of corruption.

6 The fundamental weakness of development goals (such as the Millennium Development Goals) is their lack of focus on how targets are actually to be achieved. To what extent do you agree with this claim?

Examiner hints

Better answers will demonstrate an excellent understanding of the concept of development and may also contain explanations of concepts underlying particular goals such as environmental sustainability, poverty or hunger. Answers may focus on the example provided of the Millennium Development Goals and the setting of development targets for realization in 2015, or they may focus on other examples of development goals.

Arguments that this is a fundamental weakness of development goals may include:

- the lack of focus on methods

- the lack of defined responsibilities for rich countries.

Answers may also identify other weaknesses of development goals, such as to the need to further develop some targets, for example, equality and gender issues, or to the need to respond to the changes in the political climate since 9/11.

Arguments that this is not a fundamental weakness of development goals may include:

- it was justifiable to set the MDGs without guidance on how to achieve them because they were intended to raise consciousness about development issues

- development goals help with the classification of issues into defined categories

- they provide a focus for political consensus at international level.

Answers should make reference to specific examples, which could for instance be drawn from the UN Secretary General's annual progress report, or from the experience of individual countries.

Responses may end with a conclusion/judgement on the extent to which it is helpful to set such targets without specifying the means of achieving them.

3.7 References and further reading

[1] From OECD, www.OECD.org, accessed 20 March 2016.

[2] Data as of 1998, obtained from "History of Education, Selected Moments of the Twentieth Century".

[3] Obtained from www.davidharvey.org.

[4] "Beyond the Millennium Development Goals: What could the next global development agenda look like?", Auckland, 19 August 2013.

[5] See "David Kang: Iraq was the first 'resource war' of the century", *The Guardian*, 12 February 2009.

[6] "Inequality Rising, Vision of Humanity", http://www.visionofhumanity.org/#/page/news/1167.

[7] "European Commission Democracy and Human Rights Democracy, Human Rights and Development".

[8] "Human Rights Watch 2014", http://www.hrw.org/world-report/2014/country-chapters/.

[9] Albrow, Martin and King, Elizabeth (eds). 1990. *Globalization, Knowledge and Society*.

[10] United Nations Development Programme, "Humanity Divided: Confronting Inequality in Developing Countries", 29 January 2014.

[11] Allen, Tim and Thomas, Alan. 2000. *Poverty and Development into the 21st Century*. OUP, pp. 348–349.

[12] See UN Sustainable Development Knowledge Programme, "Open Working Group Proposal for Sustainable Development Goals", sustainabledevelopment.un.org/sdgsproposal

[13/14] For this and more, see Haynes, pp. 20–24.

[15] Clemens, Walter C., Jr. 2004. *Dynamics of International Relations*, pp. 433; 436–437

[16] World Health Organization, Structural Adjustment Programmes, who.int/trade/glossary/story084/en/

[17] World Bank, "Evaluating the Washington Consensus".

[18] See "Environmental Protection Index", epi.yale.edu.

[19] O'Connor, DE. *The Basics of Economics.*, pp. 223–224.

[20] Kanbur, Ravi, "What's Social Policy got to do with Economic Growth?"

[21] UNDP, Human Development Report 1997, p 2.

[26] World Bank, Deepa, Narayan et al., "Voices of the Poor, Can Anyone Hear Us? Voices from 47 Countries"

[23] World Bank, "What is Development?", worldbank.org/depweb/beyond/beyondco/beg_01.pdf, p. 2.

[24] Ranis, G. Stewart, F. and Ramirez, A. Economic Growth and Human Development in *Oxford*, p. 61 and Mahbub ul Haq, The Birth of the HDI, p. 127.

[25] Human Development Report 1990, http://hdr.undp.org/sites/default/files/reports/219/hdr_1990_en_

complete_nostats.pdf, Box 1.1, p. 10.

[26] Anand, Sudhir and Sen, Amartya. "HDI: Methodology and measurement" in *Oxford Handbook*, p. 138.

[27] Jahan, S. "Evolution of the HDI", *Oxford*, pp. 152–153.

[28] ul Haq, Mahbub. "The human development paradigm" in *Oxford Handbook*, p. 31.

[29/30] "Beyond Economic Growth", worldbank.org/depweb/english/beyond/global/glossary.html#37

[31] *Oxford Handbook*, pp. xxv, 132–134

[33] GPI 2006, p. 2.

[34] Robert F. Kennedy Speeches, Remarks at the University of Kansas, 18 March 1968

[35] See Talberth, J. Cobb, C. and Slattery, N. "The Genuine Progress Indicator 2006"

[36] For details, see http://inclusivewealthindex.org/inclusive-wealth/#our-approach

[37] UNEP News Centre, "A New Balance Sheet for Nations: Launch of Sustainability Index that Looks Beyond GDP"

[38] See Happy Planet Index 2012 Report

[40] See "Evo Morales has proved that socialism doesn't damage economies", *The Guardian*, 14 October 2014

[60] UN Human Rights and Center for Economic and Social Rights, "Who Will Be Accountable? Human Rights and the Post-2015 Development Agenda"

[41] World Bank, http://www.worldbank.org/depweb/english/beyond/global/glossary.html#37

[42] http://www.investopedia.com/terms/c/credit.asp

[43] http://www.nber.org/papers/w9682.pdf

[44] UNESCO, "Diversity of Cultural Expressions", https://en.unesco.org/creativity/cdis/dimension/economy

[45] "Tata to move car plant from West Bengal", *The Financial Times*, 3 October 2008

[46] UNICEF, Glossary of Migration Related Terms

[47] www.unesco.org/uil/litbase/?menu=4&programme=3

[48] Todaro, M. and Smith, S. *Economic Development*, p. 476.

[49] Haque, M Shamsul. 1999. "The fate of sustainable development under neoliberal regimes in developing countries". *International Political Science Review*. Vol 20, number 2, p. 203.

[50] Fischer, S. Chapter 2, The Washington Consensus, Peterson Institute for International Economics

[51] Elliott, J. *An Introduction to Sustainable Development*

[52] Musaccio, A. and Lazzarini, S. "Reinventing State Capitalism: Leviathan in Business, Brazil and Beyond"

[53] For more, see http://blogs.reuters.com/ian-bremmer/2012/07/03/are-state-led-economies-better/

[54] Sendrowski, S. "China's Global 500 Companies are Bigger than Ever", 2015, fortune.com/2015/07/22/china-global-500-government-owned/

[55] West, Darrell M. *Billionaires: Reflections on the Upper Crust*. The Brookings Institution, p. 103.

[56] Sen, Amartya. "Development as Capability Expansion" in Sakiko Fukuda-Parr and AK Shive Kumar (eds). *Oxford Handbook of Human Development*, p. 4.

[57/58] Robeyns, Ingrid. *The Capability Approach: An Interdisciplinary Introduction*, p. 6.

[59] See http://www-personal.umd.umich.edu/~delittle/nussbaum.htm

[60] See Joel Krieger and Margaret E. Crahan, *The Oxford Companion to Politics of the World*, pp. 270–272

[61] Clemens, Walter, Jr. 2004. *Dynamics of International Relations*, p. 440.

[62] "World Tourism Highlights 2015", http://www.e-unwto.org/doi/pdf/10.18111/9789284416899, p. 4.

[63] Joseph Schumpeter, 1911

[64] http://www.oecd.org/sti/sci-tech/1913021.pdf, p. 7.

[65] Powell, Walter W. and Snellman, Katsa, "The Knowledge Economy"

[66] World Bank, "Knowledge Economy"

[67] For more on this, see http://siteresources.worldbank.org/INTUNIKAM/Resources/2012.pdf

[68] For details, see interactive diagram http://www.ellenmacarthurfoundation.org/circular-economy/circular-economy/interactive-system-diagram

[69] European Commission, "Moving towards a Circular Economy"

[70] UNESCO, "Teaching and Learning for a Sustainable Future"

[71] Ministry of Education, Singapore, 2014 Syllabus, Character and Citizenship Education, Primary

[72] UNESCO Global Citizenship Education, *Preparing Learners for the Challenges of the 21st Century*. 2014, p. 16

[73] Education for Sustainable Development, UNESCO

Acemoglu, D. and Robinson, J. "The Role of Institutions in Growth and Development", WB, 2008

Anup Shah, "Structural Adjustment: A Major Cause of Poverty", http://www.globalissues.org/article/3/structural-adjustment-a-major-cause-of-poverty

Arnold, Roger A. 2005. *Economics*

Barro, Robert J. 2008. "Democracy and Growth".

Blair, Tony. "'Doctrine of the International Community' Economic Club of Chicago", 22 April 1999

Desai, Meghnad. "Measuring Political Freedom".

"End Poverty: MDGs and Beyond 2015" http://www.un.org/millenniumgoals/pdf/Goal_1_fs.pdf.

European Commission, "Moving towards a Circular Economy".

For more details on the WTO, see https://www.wto.org/english/thewto_e/whatis_e/tif_e/dev1_e.htm.

Friends of the Earth briefing, Development and the Baku-Ceyhan Pipeline, http://www.foe.co.uk/sites/default/files/downloads/aidingthebakupipeline.pdf.

Furth, S. "High Debt is a Real Drag", The Heritage Foundation, heritage.org/research/reports/2013/02/how-a-high-national-debt-impacts-the-economy.

Hallaert, J. 2010. "Increasing the Impact of Trade Expansion on Growth: Lessons from Trade Reforms for the Design of Aid for Trade".

Halperin, Siegle and Weinstein, *The Democracy Advantage*.

Helen Clark. 2013. "Conflict and Development: Breaking the Cycle of Fragility, Violence, and Poverty".

Hoffman, D., "Complementary Currency".

IMF, https://www.imf.org/external/np/exr/facts/imfwb.htm.

Jefferson, Philip N. (ed.). 2012. *The Oxford Handbook of the Economics of Poverty*, OUP.

Jennifer C. and Elliott, A. 2006. *An Introduction to Sustainable Development*.

Ministry of Education, Singapore. 2014 Syllabus, Character and Citizenship Education, Primary.

Radelet, Steven. 2010. *Emerging Africa: How 17 Countries are Leading the Way*.

Ramphal, S. *Debt has a Child's Face*, unicef.org/pon99.

"Report of the UN High level Panel on the Post 2015 Development Agenda".

"Rights based Approach to Capacity: Sustainable Capacity International Institute, sustainable capacity and human rights", sciinstitute.org/capacity.html.

Sen, Amartya, "Development as Freedom".

Sud, Inder. "Poverty: A development perspective".

The Baku-Ceyhan Pipeline, http://www.foe.co.uk/sites/default/files/downloads/aidingthebakupipeline.pdf.

UNESCO, "Poverty".

UN Statistical Annex", http://www.un.org/en/development/desa/policy/wesp/wesp_current/2013country_class.pdf.

"World Bank, Globalization and International Trade", worldbank.org/depweb/beyond/beyondco/beg_12.pdf.

World Bank, Global Monitoring Report 2014, "Ending Extreme Poverty".

World Bank, 1992. "Governance and Development".

World Bank, "Poverty Headcount Ratio at 1.25 a day (PPP)", data.worldbank.org/indicator/SI.POV.DDAY.

World Bank, "Poverty Reduction and Equity".

www.brettonwoodsproject.org/2005/08/art-320869/.

4 PEACE AND CONFLICT

Key concepts
→ Peace
→ Conflict
→ Violence
→ Non-violence

Learning outcomes
→ Contested meanings of peace, conflict and violence
→ Causes and parties to conflict
→ Evolution of conflict
→ Conflict resolution and post-conflict transformation

Political interactions between countries are often viewed in terms of peace or conflict, or a combination of both. In fact, the various case studies of these interactions almost without exception revolve around a (perceived) clash of interests between the parties involved. Unpicking the dynamics between these parties, how history has shaped their relations, how an imbalance or balance of power influences them and how IGOs (intergovernmental organizations), NGOs (non-governmental organizations) and legal frameworks enable or restrict them is a challenging task. It is, however, important not to oversimplify the causes of conflict. It is never just "religion" or "scarcity" that motivates people and as a conflict moves further away from its original "trigger" many more issues will have arisen that will further complicate matters.

The study of peace and conflict in global politics does utilize a number of conflict models that in the first instance could be seen as an overgeneralization of these conflicts. They do, however, allow us to identify the root causes of conflict and should be seen as a useful tool for better understanding the conflict and as a starting point to further explore its intricacies.

The study of peace and conflict allows for an interdisciplinary approach, using methods and knowledge from geography, history, politics, psychology, law, environmental studies, the sciences, mathematics, and so on. However, this sometimes leads to the criticism that it is not a "pure discipline" and that it may involve people with an expertise in one area making claims about another. Furthermore, the often-practised normative approach in the discipline of valuing peace over violence and non-violent protest over violent protest, is similarly criticized, as it is claimed that this reduces the academic character of the discipline. Regardless of the criticism, the study of peace and conflict does allow for a deeper understanding of human interactions and ways to understand, and perhaps resolve, conflicts.

Key questions

1   What are the types of power used in resolving conflict situations?
2   What is the role of the United Nations Security Council in mediating conflict?

A large anti-war rally, opposed to the Vietnam War, in Washington DC, USA

Key concepts and links with other units

Power, sovereignty and international relations

Power plays an important role in peace and conflict, as a power imbalance can itself create conflict. Power is often used to forcefully attempt to resolve conflicts through, for example, humanitarian intervention. The emergence of humanitarian intervention has also led to the erosion of state sovereignty. Terrorism and migration are two examples that have a global impact. Conflict often emerges when the legitimacy of particular leaders is called into question. Non-violent protesters often challenge the legitimacy of their country's rulers and try to undermine the support for the ruler. It is increasingly difficult to see conflicts in isolation, and they often require a global response. The interdependence of the various actors therefore plays an important role in peace and conflict.

Human rights

Human rights are at the centre of many conflicts. Certain interpretations of violence include in their definition withholding rights from a person or group. The emphasis on "positive peace" reinforces the need for equality to achieve a durable, sustainable peace. Post-conflict societies often struggle with coming to terms with their past, and it often seems as though justice may lose out against peace in post-conflict peacebuilding through amnesty or forgiveness.

Development

In the wider interpretations of peace and conflict development plays an important role in that the structures through which some countries appear to have become more developed than others are considered "structurally violent". The media and transport developments related to globalization impact on how much we know about conflicts across the globe and how quickly certain nations can respond to them, thus impacting on how conflicts come into being and how they can be resolved.

Theoretical foundations

Although the main theoretical foundations of global politics differ in their interpretations of what motivates human beings, they all acknowledge the central role of conflict in the relations between the various global political actors.

Levels of analysis

Issues of global importance are not just those that are on a grand scale; problems that arise on a community level can also become global issues. For example, the widespread practice of domestic violence and how the perpetrators justify their actions make it of global importance. Without safety and security in the home, how can a society really be at peace? Many conflicts that used to mainly affect a single community or country can nowadays have a profound impact on other regions through migration, acts of terrorism or simply the media reporting about it. Issues that were traditionally considered the internal problems of a state are now increasingly considered of global importance.

Structural violence

This term refers to any type of inequality embedded into a society that prevents people from meeting their basic needs.

Introduction

Terminology related to peace and conflict is often highly contested. The definition of, for example, "peace" or "terrorism" seems to be "in the eye of the beholder" – for example, a person's position may influence whether or not they see someone as a terrorist or a freedom fighter. Achieving universal acceptance of any definitions has proven to be challenging, as various stakeholders have different interests. States may want to see a narrow definition of violence so as not to be too easily labelled violent themselves. Similarly, environmental NGOs may argue in favour of a broad definition of peace, to include sustainable and harmonious living, in order to be able to claim that societies are not yet as peaceful as they think they are. There are also different cultural traditions that influence the understanding of these terms. Despite these issues, people's interpretation of peace or violence can influence their behaviour drastically, and so it is important to understand how they define these concepts.

Many of the main thinkers in this topic are often driven by what they think ought to be rather than what actually is, and so their definitions are influenced accordingly. Another complicating factor is that terms are often used differently in different contexts. An aid worker describing their peacebuilding efforts is talking about a different form of peace from a historian talking about the Pax Romana, a 200-year period of relative peace experienced by the Roman Empire. Lastly, the key terms related to peace and conflict are often so interrelated that it seems impossible to define one term without agreeing on the other. Particularly, each of the main concepts of peace, conflict, violence and non-violence seem to be undefinable without using one or more of the other concepts. And if we can't agree on the definition of one, it is difficult to agree on the other.

Different definitions of peace, conflict and violence

The word "peace" is used in many different ways and in many different contexts, from the casual Arabic greeting *"As-salamu alaikum"* (meaning "Peace be upon you") to the formal announcement in a press conference of an inter-state peace accord between two warring countries. Clearly the two ways of using "peace" are not the same.

For examples of the usage of "peace" one can go back hundreds of years to, for example, *Leviticus*, the third book of the Torah or Old Testament. In Chapter 26, verse 6 it states:

> *I will grant peace in the land, and you will lie down and no one will make you afraid. I will remove savage beasts from the land, and the sword will not pass through your country.*

Peace and conflict

A person's definition of peace and conflict terminology can, among other factors, be influenced by their

· position

· interest

· culture

· aims

· contextual situation

· definition of other terms.

Thinking and research skills

1 Write down your definition of peace. Compare it to a classmate's definition. How do they differ? Why are they different? Is it because of one of the six elements mentioned in the box above?

2 Look up an NGO or IGO that claims to promote peace. How do they interpret peace? What would have influenced their definition? How different is it from yours?

143

Although religious texts can be interpreted in different ways, this one seems to interpret peace as a situation where one does not have to fear physical violence. In about the same time (600 BCE) in China the Tao Te Ching (a fundamental text of Taoism) emerged, which explains that there would be peace when:

> *[p]eople would be content with their simple, everyday lives, in harmony, and free of desire. When there is no desire, all things are at peace.*

Whereas Leviticus supposedly equals peace to a lack of physical violence, the Laozi equates it to a lack of desire – a state of internal harmony.

In "Creating Global-Local Cultures of Peace" (1996), Linda Groff, Professor of Political Science and Future Studies at California State University, and Paul Smoker, formerly Professor of Peace Studies at Antioch University, argue that there are six stages "in the evolution of the peace concept". Their very use of the term "evolution" reveals that they may regard the final and broadest interpretation of peace as the most desirable and perhaps inevitable interpretation of peace. Regardless of their own preferred definition, they do provide a clear overview of interpreting peace from a very narrow to perhaps the broadest form.

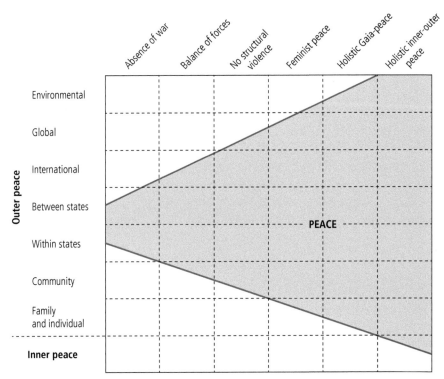

▲ From a narrow to a broad definition of peace.
   Source: "Creating Global-Local Cultures of Peace" by Paul Smoker and Linda Groff (1996), *Peace and Conflict Studies*

Examiner's hint

Be aware of the background of your sources and how this influences their views and reliability. In the highest markband for Paper 2 it is expected that different views are evaluated. In this case, you could investigate who Paul Smoker is and how, among other factors, his British background and professorship may have influenced him.

Narrow forms of peace

Peace in its narrowest forms could be interpreted as "negative peace" (in the diagram on the previous page called "absence of war") or the slightly broader "balance of forces". Both interpretations view peace in relation to war. When there is no war or not even a likelihood of war erupting due to an imbalance of power in the world, there is peace.

Someone enduring the horrors of a war could very well share the negative peace interpretation. They could consider "the bombs no longer dropping" as peace. Groff and Smoker argue that this is the most widespread interpretation of peace. It also ties in with the original interpretation of "peacekeeping". The first deployment of armed United Nations "peacekeepers" in 1956 in the Egyptian Sinai desert to separate Israel and Egypt successfully established peace, in the sense that it separated two warring parties and prevented war between them. The peacekeepers "kept the peace" for 10 years and their withdrawal in 1967 paved the way for the outbreak of the Six Day War between the two countries. The fact that peace treaties often signal the official end of a war further confirms the widespread use of this narrow interpretation of peace.

▲ UN Secretary General Dag Hammarskjöld visits United Nations Emergency Force (UNEF) forces in the Sinai desert, the very first UN "peacekeepers". This is the Brazilian contingent.

"Balance of forces" goes beyond the negative peace interpretation by also identifying how war could be prevented. Internationally, this refers to a lack of an imbalance of power between various global power blocs or the lack of a power vacuum. Though hegemonic stability theory (the theory that peace is more likely with the presence of a single dominant power on the global stage) argues the opposite – that the existence of one global superpower furthers stability and hence peace – it can still be related to the balance of forces view as it also interprets peace as the absence of war and the prevention of it through stability. The large amount of proxy wars fought throughout the Cold War, when there was no single supreme leader, could support this interpretation.

Within the state, "balance of forces" refers to a certain balance between various groups within a country that could prevent the outbreak of civil war. For example, in the past 10 years Ukraine saw both pro-Russia and pro-European Union governments, but when in 2014 the pro-Russian prime minister decided not to sign an association treaty with the European Union, protests led to his departure and the outbreak of violence that is still ongoing today. Some would argue, however, that the absence of war and even the presence of internal and international stability could not possibly be interpreted as peace if it still means that people are suffering from domestic violence, discrimination or other forms of oppression.

Wider forms of peace

Two wider interpretations of peace are "positive peace" ("the absence of structural violence" in the diagram above) and "feminist peace".

Martin Luther King (1963) equated positive peace with justice, a system in which people respect one another"s dignity and worth.[1] One of the "fathers of peace research", Professor Johan Galtung, further developed this by arguing that peace is the absence of violence, both direct, physical violence and indirect, structural violence, and that positive peace is the presence of social justice; for example, the equal or "egalitarian distribution of power and resources" (*Journal of Peace Research* no. 23:9).[2] This would indicate that without development, there would not be peace – and not just economic development, but the removal of any form of inequality.

Assessing the development of states, Economics Professor Paul Streeten maintains that "life expectancy and literacy could be quite high in a well-managed prison. Basic physical needs are well met in a zoo" (1995: xiv).[3] Countries that could be considered "prisons" or "zoos" in terms of

NGOs claiming to aim for peace: Greenpeace

Greenpeace is one of the most well-known non-governmental organizations aiming

to expose global environmental problems, and to force the solutions which are essential to a green and peaceful future   Greenpeace mission statement

The organization claims to be committed to non-violence and, in line with Gandhi's tactics of actively opposing and challenging one's enemy (see 4.2), it has sparked controversy over what some see as the aggressive way in which it carries out some of its campaigns. Greenpeace itself suffered from violence, one of the most notorious incidents being the sinking of the *Rainbow Warrior* by agents of the French secret service, which resulted in the death of a photographer.

Greenpeace's goal is to ensure the ability of Earth to nurture life in all its diversity. Therefore, it seeks to

- protect biodiversity in all its forms
- prevent pollution and abuse of Earth's ocean, land, air and fresh water
- end all nuclear threats
- promote peace, global disarmament and non-violence.

their development and human rights record may be considered peaceful if you follow the "balance of forces" interpretation. They would be far from peaceful if you advocate "positive peace" as the correct interpretation of peace.

By focusing on the individual level, rather than just global or state structures, "feminist peace" further extends the interpretation of peace to include the removal of any form of discrimination. Even though a lot of discrimination occurs based on gender, "feminist peace" does not emphasize this form of discrimination over other forms. It simply refers to the feminist peace researchers who put this interpretation forward. Even though this further stretches the definition of peace, it probably does not satisfy those people who argue that we should strive to live more in harmony with nature and ourselves.

Perhaps the widest interpretations, "holistic gaia-peace" and "holistic inner-outer peace", relate peace to living in harmony with the environment and being at ease with yourself.

Groff and Smoker explain how "holistic gaia-peace" is a "holistic peace theory, where human beings are seen as one of many species inhabiting the earth, and the fate of the planet is seen as the most important goal". From this point of view, peace means living sustainably and harmoniously with the environment.

The second interpretation, holistic inner-outer peace, also includes the spiritual, often religious, dimension of peace. The often-heard phrase "if you don't love yourself you can't love someone else" is here applied to peace. If you're not at peace with yourself, your own shortcomings, temptations and abilities, how can you further peace towards others? This can, for example, be related to the concept of the Greater Jihad in Islam. The Greater Jihad entails the internal human struggle of dealing with disappointment, strong emotions and temptations.

Holistic inner-outer peace is also used in other ways. Former UN Ambassador for Singapore Kishore Mahbubani (2015) argues that

[f]irst, introspection, reflection, humility, and innovation are needed to design new institutions or adapt current institutional arrangements and develop new financing mechanisms, with international solidarity and clear prioritisation of objectives and goals.[4]

Here he identifies what could be seen as "inner peace" as a catalyser for global human well-being.

The ambiguity of the term "peace" can be further explored through frequently used conflict resolution terminology: peacekeeping, peacemaking and peacebuilding. We may think that these are working towards the same "peace", however, as the diagram below shows, they do not.

Peacekeeping in its original interpretation addresses a physically violent conflict to achieve the end of fighting between two parties, in other words, negative peace. Peacemaking would then be working towards a peace treaty to ensure that negative peace will be maintained for the foreseeable future. Peacebuilding interprets peace as positive peace, the establishment of justice and equality.

Research skills

Visit the Global Peace Index website (www. visionofhumanity.org). They interpret peace as "a process which underpins the optimal environment for human potential to flourish." (Global Peace Index 2015: 83).

1 What indicators do they use to measure peace? Do you agree with them?

2 Pick a country and apply narrower and broader interpretations of peace to it. Would you think that country would rank lower or higher, if a broader rather than a narrower interpretation of peace was applied?

Research and thinking skills

Revisit the IGO or NGO you researched on page 143. Does it fit into one of Groff and Smoker's six stages of peace (page 144)?

Thinking skills

When can conflict be "good" or "productive"? Think of an example, personal, local or global, where conflict ultimately led to a better situation. Do your classmates agree?

TOK

What role do the emotions of individuals play in influencing events and decisions in global politics?

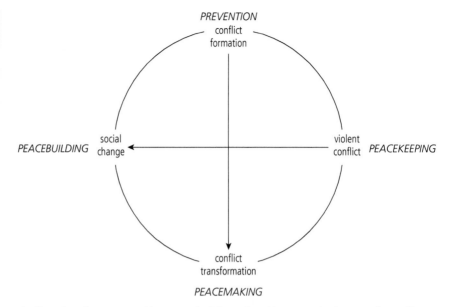

Peacekeeping, peacemaking, peacebuilding; all working towards the same "peace"?

Though the narrow interpretation of peace – the absence of war – is still the most widely used one, other, wider interpretations are being more frequently used as it is increasingly understood that the absence of war would not necessarily make the world a peaceful place.

Conflict

TOK

How can we know that something is a cause of something else?

"Conflict" as a concept may not be interpreted in as many ways as "peace", however, it is nonetheless understood in many different ways. Galtung defines conflict as "actors in pursuit of incompatible goals".[5] The aims of two or more parties seem to be contradictory and as they seek to achieve these aims, they clash or "strike together" (*confligere*, in Latin).

The meaning of the term "conflict" is clouded by its different uses (see left).

The causes of conflict are often generalized through comments such as "it's all about oil or power" or "religion is the cause of most conflicts". This can lead to the misunderstanding that the causes of a conflict can easily be generalized and reduced to one single factor. This is connected to another misunderstanding: conflict parties are unitary actors, that is, all those who are part of one conflict party are involved in the conflict for the same reason, are aiming to achieve the same goal and are all working towards that goal.

Often, we only become aware of a conflict when people express their dissatisfaction with how they are being treated, from complaining at work about a nasty boss to a large demonstration for equal rights for indigenous people. This fuels the misperception that we can only speak of a conflict when this dissatisfaction becomes visible. Conflict is often associated with violence or war, or at least disharmony – whether in personal or international relations – and is therefore seen as undesirable. The news is saturated with horrendous images of conflict, and so it's easy to conclude that conflict is always bad. However, if conflict is (mis)perceived as always undesirable, then it naturally leads us to think that we always need to resolve the situation. Stability, order or harmony needs to be restored, and we can't trust the conflict parties

Six common (mis)conceptions about conflict

1 Conflict is caused by single factors.

2 Conflict parties are (rational) unitary actors.

3 Conflict is always visible.

4 Conflict is always undesirable.

5 Conflict always needs to be settled.

6 Conflict always requires "third-party intervention".

to satisfactorily resolve the issue, therefore, intervention is required by "third parties" – parties not directly involved in the conflict. On a personal level, mediators may be called in to resolve a marriage crisis; on an international level, "the United Nations Security Council meets to address the conflict in South Sudan". But is the third party's role always constructive and do we always need them to resolve the conflict?

We often tend to point to one factor in the cause of conflict. Over the past decades any external involvement in the Middle East is immediately linked to "access and control over oil"; or if it's not oil, then "it's power politics" or "it's religion". However, blaming everything on one single factor is reductionist and fools us by taking such a complex issue as conflict and overgeneralizing its causes. In *For God's Sake: A Jew, a Christian and a Muslim Debate Religion (2013),*[6] four authors ask themselves what the role of religion is in the contemporary world. Woodlock argues that "[r]eligion, unfortunately, provides a useful cover… for the evil-hearted" and Smart adds that the idea that "most of the wars of history have been caused by religion is demonstrably false". They seem to suggest that it's too easy to blame "religion" for conflict.

While religion, power, water, and so on play an important role in many conflicts, it would be impossible to connect all conflict parties, their motivation and their goals to a single factor. We have to appreciate conflicts as they are: incredibly complex issues that require laborious work to unearth the various motives, links and roles of conflict parties.

Overgeneralizing causes of conflict also leads us to assume that those people making up a conflict party all agree on the "what, why and how" of the conflict. The Realist tradition often views conflict parties, whether states or non-state actors, as unitary actors. However, if you look at the historic disagreements between the Pentagon (United States Ministry of Defense) and the US State Department (Ministry of Foreign Affairs) it's rather difficult to make statements such as "the United States foreign policy concerning Syria…" when various actors within the United States are pursuing different or even contradictory policies. *The Wall Street Journal* reported in 2014 how US Secretary of State John Kerry did not see eye-to-eye with the Pentagon about their approach to the Syrian opposition.

And then those in power may have wholly different motives for their role within a conflict. One possible reason for George W. Bush invading Iraq in 2003 was to avenge Saddam Hussein's alleged attempt to murder his father.[7] It's at best doubtful, however, whether the entire conflict party, the United States, would share this view. Once more it seems wise to acknowledge that conflict parties are more complex than we make them out to be.

We often become aware of conflicts around the world once groups clash, for example, in demonstrations or through a terrorist attack. This can lead us to believe that we can only refer to a conflict when it becomes visible. For example, in 2011 Bolivians started demonstrating against a road that was supposed to go through an area largely inhabited by indigenous people. Other demonstrations then followed

TOK

Look up the article in *The Guardian* and read about the authors' views on the role of religion in conflict:

http://www.theguardian.com/commentisfree/2013/jul/02/religion-wars-conflict

1   With which author do you agree the most? What are your reasons?

2   What is the influence of the authors' *personal knowledge* on this topic and what is the role of shared knowledge?

3   Can someone who does not follow a particular relgion *really* know that religion?

▲ Bolivian police clash with protesters during a march towards La Paz against a road project through indigenous land.

"against [the] government's violent crackdown on demonstrations".[8]

Before the actual confrontation there has already been a stage of dissatisfaction of one or more conflict parties with the other. We often don't hear about this stage of invisible, or "latent", conflict and therefore sometimes exclude this stage from our conflict analysis, but it is crucial to understand how a lingering, muted, deceivingly calm situation has turned into an outright clash. And since we're aiming to fully understand conflict, we need to go beyond the apparent silence and identify the "latent conflicts" that could at any time burst into "overt conflict". Those conflicts are already very real, but just haven't shown themselves in a way that reaches the mainstream news.

We often identify conflict with negative images such as frustrations, anger and bloodshed, and many conflicts lead to unimaginable misery

POWER		Unpeaceful ◄······· Relations ·······► Peaceful		
		Static	**Unstable**	**Dynamic**
	Balanced		3. Conflict settlement	4. Sustainable peace
			Conciliations	*Peaceful development*
	Unbalanced	1. Latent conflict	2. Overt conflict	
		Conscientisation	Confrontation	
		Low ◄····················►High		
		Awareness of conflict		

▲ The progression of conflict in unbalanced relationships (adapted from Curle 1971)

and seem pointless or to be pursued for reasons we don't agree with. The homepage of the Armed Conflict Database (https://acd.iiss.org/) of the International Institute for Strategic Studies states the death toll

from armed conflicts. For 2015 it was estimated at 167,000. When we are then also confronted with plenty of countries claiming conflicts need to be "contained", "resolved", "neutralized", "prevented" and so on, it could easily lead us to think that conflict is undesirable. However, if we look at what Arundhati Roy calls "the high priests of non-violent resistance",[9] Nelson Mandela, Mahatma Gandhi and Martin Luther King, Jr we can conclude they were actively pursuing conflict. They were confronting their adversary and through their actions arguably increasing the tensions, therefore, creating more conflict. It seems then that conflict is not necessarily bad, as it can also be seen as a road to "sustainable peace".

Joe Gerstandt, an American war veteran, neatly summarizes our options whenever we disagree with someone.[10] We can remain in the "latent conflict" phase by not raising the issue, which according to Gerstandt leads to "fake harmony". We can take the option of "destructive conflict" by, for example, withholding information from a colleague or we can find a way in which we can address our differences in a "constructive" way, perhaps in the spirit of Mandela, Gandhi or King.

Therefore, it is difficult to claim that conflict is always undesirable. It all depends on how we and the other party approach the conflict.

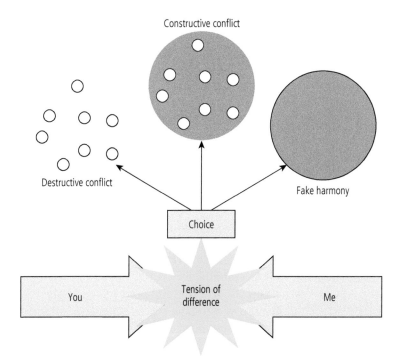

▲ Our options when we are confronted with the "tension of difference"

TOK

What constraints and limitations are there on the methods that can be used to gain knowledge in global politics?

Related to the general misconception that conflict is always bad is the apparent need to settle a conflict, ideally immediately. "Settling" the conflict could then very well mean that whichever tensions have come to the forefront are to be contained or neutralized. For example, Bahraini Major-General Tariq al-Hassan responded to widespread pro-democracy demonstrations in his country issuing the warning, "Action would be taken against those who spread terror among citizens or residents, put the safety of others at risk or try to disrupt the nation's security and stability".[11]

The Bahrain pro-democracy protests, 2011

"Security and stability" surely sound nicer than "conflict" and "demonstrations", but it is clear in whose interest it is to "settle" this conflict by cracking down on the protestors. Other countries may then express their worries about the increased tensions in Bahrain and demand that everything returns to normalcy. However, here it seems the conflict can only really be resolved when the parties find a way to satisfy both parties' aims. And as long as the deeper lying issues are not addressed and protests are met with violence and arrests, surely the conflict is not really "settled". Therefore, before we rush to settle a conflict, we may first have to see what it is about and whether or not we are "neutralizing" a legitimate claim and instead of resolving it, we are simply pushing the conflict back to the "latent phase" or into "fake harmony".

When conflict parties confront one another, it often seems that it should be up to a third, supposedly uninvolved, party to intervene, as the conflict parties themselves cannot be trusted to find a constructive agreement. Third parties can indeed play a very constructive role in bringing two conflict parties together. One example is former US Senator George Mitchell, who was crucial in bringing the two conflict parties in Northern Ireland together by Good Friday, 1998. Colum McCann applauds him for his "ability to deal with the mighty weapon of language" in the negotiations as he reminisces about those days in a recent article in *The New York Times*.[12] Yet all too often third parties have their own interests, and these may not necessarily lead to sustainable peace. After the horrors of Rwanda and Srebrenica it seemed the world's leaders agreed that the international community should intervene when civilians are attacked by (their own) government forces. However, almost immediately critics such as the Nicaraguan priest and former president of the United Nations General Assembly Miguel d'Escoto Brockmann voiced their concern that this agreement would be "misused, once more, to justify arbitrary and selective interventions against the weakest States".[13]

Brockmann argued that third parties cannot always be trusted to intervene selflessly and constructively in a conflict. Additionally, the conflict parties themselves may want to resolve their conflict without external interference, and why wouldn't they have the right to do

TOK

Why might language be described as a "mighty weapon"?

so? Other drawbacks of third-party mediation are that it "inevitably causes delays… and carries the risk that messages may be garbled in translation" (Berridge, 1994).[14]

Similarly to Galtung and many other conflict theorists, the University for Peace defines conflict as "a confrontation between one or more parties aspiring towards incompatible or competitive means or ends" (Miller, 2005).[15] So even though the many misconceptions about the term can influence our interpretation of conflict, there does seem to be a generally accepted definition.

Violence, including structural violence

Like peace, the term "violence" can be interpreted in different ways. As we saw earlier, peace is often equated with the absence of violence, and so it seems the wider our definition of peace, the wider our definition of violence.

Once again the most widely used interpretation of violence is the narrower variant: physical violence – also known as direct violence. We normally associate violence with physical force and so do most dictionaries. This is generally the most visible form of violence and we are often directly or indirectly confronted with it. Some of the main debates about physical violence pose the question of whether aggression is learned or innate, that is, "simply" part of our nature.

Many conflict theorists go beyond the narrow interpretation of violence and argue that discrimination and the unequal global distribution of power, resources and food should also be considered "violence", which they call "structural violence". The way in which society legitimizes direct or structural violence is called "cultural violence", and the use of this term further stretches the interpretation of violence.

▲ Campaign against domestic violence in India. Bell Bajao or "Ring the Bell"

Research skills

Look up statistics for domestic violence in your country, for example, through the World Health Organization or the national statistics bureau.

1 Are they similar to any of the (parts of) countries in the chart below?

2 What would be the reason for those numbers?

3 What are the difficulties of obtaining reliable statistics about domestic violence?

Perhaps the most visible forms of physical violence are displayed in wars. Each party may justify their violence in one way or another; they would acknowledge they have used some physical violence against, in their eyes, legitimate targets. A less visible and (by the perpetrators) more contested form of physical violence is domestic violence – physical, sexual or emotional violence between intimate partners or against children.[16] A study by the World Health Organization shows that this form of violence is widespread. Assistant Director-General Joy Phumaphi says, "Each culture has its sayings and songs about the importance of home, and the comfort and security to be found there. Yet for many women, home is a place of pain and humiliation."[17] As this report clearly shows, violence against women by their male partners is common, widespread and far-reaching in its impact. The data (see below) show this is an issue of global importance, yet many of the perpetrators would probably not consider their behaviour as "violent" and the victims often state some of the violence may be justified.

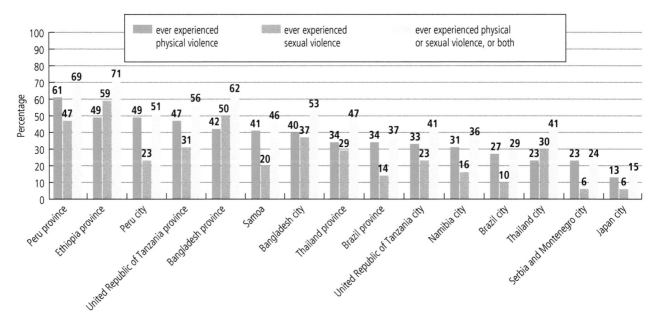

▲ Prevalence of lifetime physical violence and sexual violence by an intimate partner.

In its *2015 Intimate Partner Violence Surveillance* the US National Center for Injury Prevention and Control states:

Physical violence includes, but is not limited to: scratching, pushing, shoving, throwing, grabbing, biting, choking, shaking, hair-pulling, slapping, punching, hitting, burning, use of a weapon (gun, knife, or other object), and use of restraints or one's body, size, or strength against another person. Physical violence also includes coercing other people to commit any of the above acts.

They expand the interpretation of violence by adding that "coercing" or forcing someone to be violent should also be considered as "violence". The Duluth Model of Violence (see below), also developed in relation to domestic violence, further expands the interpretation of violence by highlighting how "power and control" are at the heart of violent behaviour. They (the Domestic Abuse Intervention Programs) include "the pattern of actions that an individual uses to intentionally control or dominate his intimate partner" in their interpretation of violence.

The Duluth Model of Violence

The wheel contains the following sections arranged around the center "POWER AND CONTROL":

Outer ring labels: PHYSICAL VIOLENCE SEXUAL (top) and PHYSICAL VIOLENCE SEXUAL (bottom)

Using coercion and threats
Making and/or carrying out threats to do something to hurt her • threatening to leave her, to commit suicide, to report her to welfare • making her drop charges • making her do illegal things.

Using intimidation
Making her afraid by using looks, actions, gestures • smashing things • destroying her property • abusing pets • displaying weapons.

Using economic abuse
Preventing her from getting or keeping a job • making her ask for money • giving her an allowance • taking her money • not letting her know about or have access to family income.

Using emotional abuse
Putting her down • making her feel bad about herself • calling her names • making her think she's crazy • playing mind games • humiliating her • making her feel guilty.

Using male privilege
Treating her like a servant • making all the big decisions • acting like the 'master of the castle' • being the one to define men's and women's roles.

Using isolation
Controlling what she does, who she sees and talks to, what she reads, where she goes • limiting her outside involvement • using jealousy to justify actions.

Using children
Making her feel guilty about the children • using the children to relay messages • using visitation to harass her • threatening to take the children away.

Minimizing, denying and blaming
Making light of the abuse and not taking her concerns about it seriously • saying the abuse didn't happen • shifting responsibility for abusive behavior • saying she caused it.

▲ The Duluth Model of Violence

The Duluth Model

The makers of the Duluth Model of Violence have decided not to make their wheel gender neutral as "[m]aking the Power and Control Wheel gender neutral would hide the power imbalances in relationships between men and women that reflect power imbalances in society. By naming the power differences, we can more clearly provide advocacy and support for victims, accountability and opportunities for change for offenders, and system and societal changes that end violence against women."

1   Do you agree with their decision? Why (not)?

2   Are they similar to any of the (parts of) countries in the chart above?

3   What would be the reason for those numbers?

4   What are the difficulties of obtaining reliable statistics about domestic violence?

Many psychologists have weighed in on the debate of whether aggression ("any behaviour intended to harm another person who does not want to be harmed") is a natural phenomenon or whether it is learned. This was largely motivated by the question of whether a perfect society (for example, a society achieving positive peace) is actually possible.

If people are inherently aggressive, then aggression will always be with us and society or culture needs to find a way of living with it.

R. Baumeister and B. Bushman, 2014

The instinct theorists, from Freud to Lorenz, argued that aggression is indeed a part of our nature. They often compared human to animal behaviour and used examples of "instinctive" aggressive behaviour of humans to support their hypothesis. Various learning theorists used examples of education, how children are raised and the influence of media or video games to argue the opposite: aggressive behaviour is learned. Baumeister and Bushman favour a middle ground in this nature versus nurture dispute, arguing that both learning and instinct are relevant for understanding human aggression.[18] The nature–nurture debate has often been politicized by supporters of one interpretation or the other. A concerted attempt to neutralize the "nature" camp was made by a number of scientists through "the Seville statement on Violence" (see below). Even though they presented their argument (that violence is not natural) in a rather bold and firm way, the debate is far from over.

Seville Statement

"Believing that it is our responsibility to address from our particular disciplines the most dangerous and destructive activities of our species, violence and war; recognising that science is a human cultural product which cannot be definitive or all encompassing; and gratefully acknowledging the support of the authorities of Seville and representatives of the Spanish UNESCO [United Nations Educational, Scientific and Cultural Organization], we, the undersigned scholars from around the world and from relevant sciences, have met and arrived at the following:

1 *It is scientifically incorrect to say that violence is genetically determined.*

2 *It is scientifically incorrect to say that it comes from our animal past.*

3 *It is scientifically incorrect to say that, in the process of human evolution, there has been a greater selection for aggressive behaviour than for other kinds of behaviour.*

4 *It is scientifically incorrect to say that humans have a "violent brain".*

5 *It is scientifically incorrect to say that violent behaviour is genetically inherited.'*

Do you agree with the Seville Statement on Violence? Why (not)?

TOK

The Seville Statement was criticized for "discredit[ing] pyschology and scientists because it uses science to pursue political objectives".

Should scientists refrain from statements like this?

Galtung argues in favour of broadening the definition of violence. He acknowledges the widespread suffering from direct, physical violence, but argues that there may be more people suffering from "social injustice"– the unequal and unfair distribution of wealth and power (see diagram below).[19] This suffering may be less visible, as there is no clear perpetrator and not one obvious victim, but it is no less real. If there is enough food in the world, and we have the systems to distribute this food equally, how can people then still be dying from starvation? Perhaps the structures that society has built that "cause" this suffering can be considered violence.

Galtung states that any human-made societal structure preventing us from reaching our potential should be considered "violence". An immigrant in Denmark not invited for a job interview because of a "foreign sounding name" and a South African human immunodeficiency virus (HIV) patient dying because of a lack of access to medication would both be considered "violence" according to this interpretation.[20]

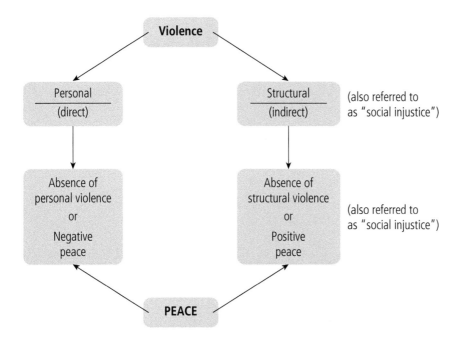

Galtung did not stop there with broadening the interpretation of violence (and peace). He also coined the term "cultural violence".

Cultural violence is the prevailing attitudes and beliefs that justify and legitimize the structural [and direct] violence, making it seem natural. Feelings of superiority/inferiority based on class, race, sex, religion, and nationality are inculcated in us as children and shape our assumptions about us and the world. They convince us this is the way things are and they have to be.

William T. Hathaway[21]

TOK

In what ways are factors such as gender and nationality "inculcated in us as children"? In what ways do these factors shape our assumptions about ourselves? In what ways do these factors shape our assumptions about other people?

There are many ways in which direct or structural violence is justified, regardless of whether we agree with the arguments put forward. We could refer to a state's monopoly on physical violence through its armed forces and police, the recruiter"s argument that "foreigners are stealing our jobs" for not inviting an immigrant to a job interview or the religious leader referring to a religious text to justify that "a women"s place is in the kitchen" (the justifications of violence are further explored on page 164). Whether or not you agree with a broad interpretation of "violence", social injustice and legitimization of violence, it is often used in conflict analysis to further understanding and will therefore be further explored in the remainder of the unit.

> ### Thinking skills
>
> Revisit your interpretation of peace. Is it similarly broad or narrow to your interpretation of violence? Why (not)?

Types of conflict

Traditionally, conflict analysis has largely focused on the state and any conflicts it had with other states or alliances of states. However, this realist focus on the state is increasingly difficult to maintain with so many non-state actors actively engaged in conflict, from terrorist organizations to non-violent protest groups.

Conflicts are often characterized by the actors who are involved with it (for example, interpersonal or inter-state) and whether or not physical violence is used in the conflict. The Correlates of War (COW) Project of the University of Michigan and the Uppsula University Conflict Data Program, two of the most renowned recorders of violent conflict, use a typology in which they subdivide armed conflict into inter-state, extra–state, internationalized internal conflict, and intra-state conflict. The most recent addition by COW is the category of conflict between "non-state actors".

Another common typology of conflict is on the basis of the main issue of contention between the parties. On the basis of his many years of conflict mediation, Dr Christopher Moore identified five areas around which conflicts appear to be centred: data, interest, value, relationship, and structure (1996: 60–61).[22]

Wallensteen, Sollenberg and Sollenberg define armed conflict as,

> *the contested incompatibility which concerns government and/or territory where the use of armed force between two parties, of which at least one is the government of a state, results in at least 25 battle-related deaths.*[23]

As we've seen, incompatibility here refers to how two or more parties' aims seem to clash. If this clash then turns physically violent and results in "25 battle-related deaths" it is considered an "armed conflict". One of the conflict parties has to be the government of a state.[24]

We may therefore divide armed conflict into inter-state, extra-state, internationalized and internal conflict.

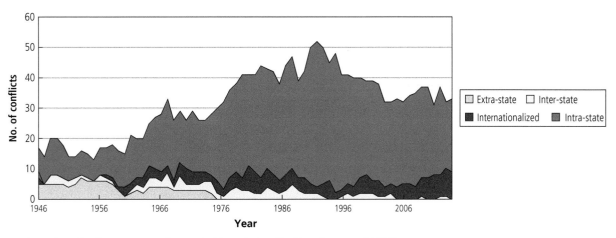

▲ Armed conflict by type according to the Uppsala Conflict Data Program (UCDP)

Inter-state conflict

In inter-state conflict the primary warring parties, who first stated the incompatibility, must be government parties. The diagram above shows this type of conflict has not been that prevalent over the past 70 years and has been rather rare in the past 10 years. However, the *2015 World Economic Forum Global Risks Report* shows that inter-state conflict is one of the main concerns of leaders and decision-makers. An example of a recent inter-state conflict is the border dispute between South Sudan and Sudan, which erupted in 2012. South Sudan was originally part of Sudan, but voted for independence in a 2011 referendum. The Director of the Advisory Board of the Centre for Risk Studies at University of Cambridge, Andrew Coburn, claims that for inter-state conflict, there are "a number of regional hot-spots, including the obvious Middle East, central and eastern Africa, the eastern European margins, the Indian subcontinent, parts of Latin America and the emerging South-East Asian powers".[25]

▲ Sudanese soldiers on a South Sudanese tank in the border region 2012

Extra-state conflict

Extra-state (or extra-systemic) conflict, as we can also see in the diagram above, has not been seen since 1975, when Indonesia conquered East-Timor. It occurs between a state and a non-state group outside its own territory and can be further subdivided into colonial war and imperial war. In the period of colonization of large parts of the world by mainly European powers and then in the period of wars of decolonization, these conflicts were rather common.

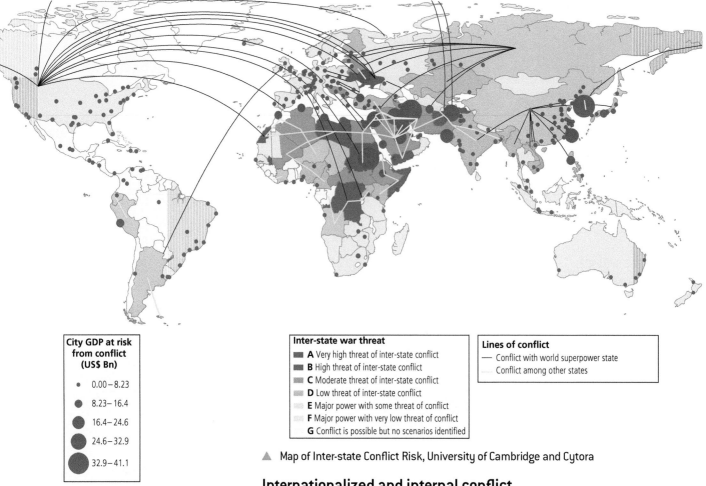

City GDP at risk from conflict (US$ Bn)

- • 0.00 – 8.23
- • 8.23 – 16.4
- • 16.4 – 24.6
- ● 24.6 – 32.9
- ● 32.9 – 41.1

Inter-state war threat

- **A** Very high threat of inter-state conflict
- **B** High threat of inter-state conflict
- **C** Moderate threat of inter-state conflict
- **D** Low threat of inter-state conflict
- **E** Major power with some threat of conflict
- **F** Major power with very low threat of conflict
- **G** Conflict is possible but no scenarios identified

Lines of conflict

- —— Conflict with world superpower state
- —— Conflict among other states

▲ Map of Inter-state Conflict Risk, University of Cambridge and Cytora

Internationalized and internal conflict

Internationalized internal conflict occurs between the government of a state and internal opposition groups with intervention from other states. This type of armed conflict has become more prominent since the end of the Cold War. The Ukrainian revolution is an example of this. The Ukrainian government is largely supported by Western powers, whereas the pro-Russian opposition has received support from Russia (the annexation of the Crimea – internationally recognized as part of Ukraine – by Russia could be considered an inter-state conflict). Over the past 200 years the most deadly civil wars, either with or without foreign intervention, were fought in the United States, Russia, Spain and China, all of which occurred before 1950.

By far the most widespread form of armed conflict is intra-state armed conflict. This occurs between the government of a state and internal opposition groups without intervention from other states.

Particularly around the time of the break-up of the Berlin Wall (1989) and the collapse of the Soviet Union (1991) there was a rise of intra-state armed conflict. Since the 1990s, Asia and sub-Saharan African have been the two regions most affected by violent conflict. In 2013, Asia had the highest concentration of armed conflicts, with 13 intra-state conflicts, including two major civil wars (Afghanistan and Pakistan).

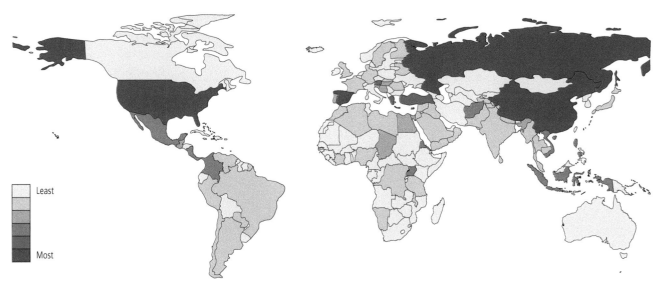

▲ Civil war deaths per country , 1816–2007, according to the Correlates of War Project

Non-state conflicts

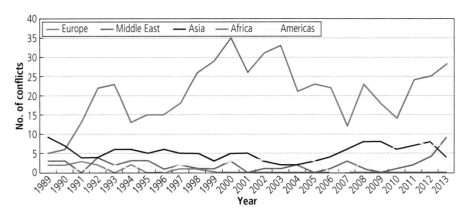

▲ Non-state conflicts by region, 1989–2013, according to the Uppsala Conflict Data Program

Non-state armed conflicts involve the use of armed force between two organized armed groups, neither of which is the government of a state. *The Human Security Report 2012* highlights the variety of groups involved in this type of conflict through the examples it provides: the Taliban in Afghanistan, Christian and Muslim groups in the Philippines, various Kenyan tribes, and paramilitary and revolutionary groups in Colombia.[26] This type of conflict has been under-researched and often ignored in traditional conflict analysis.

Moore claims that issues within conflicts are often at an "impasse" around the following areas: relationship, interest, value, structure, and data. Conflicts can easily revolve around a combination of these factors, but they don't all have to be central to the conflict.

Relationship conflicts

These types of conflicts can arise from a number of causes – when parties involved are upset with one another, when one party has a negative perception or stereotype of the other or when poor communication leads to a damaged relationship.[27] Examples can be found in those conflicts where initially positive relations have turned

Research and thinking skills

Take a hard-copy newspaper or look up a news website and go to the international/foreign section. Pick an article that is discussing a particular armed conflict.

1   Apply the five types of armed conflict to the article. Which type of conflict is it?

2   Is it difficult to identify which type of conflict it is? Why (not)?

▲ Moore's five categories of conflict

From 1915, the Ottoman government initiated the systematic extermination of approximately 1.5 million Armenians living in present-day Turkey. Many were deported through death marches leading to the Syrian desert.

TOK

How do we know whether to trust data that is presented to us?

sour, for example, in certain marriage conflicts. In other instances conflict parties could have a long history of problematic relations – or a particularly painful memory of the past – such as in cases of ethnic violence. The violence that occurred during the Sierra Leone Civil War, which lasted for 11 years until 2002, still plays a big role in society more than a decade later. Similarly, Armenians today see what happened a hundred years ago in the Ottoman Empire as an integral part of their identity. President of the International Association of Genocide Scholars William Schabas calls it "one of the three great genocides of the twentieth century",[28] but many Turkish people would disagree – and this plays a very large role in the (limited) contemporary Turkish–Armenian relations.

Data conflicts

Abramson claims "[d]ata conflicts can be caused by inadequate, inaccurate, or untrustworthy information... or different interpretations of relevant data". In conflicts there are often disagreements about what actually happened during an argument (in interpersonal non-violent conflicts) or a battle or massacre. Information can be distorted by, for example, the emotional state that the conflict parties are in, or they could very well have an interest in hiding information or downplaying its importance, and parties often highlight the events that were particularly painful for them without acknowledging the other party's strong feelings regarding other events.

The law that set up the South African Truth and Reconciliation Commission states the following aim:

[t]o provide for the investigation and the establishment of as complete a picture as possible of the nature, causes and extent of gross violations of human rights committed during the period from 1 March 1960… and the fate or whereabouts of the victims of such violations; the granting of amnesty to persons who make full disclosure of all the relevant facts.[29]

The difficulty here, especially after a long period of violence and discrimination, is in obtaining that "complete picture" and agreeing on "all the relevant facts".

Interest conflicts

Interest conflicts occur when there are perceived or actual competitive interests.

Moore

Many local groups around the world protest against the extraction of natural resources, because it may have consequences for the environment. In the United Kingdom, there is a fierce debate about fracking,

> *the process of extracting gas by drilling into the earth and injecting a high-pressure water mixture into the rock, causing the gas to flow to the surface.*[30]

Water and oil companies would have a clear financial interest in this, whereas environmental groups argue it has a significant environmental impact through the transport of huge amounts of water, chemical usage, possible minor earthquakes and it encourages a continued reliance on fossil fuels by moving potential investment away from renewable energy sources.

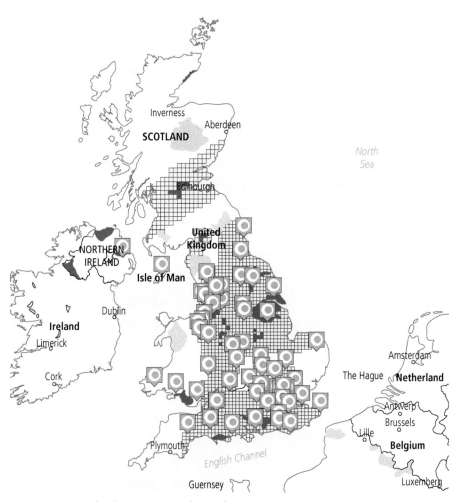

▲ Map of actual (red) and proposed (yellow) fracking sites in the United Kingdom and local Friends of the Earth groups campaigning against it

Many other conflicts revolve around (the perception of) competitive interests. The Arab-Israeli conflict is often seen as such because spokespeople of both parties lay claim to exclusive right of ownership of the land.

Research and thinking skills

Moore's categories of conflict

1   Can you think of a conflict that is mainly "structural" and one that is mainly based on "value"?

2   Why is it important to identify the main area of conflict?

Structural and value conflicts

Structural conflicts are caused by destructive patterns of behaviour or interaction, unequal control, ownership or distribution of resources [and] unequal power and authority.

Moore

The final two categories Moore identifies are structural and value conflicts. Inequality in itself can be seen as a form of conflict (structural violence) and it can often lead to tensions between those who aim to create more equality and those who may protect the "status quo".

Value conflicts revolve around "[d]ifferent criteria for evaluation ideas or behaviour… different ways of life, ideology and religion."[31] This category would be much supported by the American political scientist Samuel P. Huntington, who argued that in the post-Cold War world there was no longer a clash of ideologies, but a clash of civilizations. Regardless of the immense criticism he received – including Edward Said's thoughtful "The Clash of Ignorance" article[32] – Huntington has struck a chord with those who think in terms of "east versus west" or "Islam versus Western liberalism".

For a mediator like Moore it is important to identify the main area of conflict, as in the end that is the area where real progress is to be made, in order to solve all other related problems. We should, however, not forget that as a conflict progresses so do people's feelings, memories and goals – and it is up to a mediator like Moore to address these newly risen issues.

Justifications of violence, including Just War Theory

As violence, both direct and structural, is so widespread, societies have come up with many different ways through which they justify this violence. Some justifications, for example, honour killings, are

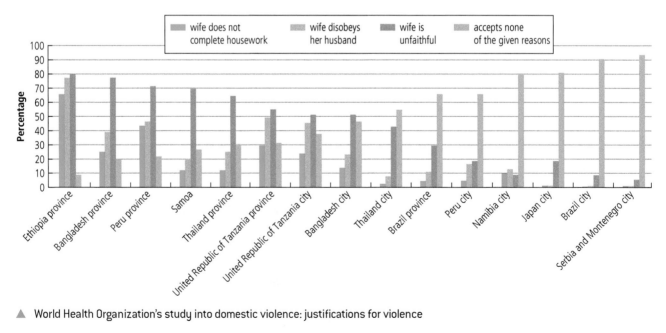

▲ World Health Organization's study into domestic violence: justifications for violence

embedded in culture and have not necessarily been integrated in the legal frameworks of countries, whereas others, such as self-defence or the state's monopoly on violence through its armed forces, are usually legalized through the country's constitution or legal framework. In the relations between countries, specifically concerning the conduct of war, a set of principles have arisen that have largely been legalized through the United Nations. These principles are known as "Just War Theory", which covers both the reasons for going to war and the conduct during war. Just War Theory has developed over hundreds of years, but more recently it is hotly debated whether it needs to be expanded. This "Responsibility to Protect" (R2P) doctrine provides new justifications for intervening militarily in conflict situations. At various levels, from the personal and societal to the international, we tend to find justifications for violence. Some may be more widely accepted than others, but the practice of justifying violence is widespread.

On the personal level, we often aim to justify our violent behaviour with references to culture, religion and human nature or by simply stating that "they deserved it". The World Health Organization's study into domestic violence shows that the victims often also indicated the violence was justified, because they hadn't completed the housework, had disobeyed their husband or had been unfaithful. In various (parts of) countries over more than 40 per cent of people saw at least one of these reasons as a justification for the violence.

Apart from their focus on peace, religious texts or the clergy claiming to represent the religion often seem to provide legitimizations for violence, from the Judeo-Christian "an eye for an eye" to the "lesser jihad" to protect Islam. Patriarchal, or male-dominated, societies often use culture or religion to justify violence. The practice of Karo-Kari, or honour killings, in Pakistan, is "primarily committed against women who are thought to have brought dishonour to their family by engaging in illicit pre-marital or extra-marital relations. In order to restore this honour, a male family member must kill the female in question."[33]

Patel, S. 2008

The Pakistani government's limited response to prevent or punish these killings, furthers the thought that this type of violence is "justified". The Global Slavery Index of 2013 reports the widespread practice of (modern)

▲ A poster showing Félicien Kabuga, wanted for his alleged role in the Rwandan genocide. Kabuga was allegedly heavily involved in the radio station RTLM, as well as *Kangura* magazine.

slavery and its justification "through culturally sanctioned or tolerated forms either of slavery or slavery-like practices that are endemic". The 2014 report gives the example of Mauritania, where "[r]eligion and slavery are closely interrelated". Other ways in which we justify our own or other people's violence is by dehumanizing the opponent. Through ascribing unhuman or subhuman characteristics to the other party, we allow ourselves to not treat the other party as humans. During the Rwandan genocide, radio station RTLM called upon its listeners (an estimated 90 per cent of the population) "to clean up the cockroaches", referring to the Tutsi minority. Portraying the other party in such a way dehumanizes them and makes it seem as though violent behaviour is justified.

Historically, it is generally accepted that the state is the one actor allowed to use violence. Police officers using Tasers or physical force to neutralize a suspect, or the riot police being called in to keep a group of football hooligans in line are both widely seen and generally accepted (though there are many concerns about the Taser and its lethal nature). Laws of a country usually allow police forces to use violence, though they're normally expected to react in a restrained manner. The death penalty is still practised in at least 22 countries and is another form of legitimized violence by the state. Even locking up people in prison, which could be considered a form of structural violence, would then be a form of justified violence. Furthermore, many legal systems around the world seem to be flawed through biases against certain minorities that can also be seen as a form of legitimized structural violence. A state's secret services are normally also allowed to use (limited) forms of violence. Torture or murder is then seen as legitimized, as the agent has performed in the country's interest, and it may even be claimed that a terrorist attack was prevented.

Many non-state actors, from guerrilla groups such as the Revolutionary Armed Forces of Colombia (FARC) to organizations like Islamic State are likely to use similar forms of violence, yet with the state's generally accepted monopoly on violence this is normally considered unjustified – regardless of whether one may agree with their objectives. However, if these actors may be successful in their struggle and establish themselves as the rulers of a particular country, then the domestic legal system is often adjusted to retrospectively legitimize the group's actions and other countries may further legitimize the original violence by accepting the new government. The military actions in Egypt that led to the removal of the democratically elected president, Mohammed Morsi, were certainly condemned by various countries, but with the leader of the military, Abdel Fattah el-Sisi, as the current president of Egypt and Morsi sentenced to life imprisonment, many countries have accepted the status quo and therefore provide legitimization of the violence perpetrated by Egypt's military leaders.

Case study of Haiti, ranked third on the Global Slavery Index 2014

HAITI

Index rank

3

Numbers enslaved

237,700

Government response

C

Vulnerability

71.9%

Index rank **3**
Estimated number of people in modern slavery **237,700**
Government response to modern slavery **C**
Vulnerability to modern slavery **71.9%**
Population **10,317,461**
GDP (PPP) per capita (Int$) **$1,703**

Prevalence

Haiti is the least developed country in the Americas, where poverty has contributed to use of the *restavèk* system. This is a common cultural practice that involves children being sent to work for other families, usually because their own parents do not have the means to care for them. The common understanding of this practice is that children will have access to school and be provided for in a way that their families cannot accommodate. However, many *restavèk* children experience exploitation in the home of their caretakers, including forced domestic service, and chronic verbal, physical, and sexual abuse.

The children come from the impoverished rural areas of Haiti, or from within poor urban areas, and labour in households in the cities. Much of the housing in urban areas is extremely basic, lacking facilities like running water and reliable access to electricity. Everyday tasks like cooking, cleaning and fetching water can be extremely arduous, and this is why many families take on a *restavèk* child. Some are forced to work very long hours, performing dangerous chores or tasks, such as carrying heavy loads, being exposed to dangerous traffic, and cooking with materials that have a damaging effect on their bodies. Many are physically abused, and some sexually abused as well. Often, they are deprived of schooling, or where

they are allowed to go sporadically, this is in such a way that they are unable to keep on top of schoolwork and fall behind or drop out. *Restavèk* children are commonly deprived of the nurturing and attention a child needs to grow and flourish.

Haitian children are also vulnerable to trafficking across the border into the Dominican Republic for domestic work, child labour and commercial sexual exploitation. Street children, often runaway or expelled *restavèks*, are vulnerable to street crime or trafficking by criminal gangs.

Although children make up the majority of victims of modern slavery in Haiti, adult victims have also been identified in forced labour in agriculture, construction and forced prostitution within Haiti, in the Dominican Republic, other Caribbean countries, the United States, and South America. Up to 200 women every year are trafficked into Haiti from the Dominican Republic, for sexual exploitation. Women living in Internally Displaced Persons (IDP) camps, which still exist following the earthquake of January 2010, are vulnerable to commercial sexual exploitation and forced labour.

1 What examples of direct violence can you find in the text above?

2 What examples of structural violence are occurring in Haiti?

3 How would these forms of violence be justified? Would you agree with these justifications?

In international relations one of the oldest accepted norms is the one that regulates war, more specifically the reasons for which it is waged and the conduct of war. Just War Theory can be traced back to Catholic scholars such as St Thomas Aquinas and St Augustine who tried to reconcile something evil (war and taking lives) with situations in which it seemed there were "conditions for permissible recourse to war". After the establishment of the just reasons to go to war, *jus ad bellum*, the just behaviour or conduct during war, *jus in bello*, was developed. If the "rules" of Just War Theory are being followed, a war

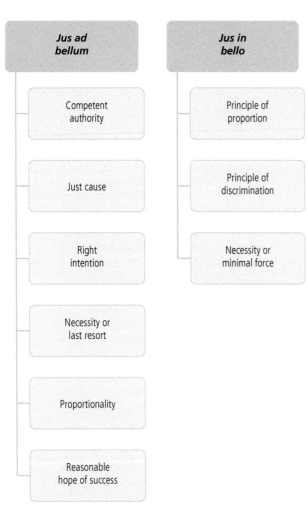

Jus ad bellum	Jus in bello
Competent authority	Principle of proportion
Just cause	Principle of discrimination
Right intention	Necessity or minimal force
Necessity or last resort	
Proportionality	
Reasonable hope of success	

▲ Just War Theory and its conditions for just reasons and principles for just conduct

can be considered legal; whereas a war not fought for the right reasons and in the right manner is considered a war of aggression.

Aggression refers to a state's use of force, or an imminent threat to do so, against another state's territory or sovereignty – unless the use of force is in response to aggression.[34]

Goldstein, 2004

The basic criteria for a war to be fought for the right reasons, or *jus ad bellum*, are:

- it requires a "competent authority" to declare and wage the war
- the war is fought in the pursuit of a "just cause"
- the war is fought with the right intention
- the war is used as a last resort
- waging the war is proportional to the act that triggered it
- there is a reasonable hope of success.

The criterion of a competent authority was originally introduced to ensure that only states could declare war and not private armies and such. O'Brien (2009) identifies some problems with this criterion: "there may be disputes as to the constitutional competence of a particular official or organ of a state to initiate the war".[35] In other words, it is often debatable as to whether the right steps were followed according to a country's constitution. The other problem is that many non-state actors claim the right to launch a war. For example, the Houthis in Yemen who rebelled against the government and took control of most of the country are considered a terrorist organization by some countries, but are supported by others. Can organizations that claim "revolutionary rights" or the right to go against a government that does not act in their interest be considered a "competent authority"? This is not clear.

Even though the United Nations Security Council is often criticized, it is generally accepted that the body is also a competent authority. Article 42 of the United Nations Charter states that the Security Council "may take such action by air, sea, or land forces as may be necessary to maintain or restore international peace and security." Since the Charter is signed by the 193 member states of the United Nations, it is close to universally accepted that the Security Council is a competent authority.

▲ Security Council session in which it voted unanimously to increase humanitarian aid in Syria

Just cause

Perhaps even more complex and debatable is the "just cause" condition of Just War Theory. One of the main, generally accepted, just causes is "self-defence". The United Nations Charter also acknowledges this in Article 51:

> *Nothing in the present Charter shall impair the inherent right of individual or collective self-defence if an armed attack occurs against a Member of the United Nations.*

However, it is often unclear how far this "self-defence" goes. In the *Joint Resolution to Authorize the Use of United States Armed Forces Against Iraq* (2002), the Bush Administration argues that

> *[w]hereas Iraq's demonstrated capability and willingness to use weapons of mass destruction, the risk that the current Iraqi regime will either employ those weapons to launch a surprise attack against the United States or its Armed Forces or provide them to international terrorists who would do so, and the extreme magnitude of harm that would result to the United States and its citizens from such an attack, combine to justify action by the United States to defend itself.* [36]

The "just cause" principle is certainly stretched here, and the legality of the war has been debated ever since.

The right intention condition means that a country can only pursue the just cause and cannot change its objectives during the war to include other, possibly unjust, causes. Also, "right intention requires that the just belligerent have always in mind as the ultimate object of the war a just and lasting peace" (O'Brien, 2009).[37] The difficulty here is clearly defining what constitutes "a just and lasting peace".

Necessity or last resort refers to the requirement that war should not be the first thing on the mind of the decision-makers. Militarism can be seen as an ideology that sees war as a natural element of society and that a state must strive for hegemony in which "military means [are not seen as] a cause for celebration but as a necessary and last resort means of achieving change" (Jabri, 1996).[38] Often it is difficult to unearth whether war was really the last option on the minds of the decision-makers, but the recent leaks of sensitive information from Chelsea (Bradley) Manning and WikiLeaks reveal war is sometimes considered as the first option and it is then considered how this can be sold to the public.

The proportionality condition dictates that the ends must justify the means. If there has been an accidental border intrusion or another minor incident, it is not acceptable under Just War Theory. O'Brien states that also "the probable good expected to result from success is weighed against the probable evil that the war will cause" (2009). Lastly, if there's no hope of success, war is not justified.

Once all the *jus ad bellum* conditions are honoured, a war-waging party still has to respect the principles of just conduct during war, or *jus in bello*. Once again, proportionality is required. In this case, the conduct during a war must be in proportion to the offence and the end goal.

▲ A Handicap International weapons clearance expert, standing by a stockpile of shells and other explosive weapons near Misrata.

The bombing of Libya by the North Atlantic Treaty Organization (NATO) in 2011, with the suspected use of depleted uranium and the confirmation that there could be more than 300 sites where unexploded bombs can be found, could be questioned in relation to the end goal – protecting Libya's citizens from Muammar Gaddafi. Under the principle of discrimination, warring parties are expected to refrain from "direct intentional attacks on non-combatants and non-military targets". Once again, these terms are debatable and it is not always clear where to draw the line. All too often, factories, media and governmental institutions may serve the military in some way, but the point when they become a legitimate military target is often unclear.

The discussion of *jus ad bellum* and *jus in bello* almost seems theoretical, as it is rather difficult to find a war that fully adheres to these criteria. The fact that the elements are open to different interpretations allows much leeway for conflict parties to justify their reasons for – or conduct during – a war. Furthermore, if powerful nations choose to ignore either *jus ad bellum* or *jus in bello*, or both, then what can be done about it?

In the past decades, it has been argued that Just War Theory should be further stretched to include justification for military intervention, as a last resort, in case of mass atrocities perpetrated within a country by its own leaders. This concept of humanitarian intervention is being used more often, but at the same time draws criticism from those who argue that it is used selectively. Regardless of the elements that are open to interpretation and the current debates about its limitations, Just War Theory is still a fundamental code in the relations among nations.

To be able to understand all the intricacies of a conflict, we often have to go back many years to unearth the deeper roots behind a situation. Whether it's an interpersonal or inter-state conflict, often there are factors in the background that greatly influence the setting as well as parties' attitudes and behaviour and the outcome of their actions. At the same time, we try to make sense of a wealth of conflict parties who are connected in various ways, pursuing unclear goals or communicating mixed messages. In this chaos, however, it is possible to identify certain factors that often seem to influence conflict, and it is possible to identify conflict parties and what motivates them. As long as we do realize that these causes and parties are not fixed – that they constantly require further study and that oversimplification may make things easier, but does not necessarily bring us closer to "the truth" – then we can allow ourselves to identify some factors that seem to influence conflict.

Causes of conflict

There are various factors that can be identified as having caused a conflict in one way or another, however, it is often very difficult to pinpoint exactly what the role of each factor is. Even a hundred years after the start of the First World War we are still debating the significance and role of the various causes. It is therefore somewhat easier to look at a variety of conflicts and to identify commonalities between them.

Conflict can often be understood by studying how we humans work, both on our own and in groups. The in-and-out groups we create and the process of dehumanization are some of the psychological factors that influence conflict. As we have seen, internal (or intra-state) wars – with or without international involvement – are the most widespread type of war. If we better understood the underlying causes of these conflicts, it would allow us to make more sense of a high number of present-day conflicts. The "greed versus grievance" debate revolves around what plays a bigger role in civil war: improving one's economic situation or issues related to identity, culture and so forth.

Many psychologists have researched the role of grouping and categorizing human behaviour. Sears, Huddy and Jervis argue the categorizing of people happens in "almost automatic fashion" and that "their similarity to their fellow ingroup members and the dissimilarity of ingroup members to outgroup members will [often] be exaggerated" (2003). Ingroups refer to the groups we believe we belong to. This categorization can range from religion or nationality to football club or hobby. Just the perception of dissimilarity can already produce conflict and depending on the circumstances this can take a more or less violent form.

> **TOK**
>
> Can other areas of knowledge, such as history, help us to understand events in contemporary global politics?

171

Many forms of discrimination seem to originate from this ingroup–outgroup hostility. Vivienne Jabri argues that conflict is defined "in terms of inclusion and exclusion". One element in the process of categorization that can lead to the worst forms of violence is dehumanization. If "the other" is not seen as human anymore, then supposedly one doesn't have to treat them as such. Studies show that social cognition or considering the "humanness" of the other can vary depending on, for example, status (Harris and Fiske, 2011).[39] A photo of a homeless person will often be met with "disgust" and there is a general habit of ignoring them as though they don't exist. Propaganda can further strengthen dehumanization, such as the hate-speeches from RTLM in Rwanda during the genocide. Widespread discriminatory practices, for example, in South Africa during Apartheid, can reinforce the idea that the other is not of similar status to oneself. As we also often fear what we don't know, separation can also reinforce the process of dehumanization. The wall or barrier that Israel built around the West Bank could have a similar effect. If groups don't meet it may be easier to believe the stories about the other and this could accelerate the process of dehumanization. Lindner's Scale of Human Worthiness uses the well-known terms of *übermensch* and *untermensch* used by Hitler to emphasize the greatness of the ingroup and the inferiority of certain outgroups. The Holocaust and other genocides of the twentieth century show what dehumanization can lead to.

Thinking skills

Greed versus Grievance: With reference to specific examples, which do you think plays a bigger role in conflict: greed or grievance?

The "greed versus grievance" debate is perhaps one of the most well-known debates concerning the causes of conflict. Collier and Hoeffler's research indicates that conflict groups are more rational than we often perceive them to be, as they calculate the "availability of finance", "the cost of rebellion", and "military advantage".[40] Critics say it is easier to quantify "greed factors" compared to factors related to grievance, but this doesn"t mean that grievance plays a minor role in conflict (Collier and Hoeffler 2004: 563–595). Michael E. Brown (1996) argues that all too easily religious or ethnic "ancient hatreds" are referred to as the cause of a conflict, for example, in the former Yugoslavia. He classifies this, according to him "widely held", view as "simple" and states that "it cannot explain why some disputes are more violent and harder to resolve than others".[41] He identifies four groups of factors "that make some places more predisposed to violence than others": structural, economic/social, political, and cultural/perceptual. If a country"s government has a lack of control over (parts of) the country then it can be classified as a weak state. This lack of governmental control can then lead to groups providing for their own security or vice versa. Brown also argues that states that lack homogenity and have ethnic minorities "are more prone to conflict than others". Brown provides the example of Somalia as a country with a weak central government and many groups that provide for their own security. In terms of ethnic geography, however, Somalia is very homogeneous.

Structural Factors	Economic/Social Factors
Weak states Intra-state security concerns Ethnic geography	Economic problems Discriminatory economic systems Modernization

Political Factors	Cultural/Perceptual Factors
Discriminatory political institutions Exclusionary national ideologies Inter-group politics Elite politics	Patterns of cultural discrimination Problematic group histories

▲ The underlying causes of internal conflict, Brown, 1996

The political factors that can cause domestic conflict to lead to war are largely related to "the type and fairness of the political system". If groups have opportunities to represent themselves through the political system and if the political system does not value a certain group over another then it's less likely that conflict will lead to direct violence. The authoritarian regime of Bashar al-Assad in Syria favoured a particular minority in the country – the Alawites – and when demonstrations were met with repression civil war broke out. Certainly, the inadequacies of the Syrian political system contributed to the outbreak of violence and economic/social factors play another role. Economic downturn can often be a bigger influence than political discrimination. When Jordan lowered its fuel subsidies in 2012 large protests erupted and it was reported that protesters asked for the abdication of King Abdullah. One banner quite rightly stated, "Raising prices is like playing with fire". The rapid process of modernization, the introduction of new technologies

▲ Cartoon in *The Times* depicting how, through social media, Tunisia "unfriended" its dictator Ben Ali

and the rise of new forms of industrialization also has a huge impact on societies. Old elites are sometimes struggling to keep up with the latest developments and this can lead to tensions. Modernization has also empowered groups who may have felt powerless before. Social media played an important role in the Tunisian Revolution of 2011 that led to the overthrow of its authoritarian regime. The cultural/perceptual factors revolve around the "ancient hatreds" mentioned earlier. Brown acknowledges that many groups have legitimate grievances. Confirming the in- and outgroup dimensions he states that "[h]owever, it is also true that groups tend to whitewash and glorify their own histories, and they often demonize their neighbors, rivals, and adversaries". From the factors identified by Brown we can learn that it is never just one element (oil prices, discrimination, dictatorship) that causes conflict, but that an interplay of various factors can provide a fertile ground for civil conflict to turn violent.

Cartoons about overpopulation

Fritz Behrendt, born in Berlin, drew many political cartoons for Amnesty International and leading newspapers across the world, such as *The New York Times* and *Der Spiegel*. One of the recurring themes in his work is overpopulation. Despite the nuclear tension during the Cold War he speaks of "the other bomb", which perhaps does not receive as much attention even though it is of similar importance. In "Growth" he identifies several elements that are growing (production, unemployment, energy problem and hunger), but the biggest concern seems to be overpopulation.

Class discussion

Do you agree with Behrendt's views as portrayed in the cartoon on the right? Is the issue expressed more important today than 40 years ago when the cartoon was drawn?

The Growing Danger—Population Explosion

Parties to conflict

Conflict often starts with a limited amount of conflict parties, but over time it can draw in many others. A conflict between a protest group and the owners of a nuclear power plant can quickly involve local or national authorities, local residents, police forces and so on. Depending on their behaviour and other factors, their role within the conflict may change. We've seen that conflict parties are often seen as unitary actors even though the people within the conflict party can have different motives for their involvement. The distinction between state and non-state actors is an important one in that states have certain rights and responsibilities, both morally and legally, that non-state actors may not have. Targeted assassinations by Israel and the United States are heavily criticized as a state is expected to "bring a perpetrator to justice". Non-state actors may not be hindered by these expectations. The types of war identified on in this chapter indicate that intra-state wars are the most widespread variant of war, and that war between states is in decline.
In violent intra-state conflicts governments are often confronted with groups labelled "terrorists" or "guerrillas". The language used to depict oneself and the other is hugely important in the perception of the conflict. It does make a difference whether reports are talking about rebels, dissident, insurgents, terrorists, freedom fighters, armed resistance or militants as many of these terms are value-laden. In American news reports the Iraqi soldiers in the 2003 war were often called "militia" or "quasi-terrorists" (Roy, 2003, p. 87). This serves to delegitimize the other party's actions and goals. Jabri claims that in conflict situations people are expected to support their country:

> *As a conflict escalates towards violence and as the "war mood" takes hold of entire populations, the dissident from either camp or the peacemaker from the onlooking external world can become subject to social contempt and censure rather than admiration.*

Jabri, 1996: 6

Encarnacion et al. (1990) developed a model that shows the proximity of various parties to the core conflict parties. These "third parties" can have a large influence on the conflict and generally the closer they are to the core parties, the better will they understand the situation but also the more biased will they be towards one or the other party. Sometimes it may be useful for a mediator to be as uninvolved as possible in order to be as neutral as possible, whereas in other cases it may be useful for the mediator to be as close as possible to the conflict parties as this may give them more power to push for a solution or their knowledge of the conflict parties can be used to resolve the issue.

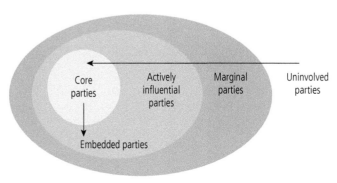

◀ "The impact of concerned parties on the resolution of disputes" in Issues in Third World Conflict Resolution by eds. Lindgren, Wallensteen, and Nordquist, Uppsala University

---

ATL Thinking and research skills

Language and conflict parties: Find a local newspaper (hard-copy or online) and look up an article about a local conflict between an NGO and a business or local authority.

1 How are the parties described in the article? Is the wording used more positive towards one party than the other?

2 Visit the NGO's website or consult leaflets or other forms of communication. How do they describe the conflict situation?

TOK

In what ways can language be used to influence, persuade or manipulate people? Are there fundamental differences between language and the other ways of knowing in the TOK course?

Conflict mapping is a process where various dimensions of conflict are analysed, from causes to conflict behaviour to outcomes. An important element within this is gaining understanding of the various parties involved in a conflict, their role and the relations between various parties. This is often a highly complex process as relations are not always obvious and the way in which parties influence a conflict may not always be that visible. *The Economist* has tried to make sense of conflict in the Middle East and the publicly acknowledged ties between the various parties (see below). This already creates a rather complex web as it has to take into account non-state actors that wield or have wielded as much power as a state – for example, Islamic State and the Muslim Brotherhood – and this web only covers the openly acknowledged relations. A conflict analyst, however, should have patience and perseverance to fully understand the conflict parties and their relations.

The main political rifts in the Middle East
Who openly backs whom

▲ The Middle Eastern mesh according to *The Economist*. 3 April 2015, 14:27 by the Data Team

Conflict parties have several options in the methods they choose to use to raise their issue. Their behaviour can evolve from restrained, or even muted, to openly and indiscriminately violent. Third parties also have a variety of ways in which they can try to influence conflict parties. All this will be discussed in the next chapter.

As we must have experienced ourselves and we can often see on the news, conflict can go through various phases of intensification and manifestation. Conflict parties have several options through which they can decide to pursue their goals, from terror tactics to non-violent protest. The dynamism of conflict adds to its complexity as conflict parties' attitudes and behaviour evolve over time. Also, behind conflict parties' statements are often deeper lying issues that are either covered up or have not yet been unearthed by the conflict party itself. The complexity further increases when third parties get involved – and they also may not always share the real reason for their intervention in the conflict. The recent emergence of the idea of humanitarian intervention seems like a positive development in that the international community can protect citizens who are targeted by their own state or are not safeguarded by it. However, it is far from generally accepted and is heavily criticized for the potential flaws of the doctrine.

Manifestations of conflict, including non-violence

The formation of in- and outgroups and the subsequent group dynamics can manifest themselves in many different ways. According to Gordon Allport (1954) our behaviour based on the prejudgments we make about the other group can start relatively harmlessly with antilocution, or hostile talking and jokes. We probably all know jokes about the inhabitants of our neighbouring country, particular minorities in our country or jokes directed at ourselves by neighbouring countries and other groups. Although this seems harmless, it can obviously be hurtful and it can create an atmosphere where it is generally acceptable to ridicule the outgroup. The prejudiced behaviour can further manifest itself through avoidance ("I never go to that part of town as it is entirely inhabited by that group") or discrimination. The first three stages can be considered forms of structural violence and could lay the foundations for the final two stages: physical attack and extermination. Though indeed it seems like a big step from a joke to genocide, if prejudice is unchecked and unaddressed it can lead to more and more extreme behaviour, and compared to the previous act the next one does not seem so severe. This so-called "foot in the door" principle explains how we may refuse an outrageous request if it comes out of the blue, but if we're gradually drawn into a system we may end up fulfilling that same request. Milgram demonstrated this in the famous Milgram experiment in which subjects were asked to inflict increasingly severe shocks on another participant "in the name of science". In the rigged experiment many subjects went as far as hypothetically administering a lethal electric shock on another person. Every increase of voltage did not seem too bad compared to the previous level. If the experimenters had asked the participants straight away to perform a lethal shock on the other participant, it is quite likely none of them would have continued. From Allport's model we can see that the sooner we address prejudiced behaviour, perhaps the bigger the chance we have to prevent further suffering in the future.

▲ Newspapers in New York report on Egyptian President Hosni Mubarak leaving office following the 2011 revolution

Prejudiced behaviour can manifest itself in increasingly severe ways:	
Antilocution	Hostile talking, including jokes
Avoidance	Keeping a distance, but without actively inflicting harm
Discrimination	Active exclusion from rights
Physical attack	Violence against the person
Extermination	Indiscriminate violence against the entire group

The violent manifestations of conflict we are often confronted with on the news are wars and acts of terrorism. Though it is difficult to define terrorism and it is often used to smear the other party (see 4.2), conventional warfare and terrorism are rather different in a variety of ways, from the use of weaponry and the legality of the actions to clothing (see table below). Guerrilla warfare seems to share characteristics with conventional warfare, as guerrillas usually seek recognition as an "official army". However, they often also employ similar tactics as terrorists, and governments who are targeted by guerrillas generally aim to label these groups "terrorists". The increase in size of violent non-state actors and their control of large territories

	Conventional war	Guerrilla	Terrorism
Unit size in battle	Large (armies, corps, division)	Medium (platoons, companies, battalions)	Small (usually less than 10 persons)
Weapons	Full range of military hardware (air force, armour, artillery, etc.)	Mostly infantry-type light weapons but sometimes artillery pieces as well	Hand guns, hand grenades, assault rifles, and specialized weapons, e.g. car bombs, barometric pressure bombs
Tactics	Usually joint operation involving several military branches	Commando-type tactics	Specialized tactics; kidnapping, assassinations, car-bombing, hijacking, barricade, hostages etc.
Targets	Mostly military units, industrial and transportation infrastructure	Mostly military, police, and administration staff, as well as political opponents	State symbols, political opponents, and the public at large
Intended impact	Physical destruction	Mainly physical attrition of enemy	Psychological coercion
Control of territory	Yes	Yes	No
Uniform	Wear uniform	Often wear uniform	Do not wear uniform
Recognition of war zones	War limited to recognized geographical zones	War limited to the country in strife	No recognized war zones, operations carried out worldwide
International legality	Yes, if conducted by rules	Yes, if conducted by rules	No
Domestic legality	Yes	No	No

▲ General Characteristics of War, Guerrilla and Terrorism. Based on Ariel Merari, from Belfer Center for Science and International Affairs paper series, "Harvard University Twenty-first Century Terrorism: The Definitional Problem of Complex Political Environments" Marcial Garcia Suarez, January 2008

sometimes make it difficult to label them (see case study about Al-Shabaab on the following page). Violent protest groups generally claim they have the right to use violence as they are often fighting a stronger opponent with more resources, weaponry and financial support. These organizations often fight against the state and they contest the state's monopoly on violence. Regardless of the difficulty in agreeing upon a definition of terrorism, A.P. Schmidt identified some characteristics of terrorism (see below). Particularly the publicity element seems vital to a terrorist. Some Norwegians have dealt with the terror attack on the governmental district in Oslo and a youth camp on an island by not mentioning the perpetrator's name anymore, as he was seeking self-glorification, among other things. A commonality between a violent and non-violent protestor is that both are seeking attention for their cause from the media and the general public.

The pamphlets or manifestos of violent and non-violent protestors often provide justifications or explanations for their decision to use violence or not. Violent protestors may refer to religious or ideological texts that justify the use of violence, or they may claim they should be able to use similar methods to their opponents, often the state. Fidel Castro argued he used violence in his successful Cuban Revolution because his opponent had not left him any other choice. The arguments used by non-violent protestors range from similar religious or ideological texts to the argument that non-violent protest is more effective.

Key characteristic elements of terrorism

1. The demonstrative use of violence against human beings
2. The (conditional) threat of (more) violence
3. The deliberate production of fear in a target group
4. The targeting of civilians, non-combatants and innocents
5. The purpose of intimidation, coercion and propaganda
6. The fact that it is a method, tactic or strategy of conflict waging
7. The importance of communicating the act(s) of violence to larger audiences
8. The illegal, criminal and immoral nature of the act(s) of violence
9. The predominantly political character of the act
10. Its use as a tool of psychological warfare to mobilize or immobilize sectors of the public

Which characteristics are highly debatable and difficult to apply? Look up a recent act of violence that was labelled "terrorism". Do all the characteristics apply to that case?

Schmidt, AP. 2004. "Terrorism, the definitional problem".
Case Western Reserve Journal of International Law.
Vol 36, pp. 375–419.

Crisis group report on Al-Shabaab's terrorist actions in Kenya

Kenya: Al-Shabaab – Closer to Home Nairobi/Brussels

25 Sep 2014

In its latest briefing, "Kenya: Al-Shabaab – Closer to Home", the International Crisis Group highlights Al-Shabaab's growing presence and increasingly frequent attacks and the muddled response of Kenya's government, security services and political elite. Anti-terrorism operations perceived to target entire communities have exacerbated feelings of marginalization and persecution, particularly of the Muslim minority, and are feeding directly into Al-Shabaab's messaging and recruitment.

The briefing's major findings and recommendations are:

— The wider danger of Al-Shabaab's tactics in Kenya lies in its ability to use existing religious and ethnic fault lines to deepen the country's political and social divides.

— Kenyan political elites need to acknowledge the domestic terror threat and form a common action plan together with the country's senior Muslim leadership to counter extremist recruitment.

— The government should put into practice the recommendations of the 2008 Special Action ("Sharawe") Committee set up to address the concerns of the Muslim minority: these include measures to end institutional discrimination against Muslims and their more proportional representation in senior public service appointments.

— The government and its security services need to identify and isolate the specific Al-Shabaab threat and not conflate the actions of extremists with specific communities – especially in the north east and the coast – whose past and present grievances make them suspect in the eyes of the state. It must reappraise its anti-terrorism practices and operations, that are perceived as collective punishment of Muslims and particular ethnic groups. It should also allow for transparent investigations and redress where operations have exceeded the law or breached constitutional rights.

"Kenya's 4.3 million Muslims have been historically marginalised, especially in the north east and along the coast", says Cedric Barnes, Horn of Africa Project Director. "If the government wants to cut grassroots support for Al-Shabaab, it has to address the widespread institutional and socio-economic discrimination felt by Kenyan Muslims".

"The blame for growing radicalisation in Kenya lies less in the weaknesses of the country's institutions than in the unwillingness of political leaders to put aside partisan divisions," says EJ Hogendoorn, Deputy Africa Program Director. "Their playing politics with terrorism compounds an already volatile situation."

1   Research the size, influence and control of territory of Al-Shabaab. Apply the general characteristics of war, guerrilla and terrorism to the organization. To what extent can they be considered a terrorist organization?

Misconceptions about nonviolent conflict

1. It is widely believed that violence always works quickly, and nonviolent struggle always takes very long. Both of these beliefs are false.

2. Nonviolent struggle is often believed to be weak, but in fact it can be very powerful. It can paralyse and even disintegrate a repressive regime.

3. Nonviolent struggle does not need a charismatic leader.

4. Nonviolent struggle is a cross-cultural phenomenon.

5. Nonviolent struggle does not require any religious beliefs (certainly no specific religious beliefs), although at times it has been practised with religious motives.

6. Nonviolent struggle is not the same as religious or ethical, principled nonviolence, but a very different phenomenon. This distinction must be made clear and not downplayed.

7. Although it is still widely believed that this technique can succeed only against humanitarian and democratic opponents, it has at times been successful against brutal regimes and dictatorships, including Nazi and Communist ones.

8. It is said by some people and groups that nonviolent struggle only succeeds by melting the hearts of the oppressors. However, it has been coercive and even destroyed extreme dictatorships.

Sharp, Gene. 2003. *There Are Realistic Alternatives*.
Boston, Massachusetts. The Albert Institution.

The stategic logic of nonviolent protest

1. It enhances domestic and international legitimacy which increases pressure on the target.

2. Regime violence against nonviolent movements is more likely to backfire against it.

    a) It can result in the breakdown of obedience among regime supporters [and] mobilization of the population against the regime

    b) and can lead to international condemnation of the regime, leading to sanctions or aid for the nonviolent campaign.

3. Nonviolent resistance campaigns appear to be more open to negotiation and bargaining because they do not threaten the lives or well-being of members of the target regime.

    a) The public views nonviolent campaigns as physically nonthreatening and violent campaigns as threatening.

    b) When violent insurgents threaten the lives of regime members and security forces, they greatly reduce the possibility of loyalty shifts.

Stephan, Maria J and Chenoweth, E. 2008.
"Why civil resistance works. The strategic logic of nonviolent conflict".
International Security. Vol 33, pp. 7–44.

Research and self-management skills

Listen to Fidel Castro
in his own words here:
https://www.youtube.com/
watch?v=67ZWBI-66H8

The effectiveness of protest was researched by Stephan and Chenoweth (2008) who found that non-violent campaigns are twice as successful as violent campaigns. One may argue that non-violent protest is normally only used against democratic or weak regimes and may therefore be more successful, but according to Gene Sharp (2003) this is one of the many misconceptions about non-violent protest (see above). Stephan and Chenoweth give a number of reasons why they consider non-violent protest to be the logical choice for the protestor. The attention it can draw to the cause of the protestor, especially when the opponent uses violence against non-violent protestors and the likelihood of supporters of the opponent joining the non-violent protestors, or at least withdrawing their support of the opponent, play a large role in the success of non-violent protest (see previous page).

As a non-violent protestor is often faced with an opponent with potentially superior power in terms of weaponry, forces and finances, a non-violent protestor is expected to find ways in which they can undermine that power. The key element is removing people's obedience to the opponent, to weaken their financial support (for example, through not paying taxes) and numerical superiority by convincing the general population or security forces to withdraw their (implicit) support to the regime. The so-called "pillars of support" are the elements upon which a regime's power is based. These can range from businesses to education to the military. In their handbook for non-violent struggle, Popovic, Milivojevic and Djinovic have visualized these pillars (figure 22). As student leaders they were involved in the non-violent protests against Milosevic in the former Yugoslavia and since then they have trained various groups in how to organize a non-violent campaign, including the student protestors in Egypt (see the case study on the following page for their analysis of the Egyptian regime's pillars of support).

As mentioned on page 151 Arundhati Roy calls Gandhi, Mandela and King "the high priests of non-violent resistance". Certainly Gandhi has laid foundations for present-day non-violent resistance by taking on the mighty British Empire, and King's struggle for racial equality has had a profound impact on the United States and similar struggles worldwide. Mandela's African National Congress (ANC) was branded a terrorist organization and his leadership of the military wing has led many to still brand him a former terrorist, but indisputably he can be largely credited for South Africa's non-violent transition from Apartheid to democracy. Roy is rather depressed about the fate of the United States, India and South Africa after the deaths of King, Gandhi and Mandela and this reminds us that building a positively peaceful society is a constant struggle.

Thinking skills

Non-violent protest and the pillars of support

1   Identify an authoritarian regime. What are its "pillars of support" and how do they support the regime?

2   How could a non-violent protest group win those pillars over to remove their support to the regime?

Analysis of some of Egyptian President Sisi's pillars of support by the Centre for Applied Non-Violent Action and Strategies (CANVAS)

1 *Security forces: The Military* The military has taken on too big a social role in Egyptian society, and the administration of Sisi seems to be a continuation of that anti-democratic trend. There have almost always been military leaders at the head of the Egyptian state, and they enjoy a fair amount of independence from the executive, and often enjoy respect from the populace. They were aligned with [former president] Mubarak until they saw the tides shift in society and decided to back the revolution instead. Most consider that the military launched the Tamarod movement that ousted [former president] Morsi, and the coup was a time of national rallying around the military. Many of the protestors chanted, "The military and the people are one hand." Further, many have considered Sisi's presidency to be restoring military order in a way that will save Egyptian society from insecurity and unrest. As previously mentioned, the military in Egypt is deeply tied into the economy. Much of the country's infrastructural and economic projects are managed by the military, including hospitals, factories, clubs, construction, and real estate. Therefore, similar to the police, the main way that the military might become estranged from Sisi is if his economic reforms are significant enough to really hurt them economically.

2 *Economic Elites* Since the Egyptian economy has become increasingly crippled by the instability following the 2011 revolution, the country is struggling to gain and keep investments. The economic elites are a diverse group, and at least partly tied in with the military and corrupt bureaucracy. They seem to support Sisi in terms of the stability he promises but, similar to the military, the support might wane if his economic reforms cut too deep into their agenda. It is possible, however, that the economic reforms he makes will mainly affect the poorest in society and will not turn the elites against him.

3 *Judiciary* The judiciary in Egypt enjoys a surprising amount of independence from other branches of government, and they can be seen exerting this power now. Most judges were appointed by Mubarak, and remain loyal to the undemocratic vision of stability through repression that his rule represents. There seems to be no clear plan for dealing with the fact that

this judiciary is very powerful and entirely inherited from the Mubarak regime. They certainly seem aligned with Sisi at the moment, but as was already mentioned, they have created massive international problems for him by their violation of international human rights standards, particularly with the jailing of foreign journalists. They also enjoy significant oversight of the election process. Ultimately, the judiciary seems to be in a cooperative tension with Sisi, and the future is uncertain.

4 *Media* The media in Egypt is a major regional player and has many prominent newspapers and television stations. Television is the most popular news source, with 2 state-run channels, 6 regional channels, and 20 new independent channels. The 2011 revolution also spurred many Egyptians to go online, and as of 2012 there were nearly 30 million Egyptians using Internet access, and 14 million using Facebook. Both Facebook and Twitter are being used by prominent political forces in society to garner support as social network use rises. During the Mubarak era, media was primarily state-run and supportive of the regime, but since the 2011 revolution there has been a resurgence of independent media sources that now compete with state-run media. Most independent sources are strongly ideologically tilted towards either the secularist liberal agenda, or the Islamist agenda. While Sisi has control of the state-run media, Pandora's Box seems to have opened and the profusion of news sources and Internet users does not seem to be getting any smaller. Sisi's jailing of prominent journalists that try to cover the suppression of the Muslim Brotherhood has had a dampening effect, but it has not stopped the resurgence of independent media. He may need to court the liberal secular independent media if he is to maintain or grow popular support. Therefore, it may be that the media is one place that can put significant pressure on him to support some of the most critical and important reforms needed in this next phase of building up Egyptian society.

See the full 30-page report here: http://www.canvasopedia. org/images/books/analysis/Egypt_Analysis_2014_11_ anex3.pdf?pdf=Analysis-Egypt

The dynamic nature of conflict makes it difficult to fully understand parties' motivations, actions and impact. Various models, which may oversimplify a conflict, offer support by allowing the analyst to focus on key elements. Galtung's conflict triangle separates attitude and behaviour from each other and explains how they influence each other and the actual conflict, or contradiction, between the parties. The Positions–Interests–Needs model separates what we say from what we want and from what we really need, allowing a conflict analyst to dig deeper and unearth the basic necessities of each conflict party. Lastly, the conflict cycle allows for the identification of the phase in which the conflict finds itself and what the appropriate response could be from a third party or conflict party.

Galtung separates the conflict, or incompatibility of goals between parties, from the attitudes parties take and the behaviour they display towards each other. These three elements can influence each other in what Galtung calls "an ever escalating spiral" (see diagram below). To understand a conflict, one must backtrack through various actions that have been influenced by attitudes (and vice versa) and have altogether changed the core conflict. If a group starts demonstrating for the closure of a nuclear power plant, the original incompatibility of goals may be that the local or national authorities would like it to remain open and the protestors would like to see it closed. If a demonstration is met with violence, then this will influence the attitudes that the groups hold of each other and therefore their subsequent behaviour. This could then draw attention from other groups and may change the incompatibility of goals into the right to protest and the apparent lack of ways to express oneself. In all its simplicity the conflict triangle visualizes the dynamic nature of conflict and its core components.

The conflict triangle

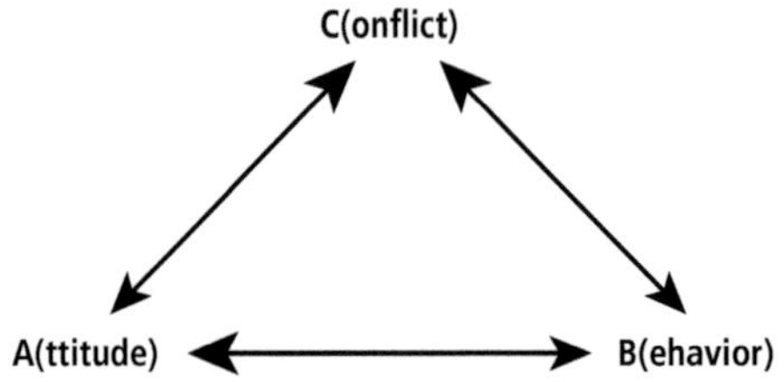

The conflict triangle. *Theories of conflict: Definitions, Dimensions, Negations, Formations* by Professor Johan Galtung, 1958

The Positions–Interests–Needs model (see below) is sometimes compared with an iceberg. When faced with an iceberg you only see the tip of it, and most of it is hiding below sea level. Similarly in conflicts, we mainly see the position of a party, or what they claim to be pursuing. However, the reasoning behind this claim, or the interest, is often hidden. Russia may claim it is defending the rights of ethnic Russians in its relations with Ukraine, but perhaps it is only using this argument to justify its actions. Maybe the deeper need for the Russian government is the need for security, which arguably has been undermined by developments such as the Baltic

States becoming European Union and NATO members, European support for an independent Kosovo and international support for the Syrian opposition. It may be that with the ousting of the pro-Russian Ukrainian president, the Russian government felt it had to draw the line. The Positions–Interests–Needs model is also often used to find "shared interests and needs" or overcome what seems to be an unresolvable conflict. Russia's and Ukraine's claims to the Crimea – annexed by Russia in 2014 – seem incompatible in that both argue they should have full ownership. However, if the deeper needs of both parties are addressed, one may be able to resolve the conflict. For both Russia and Ukraine safety is an important issue: Ukraine's security relates to its safety from Russian, but also Western, domination and, as mentioned, Russia has global security concerns. As parts of the Ukraine are pro-Russian and others pro-Western, identity is another important need for Ukraine. The (simplified) answer then maybe lies in Ukraine neither fully committing to Western organizations or to Russia. The Positions–Interests–Needs model applies just as well to global as to local or personal conflicts, as can be seen below.

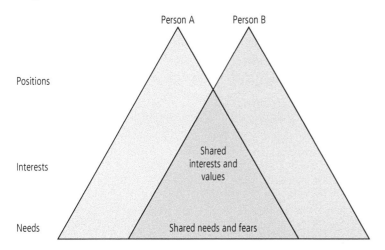

▲ Positions, interests and needs. Floyer, 1995

The conflict cycle provides a visualization of the dynamics of conflict through showing the phases a conflict can go through. From the identification of the incompatibility of goals, a conflict can turn violent and then be transformed through negotiations, and then social change may occur. Many conflicts, however, are stuck in the vicious cycle of formation and violence and in some conflicts through an outright victory of a party it may move straight from the violent phase to social change. The conflict cycle also visualizes a well-known, but important aspect: if conflict parties are fighting, you first have to separate them (peacekeeping), before you can sit them down to talk (peacemaking) and perhaps reconcile them (peacebuilding). If two pupils are fighting in the school yard, teachers first need to act as peacekeepers – separating the parties – before the principal can start with the peacemaking and the counsellor with the peacebuilding. As mentioned before, conflict models may provide clarity in complex conflicts, but they should be used with caution.

Third-party involvement in conflict, including humanitarian intervention

Third parties can be involved in conflicts in many different ways, both violent and non-violent. Violent interventions could arguably turn a third party into a core conflict party, as they actively engage in the conflict with force. The way in which a third party gets involved in a conflict often depends on their own interest in the conflict and the power they have over the conflict parties. Fisher and Keashly have identified six common ways of third-party intervention that they consider pacific or non-violent (see below). Depending on the power of the third party, and the willingness of the conflict parties to submit their case to the third party, they can act as an arbiter or judge, negotiator, consultant and so forth.

Typology of pacific third-party interventions

1   *Conciliation*, in which a trusted third-party provides an informal communicative link between the antagonists for the purposes of identifying the issues, lowering tension and encouraging direct interaction, usually in the form of negotiation.

2   *Consultation*, in which the third-party works to facilitate creative problem-solving through communication and analysis, making use of human relations skills and social-scientific understanding of conflict etiology [that is, causes] and dynamics.

3   *Pure Mediation*, in which the third-party works to facilitate a negotiated settlement on substantive issues through the use of reasoning, persuasion, effective control of information, and the suggestion of alternatives.

4   *Power Mediation*, which encompasses pure mediation but also moves beyond it to include the use of leverage or coercion on the part of the mediator in the form of promised rewards or threatened punishments, and may also involve the third-party as monitor and guarantor of the agreement.

5   *Arbitration*, wherein the third-party renders a binding judgment arrived at through consideration of the individual merits of the opposing positions and then imposes a settlement which is deemed to be fair and just.

6   *Peacekeeping*, in which the third-party provides military personnel in order to monitor a ceasefire or an agreement between antagonists, and may also engage in humanitarian activities designed to restore normalcy in concert with civilian personnel, who may also assist in the management of political decision-making processes such as elections.

Ronald J. Fisher, "Methods of Third-Party Intervention" from *Berghof Handbook for Conflict Transformation*, 2011, Berghof Research Centre for Constructive Conflict Management www.berghof-foundation.org/handbook.

As discussed previously there are only a limited number of justifications for military intervention. The United Nations Security Council may sanction it under article 42 of the UN Charter, but only if "international peace and security" are under threat. The gradual emergence of "humanitarian intervention" has undermined the realist principle of state sovereignty. The so-called "Responsibility to Protect doctrine" or R2P, argues that states forego the right to full sovereignty if they "fail to protect their populations from genocide, war crimes, ethnic cleansing and crimes against humanity"

(see below). With so many examples of states indeed failing to protect their citizens – from Sudan to Syria – it seems like an obvious choice for the international community to support this development. But with even Médecins Sans Frontières openly arguing against it, there must be more to it.

> ### United Nations 2005 World Summit: Responsibility to protect populations from genocide, war crimes, ethnic cleansing and crimes against humanity
>
> 1 Each individual State has the responsibility to protect its populations from genocide, war crimes, ethnic cleansing and crimes against humanity. This responsibility entails the prevention of such crimes, including their incitement, through appropriate and necessary means. We accept that responsibility and will act in accordance with it. The international community should, as appropriate, encourage and help States to exercise this responsibility and support the United Nations in establishing an early warning capability.
>
> 2 The international community, through the United Nations, also has the responsibility to use appropriate diplomatic, humanitarian and other peaceful means, in accordance with Chapters VI and VIII of the Charter, to help protect populations from genocide, war crimes, ethnic cleansing and crimes against humanity. In this context, we are prepared to take collective action, in a timely and decisive manner, through the Security Council, in accordance with the Charter, including Chapter VII, on a case-by-case basis and in cooperation with relevant regional organizations as appropriate, should peaceful means be inadequate and national authorities manifestly fail to protect their populations from genocide, war crimes, ethnic cleansing and crimes against humanity...
>
> United Nations, "2005 World Summit Outcome"

Successive Secretary-Generals from the United Nations have argued in favour of humanitarian intervention. Current Secretary-General Ban Ki-Moon referred to the work of his predecessors Kofi Annan and Boutros Boutros-Ghali in laying the foundations for the doctrine. Bellamy and Wheeler (2011) have identified some of the arguments for and against humanitarian intervention.[42] One of the obvious arguments in favour of intervention is "the moral case". If the media can make us aware of whatever is happening in all parts of the world and the international community has the means to intervene, why should it not "protect civilians from genocide and mass killings"? The universalist argument of "common basic human rights" is put forward to explain how we have a moral obligation to help others. Another argument put forward is the legal one. The United Nations Charter "highlight[s] the importance of human rights", which would provide some justification for Security Council-sanctioned intervention. Second, there are historical cases of what could be considered humanitarian intervention, which would provide a legal basis for future interventions. The opponents of humanitarian intervention have provided several counter-arguments: that R2P can be abused, be used selectively, can be interpreted in many different ways, that military intervention doesn't work and that the legal basis is lacking. The military intervention in Libya in 2011 was largely based on R2P principles, and though Libya's leader Gaddafi actively targeted his own citizens and a Security Council resolution formed the basis for the intervention, it could be argued that many of the reservations of the opponents of R2P also apply here.

World leaders meet in Belarus to discuss a ceasefire in Ukraine

With ever expanding interpretations of conflict, violence and peace, it is not surprising that the interpretation of "resolving a conflict" has changed. Perhaps at some point we saw "the peace treaty" or "let's shake hands" or "it's in the past" as a closure to a conflict, but, if anything, we have learned that conflict is often far from over and may even flare up again before the ink of the signature under the peace treaty has dried. Peacemaking, or bringing the parties together, is still a vital element in the process towards conflict resolution, but increasingly the argument is made that a transformation is needed by fully reconciling the conflict parties.

Peacemaking, including negotiations and treaties

As discussed previously, peacemaking can be done in many different ways, from consultation to arbitration. The role of the peacemaker can often change during the process: it may start with offering "good offices" (a neutral place to meet) and evolve into active suggestions or pressure to reach an agreement. Berridge argues that it is difficult to identify "the ideal mediator" as this is dependent on the nature of the conflict and the stage it is in. Based on his experience, however, he has identified some characteristics that generally benefit a mediator (see left). This ideal mediator may be closer to one party than the other, but is ideally impartial or seen as impartial on the particular conflict. A powerless mediator may work in certain cases, but often it is an advantage when the mediator can offer pressure when needed. As negotiations can take a long time, it is important for a mediator to be able to commit sufficient energy and time to the conflict. In 1978, US President Jimmy Carter devoted 13 days in a row to the negotiations between the Egyptians and Israelis, and even though this may seem like a minor commitment, it was far from it, considering that he also had to deal with other pressing national and international issues. However, as soon as the Egyptian–Israeli Peace Agreement between Egypt and Israel was reached, Carter's focus was on other issues such as the situation in Iran and therefore he did not "devote the sustained attention" to the vaguely formulated parts of the treaty that concerned the Palestinians. Berridge argues the mediator should generally be available over many years. As negotiations tend to be "lengthy, trying and costly" it is important the mediator has a strong motivation to stay involved. The Harvard Negotiation Project offers a number of additional suggestions to the "ideal mediator", which include the all-important creative approach, "focus on underlying interests" and needs (as in the Positions–Interests–Needs model – see page 185), and the art of listening rather than talking.

Mediation

The ideal mediator

1   should be perceived as impartial on the specific issues dividing the parties to a conflict

2   should have influence, if not more effective power, relative to [the conflict parties]

3   should possess the ability to devote sustained attention to the dispute

4   should have a strong incentive to reach a durable agreement

Berridge, GR. 2005. *Diplomacy Theory and Practice*, pp. 204–206.

Some principles of "Interest based negotiation"	
1 Separate the people from the problem and try to build good working relationships	4 Avoid zero-sum traps [mutually exclusive goals] by brainstorming and exploring creative options
2 Facilitate communication and build trust by listening to each other rather than by telling each other what to do	5 Anticipate possible obstacles and work out how to overcome them
3 Focus on underlying interests and core concerns, not demands and superficial positions	Ramsbotham, Oliver. 2010. *Transforming Violent Conflict, Radical Disagreement, Dialogue and Survival.*

For an outsider it is not always easy to fully understand what has gone on during negotiations. Even with the memoirs and interviews of those individuals involved the picture is never complete. The German news magazine *Der Spiegel* provides an interesting insight into the coming about of the Minsk II treaty regarding Ukraine, and the stakes, personal relations between the parties and their approach to the conflict. The subsequent events and ongoing conflict in Ukraine make it clear that with two treaties (Minsk I and II) there's no guarantee for lasting peace. Peacebuilding aims to address that.

The Minsk negotiations and Minsk II Treaty

The War Next Door: Can Merkel's Diplomacy Save Europe?

By SPIEGEL Staff, 14 February 2015

[German] Chancellor Angela Merkel has often been accused of hesitancy. But in Minsk this week, she committed herself to helping find a way to quiet the weapons in Ukraine. The result was a cease-fire. But it is fragile and may ultimately be disadvantageous for Ukraine... Debaltseve is a small town in eastern Ukraine, held by 6,000 government troops, or perhaps 8,000. Nobody wants to say for sure. It is the heart of an army that can only put 30,000 soldiers into the field, a weak heart. Until Sunday of last week, that heart was largely encircled by pro-Russian separatists and the troops could only be supplied by way of highway M03. Then, Monday came.

▲   Pro-Russian rebel fighters launch artillery grad rockets towards Debaltseve, Ukraine

Separatist fighters began advancing across snowy fields towards the village of Lohvynove, a tiny settlement of 30 houses hugging the M03. The separatists stormed an army checkpoint and killed a few officers. They then dug in —and the heart of the Ukrainian army was surrounded...

Given the intensity of the situation, Germany and France together took the initiative and forced the Wednesday night summit in Minsk, Belarus. The long night of talks, which extended deep into Thursday morning, was the apex of eight days of shuttle diplomacy between Moscow, Kiev, Washington and Munich. With intense focus during dozens of hours of telephone conversations and negotiations across the globe, the German chancellor helped wrest a cease-fire from the belligerents. It is a fragile deal full of question marks, one which can only succeed if all parties dedicate themselves to adhering to it. Whether that will be the case is doubtful. The Minsk deal is brief respite. Nothing more. But it is a success nonetheless.

During the 17 hours in Minsk's Palace of Independence, there was much at stake. First and foremost, the focus was on demarcation lines and local elections, it was on ending the killing in eastern Ukraine. But there were several larger questions on the table as well, questions focusing on Russia's relationship with Europe and whether it will be possible to avoid an extended conflict with Vladimir Putin's Russia. They were questions focusing on how to deal with an aggressor: Is it wise to make concessions to Putin? And at what point does compromise become appeasement?

Above all were questions of international diplomacy: What is diplomacy capable of? Is the threat of violence necessary to make diplomacy work? What is the correct path: American weapons deliveries or European diplomacy? And, perhaps most crucial of all, the focus was on European emancipation: Is Europe able to solve its own conflicts without help from the United States?…

The low point of the Minsk negotiations was reached on Thursday morning. At 8 a.m. local time, Organization for Security and Cooperation in Europe (OSCE) special envoy Heidi Tagliavini climbed into a car at Vajskovy Street 4 to deliver a piece of bad news. The rebels no longer wanted to sign the closing document.

Following their arrival in Minsk, the German and French delegations initially holed up in the German Embassy before then coordinating with the Ukrainians. It is the same pattern that had been followed in the previous days' talks: total consensus between Germany and France followed by close accord with Ukraine before beginning talks with the Russian side.

Talks continued through the entire night, without a break. At times, one of the participants would nod off, head on the table. There was plenty of alcohol available, but Merkel didn't touch it. Participants said that the tone was measured. At one point, it did become loud, with Putin and Poroshenko becoming involved in a polemical battle of words, but they quickly calmed down again. They would occasionally stand up to talk through a particularly thorny issue privately, before coming back and continuing the talks. The personal relationship between the two is a good one and they address each other with the familiar form of "you."

Large groups, smaller groups, two leaders whispering in the corner, coffee, snacks: It went on like that through the entire night. Everyone knew what was at stake and they all, participants reported, seemed to want to reach an agreement.

The Russians took a tough line. They saw themselves as being in a position of strength, partly because of the situation in Debaltseve. The Europeans, for their part, insisted on an immediate cease-fire out of concern for the volatile situation facing the Ukrainian military. The separatists, not surprisingly, wanted to delay the beginning of the cease-fire for as long as possible so as to give themselves time to completely conquer Debaltseve. Poroshenko, too, seemed to prefer a delayed cease-fire — apparently not fully understanding the situation facing his military. The Europeans were trying to protect the Ukrainians from themselves.

The European duo had already pried an important concession out of the Russian president in Moscow during the week prior to Minsk: The elections in the separatist areas will only be held within those areas behind last September's demarcation line. The hundreds of square kilometers separatists have since taken will not be considered as part of their territory. Kiev managed to assert itself on another issue as well: Direct talks with the separatists, as Moscow had been demanding, will not take place. Putin, though, got the upper hand in a different area: The border between Russia and the separatist-held regions in eastern Ukraine will be observed neither by the Ukrainians nor by international forces. This issue will only be revisited after the elections, if at all. Even before the arrival of Tagliavini, the talks had already twice threatened to collapse. Particularly contentious is the withdrawal of heavy weaponry. In the end, agreement was reached that all heavy weapons would be withdrawn from the firing lines. For the Ukrainians, the firing line refers to the front where it now stands. For the rebels, it is the front line from last September. The result is a broad buffer zone, a zone that broadens to 140 kilometers (87 miles) for heavy rocket launchers. That means that the separatists will have to withdraw their equipment deep into the territories they hold, in some cases almost to the Russian border.

That is the deal that was presented to the separatists in Dipservice Hall early in the morning. Not long later, Tagliavini returned with their rejection of the agreement. Were the talks all for naught?

The negotiators refused to give up. They returned to the vast hall inside the Palace of Independence and continued talking. Merkel, Hollande, Poroshenko and Putin retired to a smaller room off the main hall, where Putin was informed that everything now depended on him. It was a point at which the collapse of the talks was a very real possibility. Putin withdraws to an office that had been set up especially for him on the third floor of the palace to telephone with the separatist leaders waiting in Dipservice Hall. The Germans and French did not learn what exactly he said to the two — Igor Plotnitsky of the Luhansk Republic and Alexander Zakharchenko of the Donetsk Republic. But two hours later, the pair agreed to the cease-fire. At 11 a.m. local time, the marathon negotiations came to an end.

Two documents were prepared. The first was a declaration from the national leaders present. The other was the Contact Group paper regarding the implementation of the first Minsk Agreement, which was signed five months ago. Even the name of the document was the object of extended and bitter debate. Kiev and the Europeans insisted that it make reference to the first Minsk deal reached last September.

Once the talks were finished, there was no press conference held. Just before noon, Merkel, Hollande, Putin and Poroshenko left the Minsk palace. "We are hopeful" is all the German chancellor would say of the result of the long night of talks…

It is always good when the weapons go quiet, but Merkel has achieved little beyond that. Separatist leaders along with a determined Putin, who knows that the West is not prepared to spill the blood of its soldiers to defend

Ukraine's integrity, have shown her the limits of her influence. But the European order is not constructed in Berlin alone. What was achieved in Minsk has little to do with Merkel's power. It has more to do with her political skill and her persistence.

1 To what extent was Merkel an "ideal mediator" (see p.188) and did she follow the principles of "interest-based negotiations" (p.189)?

Peacebuilding, including reconciliation and work of justice institutions

After peacekeeping (separating the violent conflict parties) and peacemaking (reaching an agreement between the conflict parties) comes peacebuilding. This has often been overlooked, and still is. Susan Opotow describes reconciliation as a process that "can move people from antagonism to coexistence. It can foster mutual respect, and, at its most ambitious, it can foster forgiveness, mercy, compassion, a shared vision of society, mutual healing, and harmony among parties formerly in conflict". But "[t]here is no one-size-fits-all blueprint for reconciliation" (2001).[43] The four basic options for post-conflict societies are to altogether ignore the conflict, to bring the perpetrators of crimes to justice, to offer amnesty via, for example, a Truth and Reconciliation Commission, or a combination of any of these. Looking at how Sierra Leone dealt with its violent past, through a combination of a war crimes tribunal *and* a Truth and Reconciliation Commission, Lydia Apori-Nkansah (2011) identifies the differences between justice through retribution, or revenge, and through restoration, or repairing the harm done (see right). There are many local ways in which offenders are offered a form of restorative justice. One example is the practice of ho'o ponopono in Hawaii (see following page). Opotow argues that each system has its advantages and disadvantages. Truth and Reconciliation Commissions aim to unearth the truth of what has happened and provide a chance for both perpetrators and victims to have their say as they can "formally acknowledge a silenced and painful past". But some of the disadvantages are the costs involved in the research, "the normalization of extreme violence" and "the bureaucratization of the reconciliation process" when victims are repeatedly faced with questions about how often they were beaten or how many corpses they counted in the street. Lastly, people may not feel like actual justice has been done when the murderer of their relative receives amnesty and returns to his house opposite theirs. Sierra Leone established a Truth and Reconciliation Commission and

Development trends in restorative and retributive justice	
Justice as retributive	Justice as restorative
Justice as punishment	Justice as healing
Justice according to law	Justice according to truth
Justice as adversarial	Justice as reconciliatory
Justice as retaliatory	Justice as forgiveness
Justice as condemnation	Justice as merciful
Justice as alienation	Justice as redemptive
Justice as impersonal	Justice as human centered
Justice as blind	Justice as sensitive
Justice as humiliation	Justice as honor

▲ Restorative and retributive justice. Apori-Nkansah, Lydia. 2011. "Restorative justice in transitional Sierra Leone". *Journal of Public Administration and Governance*. Vol 1, number 1.

encountered the problem that in parts of the country it was customary to forget events from the past, rather than address them.

The Ho'o ponopono approach

A man is asleep in his home. He is awakened by some noises, and he gets up in time to catch a young boy fleeing the home with some stolen money. The police are called. The young boy is known to the police, obviously a "delinquent" and as they say: "Three strikes and you're out."

The place is Hawaii. In Polynesian culture there is a tradition combining reconstruction, reconciliation, and resolution. The ho'o ponopono (setting straight) is known to others through cultural diffusion, for example, to the owner of the burglarized house. He looks at the boy and thinks of him spending 20 years in prison. He suggests to the police, "Let me handle this one." It transpires that the boy's sister is ill, and the family is too poor to pay for medical care. Every dollar counts.

Ho'o ponopono is organized. The man's family, neighbors, and the young boy and his family sit around a table: there is a moderator not from the families and neighbors, but the "wise man/woman." There are four phases: facts, sharing responsibility, joint reconciliation, and closure. Each one is encouraged to *sincerely* present his or her version: why it happened, how, and what would be the appropriate reaction. The young boy's reason is questioned, but even if the reason is accepted, the method is not. Apologies are then offered and accepted: forgiveness is demanded and offered.

The young boy has to make up for the violation by doing free garden work for some time. The rich man and neighbors agree to contribute to the family's medical expenses. And in the end the story of the burglary is written up in a way acceptable to all. *That sheet of paper is then burnt* — symbolizing the end to the burglary but not to the aftermath.

Is this rewarding the burglar? If this restores all parties, reconciles them, and resolves the conflict, then what is the harm?

Abu-Nimer, Mohammed, ed. 2001. *Reconciliation, Justice and Coexistence. Theory and Practice.* Lanham, p. 18.

1 Do you know of any local forms of restorative justice? What would be the advantages and disadvantages of such systems?

2 Would it also be possible to apply ho'o ponopono to more serious crimes, for example involving murder? Why (not)?

TOK

How can the emotional testimonies of victims of relatives in Truth and Reconciliation Commissions create more knowledge in the path to discovering the truth of what happened? Are they more or less valid than clinical evidence, such as DNA?

Some of the advantages of establishing a criminal tribunal are that "it can diminish individual vengeance and avoid a continuing cycle of violence. In addition, it can enhance respect for the rule of law". Disadvantages are that tribunals can be seen as justice imposed by the victors on the defeated, that they can be slow, partial, narrow, and like the Nuremburg and Tokyo trials, be criticized because individuals were prosecuted for acts more properly attributable to governments. Courts are also a costly affair and could very well lead to many perpetrators denying their involvement in acts of violence, preventing the relatives from learning the details of the event and receiving an apology.

Rethinking Truth and Reconciliation Commissions: Lessons from Sierra Leone

- After an eleven-year civil war that became internationally notorious for mutilation, sexual violence, and the targeting of children, a Truth and Reconciliation Commission (TRC) began its public hearings in April 2003. Increasingly, truth commissions are regarded as a standard part of conflict resolution "first aid kits."

- Despite pressure from local NGOs and human rights activists for a TRC, there was little popular support for bringing such a commission to Sierra Leone, since most ordinary people preferred a "forgive and forget" approach…

- In northern Sierra Leone, social forgetting is a cornerstone of established processes of reintegration and healing for child and adult ex-combatants. Speaking of the war in public often undermines these processes, and many believe it encourages violence.

- In Sierra Leone's TRC, however, sensitization materials and commissioners' speeches promoted the healing and reconciliatory powers of verbal remembering, often explicitly discounting local understandings of healing and reconciliation in terms of social forgetting.

- People in both urban and rural locations were divided about the TRC, and in several communities people collectively agreed not to give statements.

- Before a truth commission or TRC is initiated in a particular setting, it is important to establish whether such an exercise has popular support—not only among local NGOs but also among ordinary survivors.

- Truth commission reports can provide crucial frameworks for debates about violence and repression, and can foster the development of stable national institutions. Sierra Leone's Truth and Reconciliation Report offers this framework. But where there is no popular support for a truth commission, we need to find alternative ways of producing such reports.

- Where a truth commission or TRC is initiated, it will be more effective if it builds upon established practices of healing and social coexistence. If we discount or ignore such processes, we may jeopardize any form of social recovery.

Shaw, Rosalind. February 2005. *Rethinking Truth and Reconciliation: Commissions from Sierra Leone.* United States Institute for Peace special report 130.

This is a summary of the report. The full report is available here: http://www.usip.org/sites/default/files/sr130.pdf

The International Criminal Court offers another option to prosecute those perpetrators involved in the most serious crimes. According to its founding document, the Rome Statute, it deals with the crime of genocide, crimes against humanity, war crimes and the crime of aggression. Genocide was defined as "acts committed with intent to destroy, in whole or in part, a national, ethnical, racial or religious group".[44] The International Criminal Court is limited by the fact that not all countries have become a member, including some of the most powerful nations, such as the United States, Russia and China. It is also increasingly criticized for its focus on Africa and the many years its procedures take up. At the same time, William Schabas, President of the Association for Genocide Scholars, calls it,

perhaps the most innovative and exciting development in international law since the creation of the United Nations… From a hesitant commitment in 1945, to an ambitious Universal Declaration of Human Rights in 1948, we have now reached a point where individual criminal liability is established for those responsible for serious violations of human rights, and where an institution is created to see that this is more than just some pious wish.[45]

TOK

In post-conflict peacebuilding, should the international community always strive for incorporating local ways of gathering knowledge (or "removing" it, through social forgetting) after a conflict?

The study of peace and conflict remains an incredibly complex yet important venture. With a better understanding of the intricacies of peace and conflict comes a more thoughtful approach to conflict situations, which in turn can lead to more constructive actions. Many of the positive change-makers have used the study of peace and conflict to learn from predecessors. An example could be how Gandhi influenced Martin Luther King who influenced Aung Sang Suu Kyi's non-violent struggle in Myanmar.

With many politicians offering us a "quick fix" to improve our lives and remove any threat to them, an evidenced, reasoned, balanced and well-intentioned approach to conflict is of the utmost importance. Many of the factors that seem to influence peace and conflict appear rather constant: the importance of resources, the search for power, the psychological dimensions of "us versus them", and so on. Yet, there are also many new developments that could well impact our approach to peace and conflict in the future.

New directions

Throughout the unit, we've argued that conflicts have been, are, and will be complex. Perhaps in the not-so-distant past global conflicts seemed less complex. The Second World War is still largely perceived as a "fascism against the rest" conflict, the subsequent Cold War is still often simplified in the "communism versus capitalism" paradigm, and according to Samuel Huntington, we not find ourselves in a "clash of civilizations" between Islam and Western liberalism.

Although these oversimplifications often bear some truth in them, they fail to recognize that all those individuals drawn into the conflict might have very different reasons for picking a side in the conflict. These could range from economical to cultural. The rise of Islamic State is often similarly explained simply through referring to religious fundamentalism. Yet many of its founders and leaders are motivated by power politics and many members could well be drawn to the organization because of financial reasons, cultural frustrations or psychological issues. Those Western nations now trying to combat Islamic State both in the Middle East and in the West will have to recognize the complexity of this conflict. Simply calling it Islamist terrorism and combating it as such will not resolve the conflict.

Terrorism is not a new phenomenon, but developments in communication through mass media and the Internet have made it seemingly easier for terrorists to spread their message. Some societies are combating this in very innovative ways. Psychologists argue that many "lone-wolf" terrorists (those acting on their own) are not particularly drawn by certain political aims, but are more guided by the pursuit of self-glory. Many Norwegians have decided to not speak out the name of the person who committed the mass murder of 69 youngsters on a Norwegian island. Similarly, German media often refrain from

mentioning the name of terrorist suspects so as not to inspire so-called "copy-cats" who also seek self-glory. So, regardless of the complexities concerning defining someone a terrorist or not, what if we chose to ignore terrorism, not giving it the attention that the terrorist was actually seeking?

There are many more questions concerning the directions of peace and conflict in the future. How will international law develop, particularly concerning state sovereignty? How long will American hegemony last and how will the nation deal with the gradual loss of power? Will social media allow for some sort of "international solidarity" between similar groups of people and will this empower them in their local struggles? Some experts are arguing that we are living in the most peaceful time ever, yet it may not feel this way because we are so exposed to the misery that is happening around the world. So, lastly, will we see (and perceive) a more peaceful future? There are no easy answers to these questions and if anything, they will probably lead to more.

4.7 Exam-style questions

1 Evaluate the success of third-party involvement in transforming one intra-state conflict away from violence and towards positive peace.

Examiner hints

Different arguments may be considered depending on which intra-state conflict is used in the answer, and it is expected that the answer will evaluate the validity of those arguments in the context of the chosen conflict. Responses are likely to include an explanation of the key terms from the question, such as third-party involvement (identifying different options for intervention, for example, armed military, diplomatic, economic), conflict transformation, intra-state conflict, violence, and positive peace. They may also highlight the importance of negative peace as an interim stage.

Reasons why third-party involvement may succeed:

- there is a supportive external environment with a strong regional and international dimension

- the parties in conflict will benefit from the transformation to peace (negative and positive) more than they can benefit from an extension of fighting

- the parties in the conflict agree to the third-party involvement

- the third party has the trust of all parties, is genuinely neutral, detached from the reasons for conflict, and is not seeking to take control in the conflict

- the third party has the necessary political, financial, and/or administrative status

- the third party has the resources and expertise (knowledge and skills) to act as a mediator between warring groups and to help lead them to a peaceful resolution

- neutral observers, for example, election observers, can change the behaviour of protagonists

- third parties have the power to transform a conflict through the use of weapon embargoes, financial freezes, and/or trade limitations or by enhancing the status of the weaker party in an asymmetric conflict, thereby bringing the stronger party to accept value in negotiation.

Reasons why third-part involvement may not succeed:

- the third-party involvement is imposed and not desired by at least one of the parties in conflict

- if the involvement includes a mediation process that is in the public domain, actors are likely to play to their constituents for domestic political gain

- extremists commit acts of violence to destroy trust in the negotiation process

- the wrong individuals from the parties in conflict are involved and they do not have the support of the rank and file engaged in the conflict – no mandate

- some conflicts are long-running and seemingly intractable, or the violence has been extreme and wounds are extensive – mediation or negotiation are not possible

- there is a failure to identify and implement the criteria that would determine success

- the third party may withdraw its involvement and leave the conflict unresolved, and possibly even less tractable.

Responses should refer to one specific intra-state conflict. While there are many definitions of intra-state conflict, examples chosen would typically have a high level of violence, within the internal boundaries of a state and with the established authority or government as one of the parties in conflict. Students may give examples of ethnic or civil conflicts which are less obviously/explicitly intra-state conflicts, however, a broad definition should be accepted.

The end of the Cold War marked a fourfold increase in the use of United Nations peacekeeping forces in intra-state conflicts around the globe. Some appropriate examples could be Kashmir, the former Yugoslavia, Cambodia, Nicaragua, Sri Lanka, Darfur, Afghanistan, Iraq or, more recently, countries affected by the Arab Spring.

Responses should include the candidate's evaluation of whether or not third-party involvement can transform a conflict towards peace, and under what circumstances.

2 "The use of violence can never be legitimate." Discuss the validity of this claim, with reference to at least one violent conflict you have studied.

Examiner hints

The focus of this question is on the moral and ethical dilemma that warfare and violence cause given that in most societies killing is regarded as wrong, and therefore if violence is to be presented as legitimate there will be religious, legal and ethical formulations needed to outline the legitimacy of war and violence. Depending on the conflict(s) used as an example, responses could look at religious perspectives, or at legal aspects, for example, the Geneva Convention, the Nuremberg Principles, or the UN Charter, or at moral perspectives.

Arguments used to legitimize violence may include:

- religious legitimacy: violence can be justified in theological terms, for example, in pursuance of a "holy war" or "physical jihad" by Judaism, Islam, Hinduism, Buddhism, Christianity, and so on

- legal legitimacy: violence as a response to a perceived international threat, following the passing of a UN resolution (for example, the UN Charter Chapter VII regarding the Iraqi invasion of Kuwait (UNIKOM), or the NATO-led intervention in Libya

- moral legitimacy: the use of violence by states could be regarded as a lesser evil to achieve a greater good, such as to avoid an undue loss of human life, or to defend its citizens, and defend justice, or in opposition to structural violence, such as unfair laws, discrimination, threat(s) to livelihood, or in response to forced migration, or lack of resources; Max Weber's ideas on the state's monopoly on violence could be relevant

- the need for self-defence by individuals or communities, for example, by indigenous groups, needing to protect themselves against outside (or local) aggression; or in revolt against an occupier, for example, the violence by Shiite groups against the US-led invasion of Iraq

- "Just War Doctrine" provides an ideal platform for analysing the legitimacy of war and violence: *jus ad bellum* provides the legitimacy for going to war. Last Resort, Legitimate Authority (State), Right Intention and Just Cause, Chance of Success, Ultimate Goal of Peace and Jus in Bello, provide the legitimacy for how the war is fought; violence must be proportional and discriminatory (not target non-combatants).

Arguments against the legitimization of violence may include:

- violence doesn't solve anything but leads potentially to more violence – conflicts may escalate and spill over into other areas, harming innocent civilians

- theological/ethical arguments against taking human life under any circumstances, or causing undue suffering

- violence often involves material destruction, for example, of infrastructure, livelihoods, and resources that may take years to normalize and be very costly to replace

- non-violent protests can be equally or more effective, and peaceful solutions through diplomatic means are likely to be more sustainable.

Responses should contain reference to at least one example of a violent conflict. This may, for example, be through the concept of a state monopoly on violence (Weber) with the formal decision of a state to go to war, or counter-examples of non-state actors who claim legitimacy, for example, that they are acting in self-defence. Non-state examples could include Northern Ireland, Israel-Palestine, South Sudan, Ukraine, the Arab Spring, Syria/Iraq, Kashmir.

Responses should include the candidate's conclusion on whether or not violence can ever be legitimate.

3   Peacebuilding is arguably more important than peacemaking, yet it is given much less funding and attention. To what extent do you agree with this claim?

Examiner hints

Responses should include the candidate's understanding of the concept of peace, and distinguish between the processes of peacebuilding and peacemaking. They may refer to negative peace, that is, the absence of direct physical violence and the end of warfare, as the essential first step in any peacemaking process. Responses may then contrast this with positive peace, which has to do with tackling post-conflict structures of violence in order to build sustainable peace.

Arguments that support the claim may include:

- peacebuilding, in which civil society is rebuilt through re-establishing social institutions such as medical facilities and schools, is essential for the promotion of social justice and the rebuilding of civil society

- in many situations the world's attention, and international efforts, are directed towards funding and supporting the earlier stages of peacemaking – that is, the achieving, monitoring and maintaining of a state of negative peace

- once negative peace has been achieved and the most visible forms of suffering have subsided, world attention tends to be directed elsewhere, and international support is forthcoming only from nations that have vested political and economic interests in the country or area in question.

Arguments against the claim may include:

- the most expensive and most important efforts have to be directed towards ending armed conflicts, as it is in these that human suffering and human rights abuses are likely to be at their worst

- establishing and then maintaining a newly achieved peace demand the greatest commitment, as the situation is likely to be at its most sensitive in the immediate aftermath of the conflict

- peacebuilding is likely to be supported in cases where direct economic and political benefits are associated with post-war reconstruction, for example, where expensive infrastructure developments are undertaken for the benefit of domestic or third parties with vested interests. However, in these scenarios, the building of low-cost social and educational institutions may be a low priority.

Responses should contain references to specific examples. These may be taken, for instance, from the break-up and reconstruction of the former Yugoslavia; the Iraq war and post-war reconstruction; the truth and reconciliation commission in South Africa; peacebuilding efforts in Rwanda or in Cambodia following the UN-backed withdrawal of Vietnamese forces and the UN-supported elections, though any appropriate examples should be rewarded.

Responses should include the candidate's view of whether peacebuilding is much more important than peacemaking, and whether it receives less funding and attention.

4 Discuss why non-violent protest is sometimes able to achieve success against even the most powerful of opponents.

Examiner hints

Responses should draw specifically on candidates' understanding of relevant key concepts, such as power, conflict, and non-violence, and may also touch on the theoretical foundation of pacifism given for this unit, or on the theoretical foundations of unit 1. Candidates may distinguish between hard and soft power. They may explore the nature of conflict, perhaps using a theoretical construct such as Galtung's conflict triangle to identify that in conflict there is always a contradiction or situational cause of conflict which is then manifested in different ways. Responses may explain that conflict can be symmetric or asymmetric (they do not have to use this exact term) and that it is in asymmetric conflicts that non-violent protest is most often used.

Arguments for why non-violent protest can achieve success against even the most powerful of opponents:

- the power of rulers derives from consent by the subjects; non-violent action is a process of withdrawing consent and thus is a way to challenge the key problems of dictatorship and other systems of oppression, genocide, and war

- in asymmetric conflicts, where the weaker party's hard power capabilities are often limited, using the soft power of non-violent protest to challenge the stronger party may be a more effective mechanism to achieve an accommodation of the weaker party's vital interests

- in certain cases, especially where open communications, publicity and the interest of the world media exist together, non-violent tactics can alter the conflict symmetry by redefining the conflict in terms of rights and by denying the use of unrestricted power to the more powerful party

- communications and modern social media have changed the ability of non-violent protest to challenge even the most powerful opponents (for example, see Erica Chenoweth and Maria Stephan's 2012 book *Why Civil Resistance Works: The Strategic Logic of Nonviolent Conflict*)

- the likelihood of success for a non-violent protest is enhanced by the fact that there is such a wide variety of methods which can be applied in different contexts (Gene Sharp's *Theory of Power* presents 198 such methods of non-violent action).

Arguments for why non-violent protest may not achieve success against powerful opponents:

- fragmentation: any divisions among the protesters will make non-violent protest ineffective against the most powerful opponents

- in asymmetric conflicts, the available violent responses are often guerrilla war or terrorism and such tactics allow the more powerful opponent to justify the use of their hard power and excessive violence to achieve their objectives; protesters turning to violence, and especially to the indiscriminate use of extreme physical violence, with no regard to international opinion or to controls (by bodies such as the International Criminal Court) will rule out the effectiveness of allied non-violent protests, by losing them the moral high ground

- closure or failure of communications and mass or social media will weaken the power of non-violent protest.

- harsh punitive measures may be taken by the powerful parties against the protestors that may effectively silence their opposition, at least in the short term: "might" may suppress "right".

Responses should contain references to specific examples. The standard examples of non-violent protests are those of Mahatma Gandhi and Martin Luther King. Unless these examples are well structured – that is, unless theory is present, backed up by the examples – they are often unpersuasive. Candidates could consider more recent examples, such as the popular movements in different countries that eventually led to the collapse of the Soviet Union; the 1990s protest against Apartheid in South Africa; or the first Palestinian Intifada, which, it can be argued, led to the Oslo Peace Process. Non-violent revolutions of the Arab Spring could also be addressed.

Responses should include the candidate's views on why non-violent protest might or might not achieve success against powerful opponents.

5 "Transforming armed conflict towards peace relies on an interrelationship of peacemaking, peace keeping and peace building." Discuss.

Examiner hints

Better answers will demonstrate an excellent understanding of the concepts of peace and conflict, and will explain the terms peacemaking, peace keeping and peace building, and how these three interrelate. Although it is expected that candidates should explain what is meant by armed conflict, it should be noted that providing lengthy definitions of terms should not form the main part of the essay. The focus should be on discussing the interrelationship between the three concepts named in the question:

- peacemaking may be described as armed intervention with the possible use of force (violence) to separate parties in conflict. Answers may discuss whether it is always and only defined as this, for example, discussing whether efforts at diplomacy may not also count as peace-making.

- peace keeping may be described as maintaining the status quo with armed force and with the use of unarmed observers between parties in conflict with their agreement.

- peace building may be described as the building of positive peace and the infrastructure of civil society, for example, education, access to health care, local services and governance structures, and the removing of psychological scars of violence. Candidates may refer to the concept of peace as often being defined as a state both of non-conflict and of harmonious relations.

Candidates should discuss the relative importance of each process to the others and how each contributes to a successful peace process. The more sophisticated answers may identify that international interest and support for the process will usually have declined or disappeared before peace building has been embarked on.

Arguments for reliance on an interrelationship may include:

- if the infrastructure and stable governance is not in place then the peace will not last

- if there is no reconciliation and reconstruction then conflict may reignite, and there may be lasting psychological resentment etc.

Arguments against reliance on an interrelationship may include:

- the view that as soon as armed conflict has stopped, peace has been achieved, so you don't need the other elements.

Candidates could also argue that lasting peace relies on other factors, such as the protection of human rights, and fair access to resources, in addition to these three elements. Answers may make reference to specific examples, such as to Afghanistan and Iraq, where the emphasis is on reconstruction, or to where the lack of all three activities for securing peace has meant that conflict has returned, or to where they have successfully been implemented together to establish peace.

Answers should include a conclusion on whether peace does rely on an interrelationship of these three. Candidates may bring in a practical reflection such as that although all three might be needed this is not always possible to implement – for example, if resources are limited, then it might be preferable to use these in more urgent peacemaking situations rather than tying them up in peacekeeping and peace building efforts.

6 "If a person died from tuberculosis in the eighteenth century it would be hard to conceive of this as violence since it might have been quite unavoidable, but if he dies from it today, despite all the medical resources in the world, then violence is present" (Galtung). To what extent do you agree with the view that those in power have an obligation to identify and prevent structural violence?

Examiner hints

Better answers will demonstrate an excellent understanding of what is meant by structural violence. Candidates may discuss the importance of understanding different concepts of peace and violence: peace as the absence of war and direct violence, or peace as the absence of all violence, including structural violence as in this reference. Candidates may include specific discussion of Galtung and the context of the 1960s and 1970s and how this is relevant today (the quotation, from 1969, comes from the context of the Cold War and the clash between different ideologies): however it should be noted that this should not be the focus of the response.

Arguments that those in power have an obligation may include:

- economic and social policies should include equal access for everyone

- those in power have a primary obligation to meet the basic needs of all people

- health care provisions like vaccinations are a basic need

- governments have more formal obligations and responsibilities than NGOs, MNCs, etc.

Arguments that they do not have an obligation may include:

- there is no such thing as structural violence

- epidemics are natural and unfortunate events rather than the responsibility of governments

- it is the responsibility of individuals to take care of themselves, and the managers of power have no obligation to do so.

Answers may make reference to specific examples, such as to places where deaths due to tuberculosis are still happening, such as in rural Haiti; or to where water is still the cause of a high percentage of communicable diseases, such as in India, or to where desertification and other negative environmental impacts, with resulting implications for health, occur due to the building of dams, for example, as in the Three Gorges Dam over the Yangtze river.

Candidates should include a conclusion on the extent to which they agree that those in power have an obligation to prevent structural violence.

[1] King Jr, Martin Luther. *Letter from a Birmingham Jail* 16 April 1963.

[2] Galtung, Johan. 1969. *Violence, Peace and Peace Research*, Journal of Peace Research no. 23 – 9.

[3] Streeten, Paul. 1995. Foreword. *Reflections on Human Development* By Mahbub ul Haq. Oxford University Press, p. xiv.

[4] Mahbubani, Kishore. 31 January 2015. "Human wellbeing and security". *The Lancet*. http://www.mahbubani.net/articles%20by%20dean/Lancet.pdf.

[5] Galtung, Johan. 1958. *Theories of Conflict*, p.24). https://www.transcend.org/files/Galtung_Book_Theories_Of_Conflict_single.pdf.

[6] *The Guardian*. 2 July 2013. "Doesn't religion cause most of the conflict in the world?" http://www.theguardian.com/commentisfree/2013/jul/02/religion-wars-conflict.

[7] King, John. 27 September 2002. "Bush calls Saddam 'the guy who tried to kill my dad". http://edition.cnn.com/2002/ALLPOLITICS/09/27/bush.war.talk/.

[8] Al Jazeera. 28 November 2011. "Fresh protests in Bolivia road row". http://www.aljazeera.com/news/americas/2011/09/2011928204718315778.html.

[9] Roy, Arundhati. 2004. *The Ordinary Person's Guide to Empire*, p. 135.

[10] Gerstandt, Joe. 5 April 2012. "Conflict: what is it good for?" http://www.joegerstandt.com/2012/04/conflict-what-is-it-good-for/.

[11] Al Jazeera. 14 February 2015. "Protests mark fourth anniversary Bahrain Uprising". http://www.aljazeera.com/news/2015/02/protests-mark-fourth-anniversary-bahrain-uprising-150214074700114.html.

[12] McCann, Colum. 30 March 2013. "Remembering an Easter Miracle in Northern Ireland". http://www.nytimes.com/2013/03/31/sunday-review/remembering-an-easter-miracle-in-northern-ireland.html.

[13] UN News Centre. 23 July 2009. "Assembly President Warns On Doctrine To Intervene on War Crimes Atrocities". http://www.un.org/apps/news/story.asp?NewsID=31562#.VaeW6PmqpHw.

[14] Berridge, GR. 1994. *Diplomacy. Theory and Practice*, p. 208.

[15] Miller, Christopher E. 2005. *A Glossary of Terms and Concepts in Peace and Conflict Studies*. 2nd edition. https://www.upeace.org/pdf/glossaryv2.pdf.

[16] See Dutton, Donald G. 2006. *Rethinking Domestic Violence*. University of British Columbia Press, p. 3.

[17] World Health Organization. WHO Multi-country Study on Women's Health and Domestic Violence against Women. http://www.who.int/gender/violence/who_multicountry_study/summary_report/summary_report_English2.pdf, p. vi.

[18] Baumeister, Roy F and Bushman, Brad. 2014. Social Psychology and Human Nature. Comprehensive Edition, pp. 294–308.

[19] Galtung, Johan. 1969. "Violence, Peace and Peace Research". Journal of Peace Research. Vol. 6, number 3, pp. 167–191.

[20] This interpretation is termed "structural violence" by Ramsbotham, Oliver, Woodhouse, Tom and Miall, Hugh. 2011. Contemporary Conflict Resolution. 3rd edition. Polity Press.

[21] Hathaway, William, T. 21 October 2013. "Varieties of Violence: Structural, Cultural and Direct". *Conflict Resolution/Mediation*. https://www.transcend.org/tms/2013/10/varieties-of-violence-structural-cultural-and-direct/.

[22] Moore. 1996.

[23] "Armed Conflicts at the End of the Cold War, 1989–1992" by Karin Axell and Peter Wallensteen, 1993, Journal of Peace Research, 30(3): pp. 331–346

[24] Gleditsch, Nils Petter, Wallensteen, Peter, Eriksson, Mikael, Sollenberg, Margareta and Strand, Harvard. 2002. "Armed Conflict 1946–2001: A New Dataset 2002". *Journal of Peace Research*. Vol. 39, number 5, pp. 615–637.

[25] World Economic Forum. Global Risks Report 2015. http://www.weforum.org/reports/global-risks-report-2015.

[26] Human Security Report 2012. http://hsrgroup.org/docs/Publications/HSR2012/HSRP2012_Chapter%207.pdf.

[27] Abramson, Harold I. 2004. *Mediation Representation: Advocating in a problem solving process*. NISA.

[28] Schabas, William. 2000. *Genocide in International Law. The Crime of Crimes*, p. ix.

[29] Truth and Reconciliation Commission. http://www.justice.gov.za/trc/.

[30] BBC News. 16 December 2015. "What is fracking and why is it so controversial?" http://www.bbc.com/news/uk-14432401.

[31] Moore, Christopher. 1996. *The Mediation Process*. 2nd edition, pp. 60–61.

[32] Said, Edward. 4 October 2004. "The Clash of Ignorance". http://www.thenation.com/article/clash-ignorance/.

[33] Patel, Sujay and Gadit, Amin Muhammad. December 2008. "Karo-Kari: A form of honour killing in Pakistan". *Transcultural Psychiatry*. Vol. 45, number 4, pp. 683–694.

[34] Goldstein, Joshua. 2004. *International Relations*, p. 295.

[35] O'Brien, William. 2009. "The conduct of just and limited war". In James E. White. *Contemporary Moral Problems*, pp. 21–32.

[36] Joint Resolution to Authorize the Use of United States Armed Forces Against Iraq. 2002. http://georgewbush-whitehouse.archives.gov/news/releases/2002/10/print/20021002-2.html.

[37] Sears, David O, Huddy, Leonie and Jervis, Robert (editors). 2003. *Oxford Handbook of Political Psychology*. Oxford University Press.

[38] Jabri, Vivienne. 1996. *Discourses on violence*. Manchester University Press.

[39] Harris, Lasana T and Fiske, Susan T. 2011. "Dehumanized Perception, A Psychological Means to Facilitate Atrocities, Torture and Genocide?" *Journal of Psychology*. Vol. 219, number 3, pp. 175–181.

[40] Collier, Paul and Hoeffler, Anke. 2004. "Greed and Grievance in Civil War". *Oxford Economic Papers* 56, pp. 563–595. http://www.econ.nyu.edu/user/debraj/Courses/Readings/CollierHoeffler.pdf.

[41] Brown, Michael, E. 1996. "The Underlying Causes of Internal Conflict". *In International Dimensions of Internal Conflict*, p. 14.

[42] Bellamy, Alex J and Wheeler, Nicholas J. 2011. "Humanitarian intervention in world politics". In John Baylis, Steve Smith and Patricia Owens. *The Globalization of World Politics*.

[43] Opotow, Susan. June 2001. "Reconciliation in Times of Impunity: Challenges for Social Justice". *Social Justice Research*. Vol. 14, number 2.

[44] Rome Statute of the International Criminal Court. 17 July 1998. http://www.icc-cpi.int/nr/rdonlyres/ea9aeff7-5752-4f84-be94-0a655eb30e16/0/rome_statute_english.pdf.

[45] Schabas, William. 2001. *An introduction to the International Criminal Court*. Cambridge University Press, p. 20.

Conclusion

The world has changed, and with it the politics that have emerged are significantly different from that of the past. This Companion has focused on contemporary politics on various geographic levels that add up to a global scale. With that are concepts that help us analyze what is happening on the ground and how to approach what we are now seeing on a daily basis. The four units that are presented here together present a holistic framework for viewing contemporary global politics. With that we have included historical background to show how action on the ground has changed and the how present day realities have evolved.

Each of the units includes key concepts that are important in understanding the relationship of the unit's subject to global politics. These are integrated into examples that further provide a grounded understanding of how politics function. This is where the important sub-focus of "people, power and politics" comes into play, for it is not only the nation states that contribute to global politics but the people who make up those nation-states, the organizations and institutions that play a role in maintaining social formations, and the people who either accept or resist the personal and organizational power that they are faced with on a daily basis.

The Global Politics Diploma Course and this Companion are designed so that teachers and students have a role in determining what examples they focus on and the parts of global politics that are of most interest to them. While the four units present the primary subject matter, within those subjects are many possibilities for study and analysis. With the approval of the course teachers, students can choose contemporary examples that elucidate the concepts and subjects presented in the course and in the Companion, and can be assessed on their individual understanding of how the concepts are related to their experience and daily life.

The way we all live now differs from the past by culture, geographic area, history and circumstances, and will continue to change as populations react to new circumstances, as globalization advances, and as geographic levels restructure themselves. The contemporary realities of global politics are complex, and will continue to require an open mind and a thoughtful analysis. Many of my students ask me at the end of the semester whether there is any hope for the world, given the many crises and conflicts, including natural disasters that seem to dominate our discussion of global politics. My answer is always that it will depend on them, their activity, their active involvement, to assure that the world remains a livable and an exciting and healthy place. There is no room anymore for apathy or dis-involvement. As these four units have shown, we have much work ahead of us, and while sometimes discouraging, it can also be exciting and will benefit all.

Index